Classroom Practices in Teaching English

NCTE began publishing the Classroom Practices series in 1963 with *Promising Practices in the Teaching of English*. The following volumes from the series are currently available.

How to Handle the Paper Load (1979), by Gene Stanford, Chair, and the NCTE Committee on Classroom Practices

Reflective Activities: Helping Students Connect with Texts (1999), edited by Louann Reid and Jeffrey N. Golub

United in Diversity: Using Multicultural Young Adult Literature in the Classroom (1998), edited by Jean E. Brown and Elaine C. Stephens

Voices in English Classrooms: Honoring Diversity and Change (1996), edited by Lenora (Leni) Cook and Helen C. Lodge

Making American Literatures in High School and College

**Classroom Practices in Teaching English
Volume 31**

Edited by

Anne Ruggles Gere
University of Michigan

Peter Shaheen
Seaholm High School, Birmingham, Michigan

National Council of Teachers of English
1111 W. Kenyon Road, Urbana, Illinois 61801-1096

Staff Editor: Tom Tiller

Interior Design: Doug Burnett

Cover Design: Pat Mayer

NCTE Stock Number 30429-3050

Library of Congress Catalog Card Number 85-644740

ISBN 0-8141-3042-9
ISSN 0550-5755

Contents

Introduction

Anne Ruggles Gere
University of Michigan

All of us who wrote for this book believe we need to rethink the ways we teach American literature. Specifically, as the first three words of our title suggest, it's time to acknowledge the "making," the forces that deliver certain texts to our classrooms; the various ways we define "American"; and the multiple and shifting meanings of "literatures." It is also time to consider how recent scholarship might contribute to the ways we teach both familiar and new works. Without such rethinking, we forfeit opportunities to participate in the continuing project of reshaping a course that is central to the English curriculum in both secondary schools and universities; we deprive our students of engaging learning experiences; and, since motion is always relative, we risk creating distances between ourselves and our colleagues by standing still.

American literature is continually being made and remade in response to shifting critical tastes; the complex interactions of economic, political, and aesthetic considerations that produce anthologies; the choices individual teachers make as they decide what to assign; and the writing that students—the next generation of authors—produce. A quick scan of articles published recently by literary critics shows that they write more about authors like Zora Neale Hurston and Frederick Douglass than they do about F. Scott Fitzgerald and John Steinbeck, on whom considerable critical attention was once focused. Similar changes are evident in the six-pound texts that students lug down the hall: The table of contents in most any recent anthology of American literature is likely to include names like Álvar Núñez Cabeza de Vaca, Gwendolyn Brooks, and N. Scott Momaday instead of Conrad Richter, Amy Lowell, and Willa Cather. The way anthologies represent authors—with a brief mention, an excerpt, or an entire selection—also shifts with time. In turn, teachers "make" American literature with every reading assignment. Telling students to skip over the anthology's new section on Native American literature helps to create American literature as surely as does bringing copies of Sharon Olds's poems to class. And students who blur genres by incorporating personal accounts into the traditional essay contribute, just as more sophisticated published writers do, to the production of new forms and topics that will "make" future American literatures. The stiff covers and sheer weight of anthologies, alphabetical reading lists, and the chronological movement from the Puritans to twentieth-century literature suggest a fixed and static perspective on American literature that needs to be countered by allowing its dynamic and changing nature, its "making," to become more visible to our students. Without this awareness, they may assume that American literature is exactly and only what they read in our classes.

The term "American" has in fact become increasingly contested. Shifting national, economic, historical, and cultural forces all contribute to the complexity of defining what "American" might mean. Does it refer to persons who live anywhere in this hemisphere, or to those who live on the North American continent, or only to those who live in the United States? What about people from the Caribbean, and both the African diaspora and the Hispanic cultures from that region? How do we categorize writers like T. S. Eliot who were born in the United States but spent much of their lives abroad? What about authors like Morris Rosenfeld who immigrated to the United States but wrote in Yiddish? How about writers like Michael Ondaatje who were born elsewhere (Sri Lanka in his case) but live in Canada and write in English about "American" topics like Billy the Kid. When "American" modifies "literature," more questions emerge. Does the term refer to texts written only in English? What about writings like those of Sandra Cisneros that include both English and Spanish passages? How do we categorize works written in Native American languages like Lakota or Cherokee? Do these count as American literature? None of these questions yields to an easy answer, but we assume that each is worth considering and exploring with students in an American literature class.

We use the term "literatures" to signal the ever growing and changing meanings that attach to what we call the literary. The computer's spell checker insists on correcting this term, but we stick with it because it signals our need to ask whether the category of the literary can be expanded to include a broader range of works. Most of us would agree that the Matthew Arnold definition—"the best that has been thought and said"—is no longer entirely adequate to describe what we mean when we say "literatures," but providing a succinct definition of this term is not easy. A quick glance at the self-descriptions of the University of Michigan's English Department in 1985 and 1995 illustrates the difficulty. In 1985 the description began, "Literature, broadly defined, represents the best that has been thought and said in the world. The literatures of England and America are not only extremely rich but are also readily accessible" (*University of Michigan Bulletin* 85). In this description the definition of literature appears succinct and clear; there seems to be little uncertainty about its meaning. Now consider the 1995 description: "The present study of literature has returned with particular force and new point to a very old consideration—that language and literature are necessarily understood as social products and agents, deeply implicated in the processes and questions that interest, and at times, agitate society more generally" (*University of Michigan Bulletin* 72). This description tells us more about the forces that help to create literature, but it offers a much less fixed view of the world in which literature exists. The distance between the two descriptions shows a shift away from the development of taste through aesthetic sensibilities and toward an emphasis on the social, political, and economic contexts surrounding texts. The 1995 description, with its emphasis upon the socially constructed and historically contingent nature of literature, invites an interrogation of 1985's Arnoldian definition with questions such as: "What does 'broadly defined' mean?" "What gets included in the category of literature?" "Who gets to decide what's 'best'?" "On what basis?" "What do you mean by 'accessible'?" "To whom is it accessible?" We believe that exploring the shifting terms that surround American literature will help students understand how literature shapes and is shaped by a given cultural context.

Teaching American literature these days means dealing regularly with complicated questions about the texts we teach. It also means asking additional questions about the approaches we take in our classrooms. What teaching challenges do new texts such as Toni Morrison's *Beloved* or Art Spiegelman's *Maus* pose, and what opportunities do they offer? How is our teaching of more familiar texts such as Nathaniel Hawthorne's *The Scarlet Letter* and Mark Twain's *The Adventures of Huckleberry Finn* shaped by recent scholarship? What are the effects of pairing a canonical work such as *The Great Gatsby* with a recently recovered one such as Nella Larsen's *Passing?* How can we call upon the resources of local archives—in libraries and historical societies—to enhance students' understanding of current debates about the concept of regionalism in American literature? How do local conventions, such as the daily recitation of the pledge of allegiance in Georgia high schools (or the absence of same in Michigan schools) shape our pedagogies? How might we identify and celebrate literary qualities in student writing? How can we convey the value of literature (however we define it) to our students? How do new technologies, particularly the Internet, reshape the ways we think about and present literature? How might our classes be enlivened by the images, out-of-print texts, author Web sites, and quantities of information available with a few clicks of the mouse?

This book does not promise to answer all of these questions, but it offers many insights from teachers who have been reading together, thinking hard, developing new approaches, and reflecting on their own classroom practices. In addition to a common interest in rethinking the ways we teach American literature, the contributors to this collection shared the experience of participating in one or more workshops that brought together university and secondary school teachers. Modeled on and developed in cooperation with the National Writing Project, these workshops were originally supported by a grant from the National Endowment for the Humanities. Making American Literatures, the umbrella project under which these workshops developed, was directed by Anne Ruggles Gere in Michigan, Donald McQuade in California, and Sarah Robbins in Georgia. Linked into an American community that extends from the Atlantic to the Pacific, touching the Great Lakes along the way, these workshops provided a forum for doing the kind of reading, writing, talking, and thinking that can transform classroom practices. Within this community we discovered many continuities that extend across institutional lines. High school and university instructors teach many of the same texts, they share common interests in pedagogy, and the first-year student at the university is just months away from the high school senior.

In particular, we realized that graduate students, who typically teach many of the lower division undergraduate courses, are in a particularly good position to develop collaborations with their colleagues in secondary schools. Steeped in the highly specialized work of their dissertations, graduate students bring to workshop discussions rich and highly useful background information about works under consideration. Secondary school teachers, usually some years distant from their own literary training, welcome the insights of their university colleagues, and, in turn, bring to the discussion the wisdom of their classroom practices. For graduate students who were much less confident about how to teach and how to represent their teaching to hiring committees, workshop discussions were invaluable to their development as teachers. Accordingly, graduate students (some now professors) number among the books' contributors.

We decided to write this book as a way of extending our conversations beyond our own workshop groups. While we have all benefited (and some of us continue to benefit) from summer meetings with colleagues who teach American literature, we recognize that our discussions are part of the much larger project of rethinking the teaching of American literature. We adapt the project name for our book title as a way of capturing issues central to recovering American literature, but this book extends beyond the project. Before we participated in this project, many of us had looked in vain for a book that suggested new ways to think about and teach American literature. By putting our ideas and experiences in written form, we could share with distant colleagues the new energy, perceptions, and enthusiasms we bring to our classes.

Because the school subject known as "American literature" is most frequently represented by the hulking anthologies adopted by school districts and carried by juniors or seniors in high school, Section I of this book explores ways of helping students see how anthologies are made, how they function in schools, and how they can be transformed. Section II focuses on what we have learned from our students, both about them as learners and about American literature. For many of us, it was a question from a student, often a rather impertinent student, that first caused us to start asking questions about what we were doing in American literature classes. A number of us began teaching when student populations were more homogeneous than they are today, and our increasingly diverse student bodies have taught us new ways of thinking about multicultural society. From here, the book turns in Section III to the issue of location—not just place or region, although that is clearly central, but also location in hierarchies of high and low culture, locations in the past that come to us through archives, and locations in the new spaces opened by Internet technology. Because our workshops led us to new and/or recently recovered texts, we also turned to the strategy of literary pairing in order to bring new voices and perspectives into the curriculum while simultaneously complicating and enriching our thinking about more familiar work. Thus Section IV includes several accounts of pairing texts in American literature courses.

"Yes," you may be saying, "this all sounds fine, but it makes me wonder if everything always went so smoothly. Didn't teachers experience any difficulties? What about the curriculum constraints teachers face?" In anticipation of such questions, Section V steps back to consider the difficulties of changing classroom practices, the implications of building bridges between high schools and universities, and the ways an individual teacher's thought and practice can begin to shape a school culture.

Some of the chapters in each section can be read during a planning period or lunch, while others will take a bit longer. We sought chapters of varying lengths to make this book accessible to a wide audience among our busy teacher colleagues. All, however, speak from and to the community of learners who teach American literatures. One of the things we have learned is the value of collaborating with other teachers. In a world where high-stakes testing, voucher plans, and political forces threaten to distract us, we found support in the steady conversations with colleagues. We learned with and from one another. As Sarah Robbins notes in her Afterword, ours is an unsettling and unsettled work. The fixed lines of print on the following pages should not be read as an indication that our work is done. Rather, we extend an invitation to you, our readers, to join us in the ongoing making of American literatures.

Works Cited

University of Michigan Bulletin: College of Literature, Science and Arts 13.12 (1984–85): 85.

University of Michigan Bulletin: College of Literature, Science and Arts 23.16 (1994–95): 72.

1 A Gathering of Flowers: Making American Literature Anthologies

Anne Ruggles Gere
University of Michigan

My first experience with American literature was, perhaps like yours, shaped by an anthology. It was my junior year in high school, and the teacher in my English A class (the one for college prep students) handed out big yellow books and assigned us to read the section on the Puritans. I don't remember the publisher or the edition of this book, but it was relatively new in 1961. Mine was a small and poor school district that didn't purchase new class sets of books very frequently.

My teacher—I'll call him Mr. Jacks—rushed us through the Puritans so that we would have plenty of time for the Transcendentalists. I had trouble understanding the introduction to that section of the book— all the language about the great oversoul was confusing, but Mr. Jacks insisted that this was central to understanding writers like Emerson and Thoreau. Mr. Jacks, who was later fired for being a Communist sympathizer and, according to local rumor, was last seen swimming toward the USSR, pushed our class through most of the selections in the American literature book. That is not what I remember about his course in American literature, however. At the same time that he urged us to answer the questions at the end of each selection, Mr. Jacks kept talking about the revolution that paperback books were causing.

I remember standing in his tiny porch/study watching him point at his library of paperback books carefully lined up on stacked bricks and boards. "These will transform reading and teaching in this country," he exclaimed. As I inhaled the fragrant stew his wife was cooking for them and their three little red-haired children, I wondered why he was making such a big deal about these paperback books. It wasn't until

I became a teacher myself several years later that I understood what Mr. Jacks was talking about. In 1967, at Princeton High School in New Jersey, I began to understand how anthologies shape teaching. If it wasn't in the anthology, I couldn't teach it. Fortunately, though, Princeton had a book depository where I could check out paperback class sets of works not included in the anthology. Mr. Jacks was right; paperback books could revolutionize teaching. But it has been an incomplete revolution.

Research tells us that many classes in American literature still rely heavily, if not exclusively, on anthologies. Applebee's 1996 study revealed that anthologies shape what is read in English classes. They also shape *how* it is read. Both writing assignments and class discussions are often directed by anthology questions that emphasize factual details of plot and vocabulary. Since anthologies are here to stay and will probably continue to influence *what* students read in American literature classes, it makes sense for teachers to address *how* that reading might be done.

When I opened my big yellow book in the eleventh grade, I assumed that the title meant what it said, that all of American literature was contained within those two hard covers. It didn't occur to me, as I suspect it does not occur to many students, that someone had made choices—Edna St. Vincent Millay but not Frances Harper; Jonathan Edwards but not Chief Seattle; poetry by women but essays by men—about what version of American literature I would see. The editors of my anthology "made" American literature for me.

One of the several goals of this book is to consider the various perspectives on American literature offered by anthologies from different eras and publishers, to consider how the convergence of economics, copyright, tradition, editorial taste, market forces, and other factors "make" literature. Scanning the table of contents in several different anthologies can be an interesting exercise, especially if one keeps track of which authors are included or excluded. Thinking about the sources and implications of these inclusions and exclusions can lead to complicated questions. How do the entailments of Faulkner's estate contribute to the fact that "A Rose for Emily" is his most frequently anthologized selection? What does it mean for a Native American student to see American Indian literatures represented only by traditional Iroquois poetry (and that in translation), with no contemporary texts and no texts by writers affiliated with other tribes, such as, say, Joy Harjo or Sherman Alexie? Anthologies don't just determine which selections students read; they also shape the ways their texts are read. If we can't abandon or change the content of anthologies, we can at least resist the fact that certain possibilities are closed off by opening up others in the apparatus of introductions, author biographies, and questions attached to individual selections. Toward this end, the articles in this section demonstrate how several teachers have analyzed, transformed, or supplemented their anthologies.

Enacting John Clifford's principle of critical literacy, George M. Seaman invited his students to analyze the audience for one of their grammar texts. This led him to undertake a similar exercise with a literature text, and, calling upon Paul Lauter's definition of the canon as "the list of works and authors believed to be sufficiently important to read, study, write about, teach—and thus transmit to the next generation of readers" (xxxiii), he encouraged his students to take a critical look at the canon offered by their literature anthologies. In concluding, he speculates that students who feel alienated from (and by) the exclusionary power of the American literature curriculum might feel more like valued members of a learning community if they were encouraged to help construct a class anthology composed of readings selected by members of the class.

Mimi Dyer implemented a version of Seaman's suggestion by asking her students to create their own anthology from the works included in their official class anthology. Instead of urging the class through a predetermined syllabus that began with the Puritans, Dyer asked her students to choose from the anthology ten selections that interested them, as well as identify literary periods and genres that they wanted to focus on. Using the students' stated preferences, she worked with them to create a syllabus that began with twentieth-century American literature, skipped around through other periods, and ended with the Puritans. Dyer says that disturbing the chronology did not prevent students from seeing literature in historical context, and, more important, her students became engaged with the material because they made choices about it and participated in the discovery process.

Linda Templeton enacted another version of Seaman's suggestion as she took up Frances Foster's definition of *anthologia* as a gathering of flowers. Specifically, Templeton asked her students to create a regional anthology. Beginning with the concepts of culture, community, and heritage, she asked students to identify changes within their corner of the Southeast and discuss how these changes affected their culture and heritage. Then Templeton sent her ninth graders on a scavenger hunt to find a variety of regional literary artifacts. From the collection of artifacts, students selected the ones that they felt were most representative of the South, with the caveat that the anthology should include a variety of genres. Then students wrote a justification for the items included in the anthology.

For Tim Murnen, a former department chair, the selections included in an anthology tell only part of the story. Murnen asks *how* authors are represented and how those representations shape teaching. Focusing on the presentation of Álvar Núñez Cabeza de Vaca in two anthologies, he demonstrates the kind of critical reading teachers can undertake to help their students understand that the way a selection is presented, the processes of excerpting, and the materials surrounding the selection all help to make American literature.

Dave Winter offers still another critical approach to anthologies by investigating the American literature course at his school since 1965. Through interviews with his colleagues, examination of anthologies used in the school over the decades, and analysis of the changing racial composition of the student body, he shows how multiple forces interact with anthologies to shape the teaching of American literature in a particular location. Together these chapters show that teachers—as well as publishers of paperback books—can revolutionize the teaching of American literature.

Works Cited

Applebee, Arthur N. *Curriculum As Conversation: Transforming Traditions of Teaching and Learning.* Chicago: U of Chicago P, 1996.

Clifford, John. "Enacting Critical Literacy." *The Right to Literacy.* Ed. Andrea A. Lunsford, Helene Moglen, and James Slevin. New York: MLA, 1990. 255–61.

Lauter, Paul, ed. *The Heath Anthology of American Literature.* 3rd ed. Boston: Houghton, 1998.

1 What Students Need to Know about the Canon

George M. Seaman
Lassiter High School, Marietta, Georgia

At the beginning of each year, the students in my British literature class complete a short lesson on the history of the English language. Typically, I rely on readings from *The Story of English*. In years past, this was my primary source for information because our literature books did not contain information on this topic. This year, however, my school system adopted new textbooks for all classes, and I was pleased to find that both the literature and grammar books included short (two- to three-page) essays on the origins of our language.

When I reviewed the selections in our new textbooks, I realized that it would be beneficial for my students to compare excerpts from *The Story of English* with readings from their new books. More specifically, I asked students to read an excerpt from *Story* and one essay from either their grammar or literature book, and then find elements in the writing that might reveal whom the writers saw as their intended audience. My students quickly discovered that the *Story* text was geared toward a more academic, specialized audience. To support this claim, my students analyzed characteristics such as the length and complexity of sentences and the level of diction used by the writer. I fully anticipated these responses. However, my students found other elements in the writing to further support their findings. For example, the excerpts distributed to the students from *Story* contained no pictures or graphics. The selections in their class texts, in contrast, seemed to offer an equal balance of information presented in text form and information contained in more visually appealing boxes or graphs. Students also noticed that the paragraphs in the *Story* selections were longer and that the text ran across the entire page, from the left margin to the right. The student texts contained smaller paragraphs that were divided more frequently by headings, and the pages were also organized into three vertical columns.

After we compared our findings, I asked my students to consider how these decisions might influence a potential reader of the texts. All of my students seemed to agree that the *Story* text (at least as rendered in the reading excerpts) did little to invite readers to the material. Several said that the writers probably assumed that any potential reader encountering this text would already have some interest in the material; otherwise, the reader would not be encouraged to continue reading, simply because of the manner in which the information was presented on the page. On the contrary, most students agreed that the books published for high school students did some very obvious things in presenting the material in order to make the information more accessible and appealing to someone not necessarily interested in the history of the English language.

As I sat and listened to my students' comments, I was pleased to find that the lesson seemed to meet my objectives. Students were able to experience this concept of audience directly by analyzing different texts to see what writers could do to engage, or possibly disengage, various types of readers. Furthermore, as I reflected on one student comment in particular, I realized further that this was an effective lesson because it allowed me to learn something new about my students and their attitudes toward reading and writing. When I asked them what factors influenced their decision in choosing the literature book reading or the grammar book reading, one student replied, "Of course, I chose the literature book. Why would anyone want to read something in a grammar book?"

I suppose this student's distaste for grammar books stems from his experiences with such texts. I imagine that he has learned that grammar books deal with rules and regulations. I imagine that he has grown weary of the authoritarian and disempowering approach that grammar books can take toward language instruction. I imagine that he is fed up with grammar books sending him the message, "This constitutes good writing." As I thought about the negative experiences that many students must have with grammar books, I wondered if their American literature anthologies were sending similar messages. Do certain rules and regulations come into play when editorial boards are making decisions about which writers to include in these anthologies? Does the authority that is the canon marginalize certain students by perpetuating the notion that to be a literate person means to read and master these selected writers? When encountering certain writers in their literature books, do students think to question the fact that someone has decided for them, "This constitutes good writing"?

My experiences in the classroom have taught me that the answer to the first two questions is a definite yes, while the answer to the third is no. Students do not stop to question the authority or legitimacy of the canon, because most of their literature teachers do not encourage them to do so. In "Enacting a Critical Literacy," John Clifford argues that "the plan of the dominant ideology has not been to alter and mend but to seamlessly weave students into the fabric of our society through the efforts of conscientious English teachers understandably more concerned with managing crowded classes than with the apparently remote abstractions of cultural hegemony" (256).

In order for my students to develop their own sense of critical literacy as espoused by Clifford, they need to have a basic understanding of the canon and the canonization process. A good starting point would be Paul Lauter's definition of the canon in his introduction to the *Heath Anthology of American Literature*: "the list of works and authors believed to be sufficiently important to read, study, write about, teach—and thus transmit to the next generation of readers" (xxxiii). Yes, students need to know what the canon *is*, as described by Lauter before the dash, but more importantly, they need to know what the canon *does*, which is addressed after the dash. Also, students need to be familiar with some of the sociopolitical forces that help shape the contents of literature books, and, as Lauter suggests, the powerful influence these contents can have in shaping future views on literature and literacy. Students need to understand that there is a certain amount of power being exercised by the editorial boards and publishers who determine whose writing they read. In describing Freire's and Giroux's views, Fingeret and Drennon claim "when adults have a critical perspective on the political and social nature of literacy, they can engage in action that uses literacy as a tool in an intentional way" (63). Similarly, high school students can also benefit from such a critical understanding.

If students are given the opportunity to critically assess the canonization process, they will be able to exercise more control in some of their literary decisions and actions. One activity that might allow students to achieve this goal would be to construct a class anthology that is made up of writers and readings selected by the individual class members. By allowing students to find writers outside the mainstream and including such writers in our curriculum, not only will we be challenging the notion of the traditional canon; we will also be legitimizing the multiple literacies that students bring to class. In addition, we will be honoring the communal nature of literacy. Finally, our selection of writers will say much more about us as individual members of a learning community and as members of a society than does simply reacting to a list of authors predetermined by a group of faceless publishing executives.

I can't imagine that E. D. Hirsch would be very fond of this activity. After all, this is no way to go about "ensur[ing] our children's mastery of American literate culture" (18). There are two very serious shortcomings, though, with Hirsch's approach. The first is that my students are not involved in deciding the standards for this culture. Unfortunately, someone else has already decided which things should be significant in determining the role of literacy in my students' lives. They are not encouraged to think critically and to question. They can't be held accountable for their decisions because they make none. Second, some of my students have no desire to belong to this American literate culture. As with my students' reaction to the reading excerpts from *The Story of English* and their realization that this text did little to invite them to the material, some of my students feel that Hirsch has done little to include them in his vision of American culture. What are we to do with them? I don't think we can simply just write them off. All of our students need to feel like they are valued members of a learning community, like they have something significant and valuable to offer to the lives of others. By accepting the exclusionary powers of the traditional canon, we allow such students to continue seeing themselves as outsiders. In James Britton's introduction to *Prospect and Retrospect*, he provides a similar message: "Gain control of a person's language and you determine his fortune, because you have usurped his natural capacity to interpret his own perceptions, indeed you narrow the very range of those perceptions" (1). Rather, students need to experience language as a means to expand their range of perceptions. By allowing students to develop a more critical perspective on the canon, English teachers can begin to use literature as a means to create a more inclusive sense of community in the classroom.

Works Cited

Britton, James. *Prospect and Retrospect: Selected Essays of James Britton*. Ed. Gordon M. Pradl. Montclair, NJ: Boynton/Cook, 1982.

Clifford, John. "Enacting Critical Literacy." *The Right to Literacy*. Ed. Andrea A. Lunsford, Helene Moglen, and James Slevin. New York: MLA, 1990. 255–61.

Fingeret, Hanna Arlene, and Cassandra Drennon. *Literacy for Life: Adult Learners, New Practices*. New York: Teachers College, 1997.

Hirsch, E. D., Jr. *Cultural Literacy: What Every American Needs To Know*. Boston: Houghton, 1987.

Lauter, Paul, ed. *The Heath Anthology of American Literature*. 3rd ed. Boston: Houghton, 1998.

McCrum, Robert, William Cran, and Robert MacNeil. *The Story of English*. Rev. ed. New York: Penguin, 1993.

2 Invitation to Anthologize

Mimi Dyer
South Forsyth High School, Cumming, Georgia

Sitting in front of my computer during winter break, I began wondering just how I could incorporate some of what Frances Foster had instilled in me when she took part in the summer workshop in which I was participating. Her two days with us had been so energizing that I was ripe for something different, anything *except* beginning with the Puritans—our stalwart yet (pardon me) boring forefathers—and marching through American Literature chronologically, reading (or in most cases skimming) every selection.

So I opened my familiar, well-worn, black-and-white composition book and turned back to my notes of that summer. Some phrases definitely stood out: "anthology user vs. anthologizer" and "anthologies *make* literature." Then I turned the page and found another question—this one asterisked: "How do we anthologize the anthology we are presented?" With these thoughts in mind, I decided to change the course of history—or rather the literature that accompanied the history—by inviting my students to resist the traditional chronological approach to American literature.

Forsyth County, like most localities in Georgia, had just gone through the arduous task of textbook adoption during the spring, and for me, like so many others, the process was painful: hours of staff development time poring over publishers' offerings and still more hours thinking about how to "use" the selected 1283-page tome (and that's the student edition!) with its myriad ancillary materials. There is more "stuff" than any one teacher could use in two years, much less one year, much *less* one semester, which is how much time I had to cover all of American literature (South Forsyth is on the 4 x 4 block system—four ninety-minute classes for eighteen weeks). I knew we could not possibly do justice to all the selected works, but I also knew that I didn't want to make the decision about what to include and exclude on my own. I wanted my students to have some choice, to be active participants in the process. That way they could become anthologizers instead of just anthology users—and thereby *make* American literature.

Now please understand that I did not come to this conclusion quite this easily, but I have a limited amount of space here. Suffice to say that this idea had been swirling around in my head since July, and, because all eleventh-grade literature classes in our school that year were taught during second semester, I had all of first semester to consider what I might do. Since our English classes are heterogeneously grouped (with the exception of honors and AP), it was possible that in a given class I might have some special education students, some students going into the workforce after graduation, some going to technical schools, and some going to colleges and universities.

Maybe I shouldn't do this with such a mix of abilities. I might confuse some of them and lose others altogether. Still others, I know, like the stability and comfort of going through a textbook in order. Then I remembered one of my pedagogical mantras: Teach to the top, and the others will follow. So I made the decision: *Go for it!*

But when I actually sat down to plan what I would say to the students, doubts came at me from all sides, like precisely placed mortar rounds: *You don't know* any *of these kids, so what makes you think you can pull this off? What will your colleagues say? How will the administration react? What happens if parents complain that their children's teacher is a lunatic?*

Well, I finally planned not to plan. *If I don't know what's going to happen, I can't prepare a talk. Moreover, I can't plan a syllabus.* Not give out a syllabus on the first day of class? Heresy! But the first day began with no plan, other than the fact that we were *not* going to go chronologically through the text. Exactly what we *were* going to do depended on what we decided as a class.

I started with what I thought was a good question: "What did you like most about your previous literature classes?" *Surely this will get some positive responses.*

"Nothin'." *Obviously the question is less brilliant than I first surmised. What do I do now?*

Not willing to abandon ship at the first threatening wave, I broached the topic in a different way. I asked students to divide their papers into two columns and label one column "Yes" and the other column "No."

"Now," I cajoled, "see if you can come up with at least five items for each column—anything at all that is appropriate in a public school classroom." (I always try to head off the less than appropriate answers.) *Ah ha! I see a few smirks, so I'm not lost after all.*

"Take about seven minutes or so." *I don't know why, but five minutes is always too short and ten is too long.*

After the allotted time, I instructed students to number their entries in order of importance, and then I invited them to write their number one ideas from each column on the white board without looking at what others had written. After everyone was finished, we looked at the results, and, sure enough, there were a number of duplicate answers.

When we tallied up the numbers, the following answers "won":

Yes	No
class discussion	lecture
variety of activities	tests
group work	group work

I can't say that I was surprised by the answers—even by the appearance of group work in both columns. What did interest me was the fact that nowhere on the whiteboard, not even as a single entry, did the word "choice" appear—nor did any synonym, derivative, or approximation thereof. Again I had assumed that students' answers would fall into the pattern I wanted, and again I was wrong.

Now what? How do I get them to go in the direction I want? After all, the idea is for them to have a voice, so if I tell them where to go and how to get there, I have defeated my purpose. My plan of not having a plan looks like it might die a very fast death.

I felt like an actress who had been given a situational prompt with no scripted lines. I was definitely on my own and feeling out of my depth. *Maybe I can use one of the activities that we discussed in the interminable staff development textbook workshops.*

"OK. These are very interesting answers, and I'll take them into consideration when I make our daily plans, but right now I want to invite you to take the rest of our time together today, which is about thirty minutes, and surf the anthology that I gave you earlier. I want you to find ten items—stories, poems, photos, paintings, anything that you find interesting. Jot down the page number, and tomorrow we will get into groups to make up a scavenger hunt for each other. The object is to allow everyone to become familiar with the textbook, so don't find things that are too buried for others to find." After they complained about having homework on the first day, they began flipping through the pages.

The next day, students came in with their lists—well, not everyone. There were those—the same ones we all have in our classes—who couldn't find the time or energy or motivation for homework. But I didn't let them off the hook. I split up what the kids call "slackers" and made them the leaders of the five groups. Then I let the others self-divide.

"OK, I'm giving you forty minutes to cull the best ten questions from your group and to type them up on the computers [I have six in my room]. We'll paste them into one document and print a copy for each team. We'll then take the last forty minutes for everyone to find the answers, and the team that finds the most correct answers will win a prize."

"Really?" asked one. "Are you serious?"

"I'm always serious about prizes," I responded without a hint of a smile.

"What is it?" they all seemed to ask at the same time. "Food?"

"No, not food. Something much more valuable than that," I offered. "You'll just have to wait and see."

So forty minutes flew by and each group developed ten questions. Most of the pieces were easily found in either the table of contents or one of the several indexes in the back of the book: titles of poems or paintings, quotations by famous authors, and dates of particular literary periods. Interestingly, the majority of questions came from the contemporary section of the anthology. *Whoa! Am I reading more into this than I should? Don't assume you know how this is going to turn out. Just let it unfold naturally. Remember what happened the other times you predicted their responses.*

When, at the end of class, we had a winning team, I handed out the prizes: Homework Passes (to be used at their discretion for a daily assignment). I could hear murmurs in the background.

"Wow! If I had known that was the prize, I would have tried harder to win."

"Randy, you slacked off and made our team lose. Look what we could have won!"

"Gosh, I can't believe it's almost time for the bell to ring!"

Indeed, I had two minutes to make the next assignment. "Guys, before you start packing up your book bags, I want to give you something to think about tonight. Take home your textbooks and look at the different periods that divide the literature. You can find the page numbers in the front of the book. Skim over the selections and see what you think about each section in general and any piece in particular. We'll talk about them tomorrow." *I sure hope this works.*

Day number three and we still had no syllabus or any clear direction of where we were going. If the students were uncomfortable, they didn't show it, and I found myself surprisingly calm, especially since Ms. Organization *always* knew what she was going to do weeks in advance. *Oh well, this is a good exercise for me too. Relax and go with the flow. No one is going to notice or care that you aren't knee-deep into the Puritans by now.*

I probably should have considered the question of students transferring into or out of my class; we were, after all, still in the first few days of the second semester, and we all know how many schedules change during that time. But I was so intent on the excitement of something different that I didn't give it a thought. Also, our school population was surprisingly stable, and I knew from experience that we would have few to transfer *into* my class from another school, especially considering the time of year.

Before we began any discussion, I asked everyone to jot down on a piece of scrap paper the literary period they liked the best. Of the twenty-five students, eighteen chose "Contemporary Literature: 1950 to Present," the very last section in the anthology—the one that most teachers never get to. Three others—those in the drama club—chose "American Drama," and four did not respond. *This is falling too nicely into place. There must be a hitch somewhere.*

"Well," I said, "this is very interesting. No one chose any of the literature before the twentieth century. I wonder why?"

"Mrs. Dyer," chimed in Marcey, one of the drama students, "it's because everything written before then is boring, in language we don't even use any more." *Here's my best chance—better take it!*

"Okay, if that's how you feel, what do you think about the idea of starting there—here—with contemporary literature?" There was utter silence, not one response. *Uh oh, you're in trouble.* "Or not," I quickly recovered. "We can start at the beginning and go straight through. It's fine." *I guess my plan has really failed this time. I'm fresh out of ideas.*

The room exploded with "NOOOO!" followed by a chorus of groans. David explained, "We're just so surprised that you asked us what we thought, we were speechless for a second. That's all. What do you say, guys, we can handle this, can't we?" David wanted desperately to start somewhere else because he had begun American literature, with the Puritans, the previous semester at another school, and he knew what to avoid. *Thank you, David!*

With an enthusiastic approval rating from my audience, I proceeded. "Great. We'll start with the present. We can then work backwards to the beginning, or we can skip around. What do you think?"

This time everyone participated in the discussion, and after a few minutes, we decided to skip around. I typed up the names of the literary periods on a piece of paper, cut the names into strips and placed them in a basket. I then allowed students to draw the strips and taped them on the wall. Finally, we had the order of study, and wouldn't you know it, by a twist of fate, "The Beginnings" was at the very end. (No kidding!)

Epilogue

I'm sure you're all wondering how it turned out. Surprisingly well. While I worried at first that students would be confused by exploring literature and historical contexts out of chronological order, I discovered that it made absolutely no difference to them. They were able to compartmentalize each period and appreciate (well, maybe not entirely) the works on their own merit. And we spent three days, which some felt was still too long, on the Puritans.

My concerns about how different levels of students would handle the unorthodox approach to studying American literature also proved to be unfounded. Because at the very beginning we made decisions together, the students supported each other and became a collaborative learning community. We shared freely with each other, and, by recognizing strengths and weaknesses, we were able to help almost everyone reach his or her potential.

Did I give students choices about what to read within each literary period? Sometimes yes and sometimes no. My main concern was to offer an alternative to the popular chronological approach while not abrogating total responsibility for the students' American Literature education. But I continued the pattern of inviting them to make choices in writing prompts and outside readings.

So how did this experience influence my ideas about anthologies? I now know that students can be anthologizers instead of anthology users and that sometimes it is better to "teach" rather than to "cover." I see that a scavenger hunt can help deconstruct an anthology by encouraging students to pull it apart at the very beginning. They gain control over the text rather than allowing the text to intimidate them. But most of all, I have confirmed once again my belief that students become engaged with the material when they have some choice, when they are treated as co-explorers in the discovery process.

I understand the constraints that prevent this approach from being successful in other classrooms—administrative requirements, logistical problems with transfer students, and exit exams, to name a few. But for now, in my classroom, I have the latitude to make the decision not to march through American literature from beginning to end.

And sometimes it's more interesting to find out where we are before we embark on the voyage of where we've come from—or where we're going.

3 Anthologia

Linda Templeton
East Paulding High School, Kennesaw, Georgia

During a summer workshop at Kennesaw State University, I had the pleasure of listening to Dr. Frances Foster of Emory University speak regarding her research on Frances E. W. Harper and her lost novels. While Dr. Foster was speaking, she used the term anthologia and explained that it meant a gathering of flowers. Anthologia so intrigued me that I coerced my daughter into creating a pastel print illustrating the term anthologia. I shared the print with my colleagues, and we agreed that it could become the cover for the collection we had begun to imagine. From there, the regional anthology was born.

Why a regional anthology created by students? Through my encouraging students to examine American literature firsthand—instead of presenting them with an anthology already bound and ready to be consumed—they get to research, dig in, wade around, and plunge headfirst into literary works that they might otherwise never have the opportunity to experience. As educators, we constantly want our students to take ownership of their learning process, and a research project such as this regional anthology provides the means for them to do just that. In addition, since students write a justification for each selection that they want to include in the regional anthology, they create their own answers for a perennial question: Why should we read this?

What class could handle this project? My ninth-grade honors English students are my guinea pigs, but I believe that this project would work well with American literature students at any level. Certainly, students need to have access to a well-stocked library, computers, and the Internet; otherwise, it would be necessary for you to bring the information to your students, which would hamper the research process. After all, we want the students doing the research—not us.

When this project first began, it was intended to focus on just literature, but as the plans solidified, I found that a regional anthology would need to encompass much more. Along with researching the literature, students need to learn about the region—know the historical facts, the populace, the language, and the culture(s)—all of the details that shape a region.

Before any of our real work begins, we explore three concepts: culture, community, and heritage. These concepts are at the heart of the regional anthology because I want the students to understand that the cultures, communities, and heritages within a region shape the region itself. Hopefully, as students realize the importance of culture, community, and heritage, they will realize the effect that each factor has on the literature coming out of a region.

After we have come to terms with definitions and guidelines for delineating culture, community, and heritage, we begin our regional anthology with a close-up look at the Southeast. Since we live in the Southeast, we work together to create the Southeast regional section of the anthology—as a model for the other regions. To get us started, we read Olive Ann Burns's *Cold Sassy Tree* during the summer. When students return in August, we study the novel and the Southern culture, community, and heritage within it. The novel is set in a small Georgia town (Cold Sassy) in the early twentieth century. Burns, a Georgia native, used her hometown, Commerce, as the model for Cold Sassy, and, as part of our regional study, students begin examining their own communities, seeking information on what shapes the communities in which they live.

Since our county is listed as one of the fastest-growing counties in the United States, students examine ongoing changes in our county community. Change is a force that the characters in *Cold Sassy Tree* battle with throughout the book, and I have designed a tiered group activity so that my students can investigate change in a variety of ways. We begin by answering the following questions as a class: What do you think of when you hear the word *change*? What kinds of things change? What is it about these things that changes? Once we have discussed these questions as a class, students break up into groups and proceed as follows:

Group 1 categorizes the insights generated from the whole-class discussion of change, putting them into groups and giving each group a heading.

Group 2 brainstorms a list of things that do not change, considering the following questions:

> What are some things that are always the same or that always happen the same way?
>
> Look back at the list of things that *do* change. While those things are changing, can you think of anything else that stays the same?
>
> What can you say about the ideas or things that do not change? How could you put them into groups? What could you call each group? Why?

Group 3 thinks about whether the following ideas and practices show change: routines or habits, rules and regulations, table manners, laws, customs of cultures. As part of their assignment, they explain their answers. Group 3 should use the following questions to guide them in their thinking process:

If these ideas do show change, would they fit into categories?
If these ideas do not show change, how would you categorize them?

Group 4 brainstorms answers to the following questions:

How is change linked to time? Why do different changes take different amounts of time?

Does change always represent progress, i.e., making things better? If, on the other hand, change can be either positive or negative, which of the changes we discussed could be called good changes? Which are bad changes? Are there any that could be both good and bad? How?

Change may be perceived as orderly or random. Can we predict change? What are some changes where you know they will happen, and how they will happen, and what are some that are surprises?

Does change happen in all areas of our world? Where have you seen changes happening in the world around you?

Change may happen naturally or be caused by people. What causes change? What are some changes that people cannot do anything about? What are some changes that cannot happen without people?

Group 5 focuses on the following question: How do our ideas about change and its generalizations apply or not apply to these items: nonliving things, traditions, religious rituals, universal truths.

Group 6 uses the class definition of change to brainstorm several examples of change from our novel *Cold Sassy Tree*.

Each group is given the opportunity to discuss their findings on change, which eventually tie in with the novel, our community, and the regional anthology.

To continue our study of the Southeast—and to help my students to get a more in-depth look at Southern literature and culture—we go to the media center at our school and have a Regional Scavenger Hunt. Students are given a list of items—all which pertain to the Southeast—to find in the library: a novel, a poem, a short story, a famous landmark, a famous author, song lyrics, a television show set in the region, a movie set in the region, an artist whose works focus on the region, a famous painting from the region, a newspaper headline about a historical event, a playwright of the region, the most famous play by that playwright, an actor from the region, an actress from the region, a famous singer, a famous dance, the colors on the flag of the largest state of the region, the number of states in the region, and the names of the states within the region. Students compete against one another for a prize (e.g., a homework pass), and we take our "found" information back to class and continue our examination of the region. I wish I could take credit for this wonderful activity, but I have to give that to a fellow teacher. Andy Smith, an English teacher at Pebblebrook High School, shared this activity with me one summer at an honors institute at Kennesaw State University—which supports my theory that teachers are the best thieves in the world!

In completing our Southeast part of the regional anthology, students select what they feel is most representative of the Southeast, and we compile copies of our selections. Each regional section should include: novel(s), short stories, poetry, drama, music, nonfiction, art, movies, dance, historical documents, and miscellaneous findings (items that are unique and do not fit into one of the categories).

The next phase of our regional anthology requires dividing the students into seven groups and assigning each group a region. The seven regions are New England, the Mid-Atlantic, the Great Lakes, the Southwest, the Central region, the Mountains, and the Pacific. Within each group, students appoint a secretary/recorder and a spokesperson. Students should begin their work by brainstorming information that they already know about their region (i.e., states, people, large cities, industries, and so on). Each group is allowed to go to the library to perform the Scavenger Hunt for the assigned region. After the initial brainstorming and fact-finding activities are complete, students begin performing their research, exploring the literature, history, populace, language, and culture of their selected region. To help with the literature research, teachers may copy the tables of contents of several anthologies so that students can examine the literary titles and select possible works to research further.

After completing the research and selection process, students are to write justifications as to why these items should be included in the regional anthology. The length of the justifications will depend on the students' abilities and on the expectations of the teacher. The completed justifications are placed in the regional anthology with the collected information for each region. Since students have to justify the works that they include in the regional anthology, they will be able to answer the question, "Why should I read this?" Let's face it: If students justify why someone should read a certain selection, won't other students listen, especially more than they would listen to an adult?

The closing activity brings students and teacher together, as all write reflective essays commenting on the project as a whole. The reflective essays should include topics such as:

> What changes would you make for future regional anthologies?
>
> What did you enjoy? What did you hate?
>
> What could you do to make it better for you? What could you do to make it better for others in your group?

These reflections provide the teacher with an opportunity to fine-tune the project based on feedback from the students. It also allows students the time needed to assess their participation and, as appropriate, to make adjustments as they take part in future projects.

Allowing students to create a regional anthology empowers them as learners and researchers. They get to explore American literature first-hand without a teacher dictating what should be read and why. Through exploration they make the decisions—they take ownership of their education. I realize that this project appears to be quite large and time-consuming; however, I believe that my students are able to examine more literature with this project than I could possibly cover in a normal class setting, and that in itself makes this project worthwhile.

4 Making Literature with the Anthology

Tim Murnen
University of Michigan

Every so often I hear stories about how some textbook company wines and dines a group of teachers or district coordinators in an attempt to get them to commit to using the company's textbook. Such stories suggest the often invisible political and economic forces that can influence everyday curriculum in countless classrooms across America. No doubt these scenarios do take place. But my guess is that most folks who are given the task of choosing textbooks do so in relative isolation, as I did several years ago when I was the newly appointed English department chair at my high school. As is the case in many districts, my high school operated relatively independently: we were free to choose what texts we deemed appropriate for our students, with approval from the school's administration. As a result, I represented no large and influential district—just teachers trying to offer their students the best curriculum they could.

There was no wine-and-dine. I was told in about February of the school year that the four-year cycle of funding had allocated a significant sum of money for use by the English department. We were to spend it wisely, since it would be the only money we would receive for four more years. The department met so that we could assess our needs collectively, but I had to admit that I knew nothing about what I was doing. I ordered sample texts from several different companies, but one anthology looked basically like the next. The American literature anthologies, for instance, all began with William Bradford and John Smith's encounters with Native Americans, although a couple were beginning to preface Bradford and Smith with traditional Native American poems and chants as well, in an attempt to be multicultural as well as chronological.

After several meetings we made our decisions. Some teachers voted for consistency, requesting the newer edition of the text they were already teaching. Others felt the text they were using was so out of date, and so out of touch with the needs of their students, that they opted for something new. We spent our money wisely that year, I suppose—as wisely as we could. But I was left with the nagging feeling that there was more surrounding literature anthologies than I knew—deeper cultural implications regarding how they were created, questions regarding how things make their way into an anthology, and how the packaging of these authors and texts within the anthology might influence what and how I taught. Were all textbooks really the same? How could my colleagues and I make the most of the anthologies we had chosen?

As we discussed this last question, we realized that there were even deeper anthology issues left unresolved by our department meetings, such as the question of "coverage." Several teachers designed their course so as to use the anthology from cover to cover. Others saw the anthology as a resource through which one might forage selectively, grabbing some things while rejecting others. The fact that we were not in agreement about the role of the anthology in our work concerned me, but choosing one approach over the other did not seem to solve the problem, since there were pitfalls in each approach. On the one hand, covering the entire anthology provides order and structure to the curriculum, but it limits the depth in which one can probe the issues in each work, and it constrains the flexibility needed to pursue the tangents that inevitably arise out of the study of literature. Time becomes the driving factor in the coverage approach, since there is rarely enough time in the school year to cover the entire anthology. On the other hand, the selective approach provides the flexibility to meet the needs of particular classrooms, but it can often operate whimsically, as teachers choose whatever they feel like choosing.

To resolve the question of how to use the anthology, we had to resolve the coverage question, but to resolve that, we needed to know how anthologies were constructed. If the anthology really represented the most important works in American literature, then maybe I was doing a grave injustice to my students by not trying to cover the entire anthology. But if I was going to use the anthology selectively, then I needed some means to guide my choices. An answer of sorts came in the form of a question asked often by students: "Why are we studying this?" The more often students asked the question, the less confident I was that my answers were satisfactory. Why *were* we studying this? I would ask myself. What makes this an important piece of American literature? Who says it is important? How did it get into this anthology when other pieces did not? My very simple, pragmatic question for myself and my colleagues—How should the anthology get used in the classroom?—was really part of a deeper philosophical question: What is the purpose of the study of literature? Do students read literature in school in order to familiarize themselves with the great works of Western culture, or are students and teachers engaged, through the study of literature, in exploration of culture?

The traditional view of literary studies saw the work of the field as perpetuating the culture—the idea that classic texts represent the excellence of Western culture, and must be passed on to the next generation in order to maintain the culture. However, in her groundbreaking study *Sensational Designs*, Tompkins argued that the status of "classic" texts were "less the result of their indisputable excellence than the product of historical contingencies" (xii). Furthermore, she argued that literary study should approach "literary texts not as works of art embodying enduring themes in complex forms, but as attempts to redefine the social order. . . . Novels and stories should be studied not because they managed to escape the limitations of their particular time and place, but because they offer powerful examples of the way a culture thinks about itself, articulating a particular historical moment" (xi). In Tompkins's conception, to engage in literary study is to do "cultural work," to involve oneself in the act of interpreting cultural artifacts for the ultimate purpose of knowing, and defining, one's culture. This approach represents a significant shift in the role of literary studies and serves to contextualize our exploration of the construction of anthologies and the role they play in the study of American literature.

To do the kind of work Tompkins called for, one would need to engage in close critical analysis of American literature anthologies. I began by looking at the work of others who had studied textbooks, but I ended up doing my own critical readings. For instance, studies by Apple and Tyson-Bernstein support and extend Tompkins's argument, illustrating that textbooks are not repositories of the indisputably excellent works of Western culture, but texts constructed by groups or individuals with particular interests or agendas. Apple argues that textbooks are economic commodities "subject to intense competition and the pressures of profit," but, as commodities regulated by state government policies, they are also subject to the competing claims of a variety of groups who have a political stake in the outcome (Apple 282). For instance, in nearly half the states in the United States, textbooks must be approved by state committees (286). Each state committee establishes a short list of textbooks acceptable for use in its state's classrooms. However, a few larger states represent the bulk of the textbook market. Since textbook publishers are concerned with profit margins, it is in their interest to take advantage of these large markets, and so they design their textbooks around the wishes of these state committees. Thus smaller states, and states without statewide adoption policies, end up with the same textbooks, designed perhaps to meet the needs of one influential state. Also, local school districts select from these approved lists, even when they are not obligated to, because they are reimbursed for doing so (286). Thus the economic market drives the production and distribution of textbooks. Tyson-Bernstein illustrates one such example of a major history textbook, influenced by the interests of one individual:

> W. Dallas Herring, a history buff and coffin maker from Rose Hill, North Carolina, was chairman of the North Carolina State Board of Education in 1966. In May of that year, when publishers were trying to get their U.S. history textbooks on North Carolina's state adoption list, Herring complained that North Carolina's role in U.S. history had been neglected.
> . . . Herring was particularly disturbed by textbooks that failed to mention the Revolutionary War battle of Moore's Creek Bridge, which lies 45 miles south of Rose Hill. . . .
> In Herring's view, the battle was important "because it delayed Cornwallis' entrance into North Carolina and kept him from gaining an early foothold in the South."
> Herring's fellow board members agreed with him and decided to put off adopting history books for a year. Harcourt, Brace and Jovanovich, whose "Rise of the American Nation" was the only book used in North Carolina at the time, produced a 1967 revision of the book with a full account of the Battle of Moore's Creek Bridge. Like many state school-board members, Herring "was surprised to see how responsive they were to my initial complaints. . . ."
> Today [1988], students across the nation still read a 250-word account [of the Battle of Moore's Creek Bridge] in "Rise of the American Nation," a book still widely used in North Carolina and elsewhere in the nation. . . . [T]hey read more about the Battle of Moore's Creek Bridge than about the Boston Tea Party or the First Continental Congress. And the battle now appears in other U.S. history books as well. (7–8)

Although this example is striking in its illustration of how textbooks can be subject to market influences and individual whimsy, it seems to reinforce what most teachers already feel deeply—that the process of choosing what gets included in a textbook seems far removed from the classroom, and that there is little or nothing the classroom teacher can do about it. However, this example does not illustrate how authors get constructed within anthologies, an issue over which teachers *can* exercise some control.

Beyond the primary question of who gets included in literary anthologies, teachers can and should be asking other questions as well:

How are these authors represented in the textbook, and how might this construction of authorship influence the way in which I implement this material in my classroom? We can say much about how an individual author is constructed within the text by examining the text ourselves. For example, the presentations of Álvar Núñez Cabeza de Vaca in two anthologies serves to illustrate the construction of authorship within a textbook, showing just how different each construction can be. Cabeza de Vaca, we should note, is an author who has recently been "rediscovered," finding his way into an increasing number of high school literature anthologies. For instance, he did not appear in the anthologies my department purchased in the early 1990s, but, by 1997, he appears in several standard anthologies, including a historical *mention* in an early section of Holt, Rinehart and Winston's *Elements of Literature: Fifth Course: Literature of the United States with Literature of the Americas*. A short passage describes the arrival of European explorers in the Americas:

> In 1528, only thirty-six years after Columbus first sighted that flickering fire on the beach of San Salvador, a Spaniard named Álvar Núñez Cabeza de Vaca (c. 1490–1557) landed with an expedition (he was its treasurer) on the west coast of what is now Florida. Cabeza de Vaca and others left the ship and marched inland. They did not return. Their fleet waited an entire year for them, then departed for Mexico, giving up the explorers for dead. Lost in the Texas Gulf area, Cabeza de Vaca and his companions wandered for the next eight years in search of other Europeans who would help them get home. Cabeza de Vaca's narrative of his journeys through what is now Texas is a gripping adventure story. It is also a firsthand account of the habits of some of the indigenous people in what is now the United States: what they ate (very little), how they housed themselves, and what their religious beliefs were. De Vaca also provides the first account of some animals and plants that the Europeans had never known existed. Cabeza de Vaca and his shipmates were alternately captives or companions of the various Native American peoples they encountered on their long trek. Here is a part of de Vaca's account of the expedition's experiences with a tribal group in the Gulf Coast area, struggling to survive a famine. . . . (7–8)

Ironically, only a tiny excerpt of Cabeza de Vaca's *La Relación*—part of one paragraph—is included in the textbook. In fact, the Holt text never even gives the narrative a title; *La Relación* has become the accepted title and the one typically used in other textbooks and anthologies. Furthermore, the passage excerpted in the Holt text describes only the plants and animals that the tribe ate in order to survive. The entire account presented in the Holt text reads as follows:

Here is a part of de Vaca's account of the expedition's experiences with a tribal group in the Gulf Coast area, struggling to survive a famine.

> Their [the Native Americans] support is principally roots, of two or three kinds, and they look for them over the face of all the country. The food is poor and gripes the persons who eat it. The roots require roasting two days: Many are very bitter, and withal difficult to be dug. They are sought the distance of two or three leagues, and so great is the want these people experience, that they cannot get through the year without them. Occasionally they kill a deer, and at times take fish; but the quantity is so small and the famine so great, that they eat spiders and the eggs of ants, worms, lizards, salamanders, snakes, and vipers that kill whom they strike; and they eat earth and wood, and all that there is, the dung of deer, and other things that I omit to mention; and I honestly believe that were there stones in that land they would eat them. They save the bones of fishes they consume, of snakes and other animals, that they may afterwards beat them together and eat the powder. (8)

In this representation, there is little sense of narrative—no *story*, with *characters* and *plot* and *dramatic tension*. What the reader never gets is the "gripping adventure story" to which the preceding historical description alludes. More importantly, however, the portrayal of the Native Americans gives the reader the impression of a culture devoid of any means of survival, a culture that (perhaps according to our post-Darwinian sensibilities) is destined to die. Because of the way the narrative has been cropped and framed, it is easy for a reader to feel nothing for the author, or the cultures it is supposed to represent.

Why Cabeza de Vaca is even included in this book—except to *mention* him long enough to get his name into the index in the back—is a mystery. To begin with, the entire historical summary has been so fragmented and obscured as to render the passage essentially meaningless. Neither the captain of the ship nor the leader of the expedition, conquistador Pánfilo de Narváez, is even mentioned, thus making it appear as if Cabeza de Vaca is the leader of the expedition. Furthermore, there is no explanation of the motives of the expedition. The scarcity of information ought to lead the reader to other questions. What were they looking for in Florida? Why did some of the men leave the ship and head inland? Why did they never return, since it is apparent that the crew that remained expected them to return? And furthermore, one must wonder, why is this in a literature anthology at all? If the account was presented as a piece of American literature worthy of study, Cabeza de

Vaca's mention in this text might be justifiable. As it is, however, there seems to be no justification for his presence in the text. This account might belong in a history textbook, but the connection to American *literature* is so oblique as to be nonexistent. Beyond the confusing biographical information and the cropped text of *La Relación*, there is no other reference to Cabeza de Vaca in the textbook. There are no questions for discussion in the student text, or even in the teacher's edition, which has the expanded marginal notes common to textbooks produced in the 1990s. In a book that weighs six pounds, and includes so much, this lack of clear context regarding Cabeza de Vaca is a great disappointment.

But there are some deeper ironies here as well. The Holt anthology is prefaced by close to twenty-seven pages of explanation of how and why it was constructed as it was. It contains essays by "noted" professors on the importance of "inclusion" and "integration," and on how to integrate the text into the teacher's plans seamlessly. There are pages listing all the contributors, editors, writers, consultants, and so on, who had a hand in the creation of the text. The sheer volume of this prefatory material is impressive; from it alone one might conclude that this text is superior to those of lesser (or less obvious) stature. But in regards to the coverage of an author such as Cabeza de Vaca, the reverse is true: the treatment given by the Holt text is void of context or literary merit. For all the weight of its review boards and its essays on the importance of inclusion—for all its physical weight too—the text does not do justice to Cabeza de Vaca the author.

If a teacher were to teach Cabeza de Vaca's narrative uncritically, as it is presented in the Holt text, the lesson would not only be short, but could be nothing other than a lesson in monoculturalism. First, as noted earlier, the portrayal of the Native Americans reinforces a Eurocentric view that the culture of the Native Americans was *destined* to fade away upon the entrance of the Europeans on the stage of America. Here I am deliberately invoking that all-too-pervasive theme of "Manifest Destiny" that has permeated American textbooks, and apparently continues to do so. Furthermore, the very fact that this Spanish narrative receives such little attention, and appears in such a fragmented form, suggests that the story of America as told through eyes other than White Anglo Saxons is of little merit. There is almost nothing else to be gleaned from Holt's construction of Cabeza de Vaca's narrative. Ironically, through its prefatory essays on "inclusion" and "integrated curriculum," Holt wraps itself in a cloak of progressive multiculturalism. However, by merely mentioning Cabeza de Vaca, the Holt text implies that the literature of the White Anglo Saxons is of prime value to American culture, and that those who know this culture and its productions possess the cultural capital. Knowing the stories of the Spanish in the United States, apparently, does not carry the same cultural weight.

Teachers who consider themselves *critical* in the generic sense might judge the narrative by its minuscule status in the text, or by the poorly written historical context, and dismiss Cabeza de Vaca as an author of no merit. However, to do so, although it might appear to be founded in a critical approach to the text, is in fact merely to accept uncritically the construction of the author perpetrated by those who compiled this anthology. This is how the textbook becomes the curriculum; it dictates teachers' reception of the author, and thus colors how teachers present that author to their students. To be truly critical, teachers must ask themselves a range of questions: Is there more to this author than the anthology suggests? How has the anthology constructed this author? Is this the construction that I want to present to my students? If my construction of the author differs from the textbook's, how will I negotiate this dilemma without undermining the future effectiveness of the textbook, or of my own teaching?

At stake in these highly constructed representations of authors in textbooks is the notion of *multiculturalism* which has become such a driving force in curriculum construction in recent years. Anthologies are clearly becoming more ethnically diverse, but that doesn't guarantee that they are more *multicultural*. Teachers must ask themselves: Are the portrayals of author and subject truly representative of the cultures being depicted? What kind of representation of Native Americans, or of the Spanish in North America, is being constructed by the fragmented clip of Cabeza de Vaca's account in the Holt text? An uncritical assessment might applaud the Holt text for its inclusion of Cabeza de Vaca, without looking closer to see the misrepresentation of the Spanish and the Native Americans. Ethnically diverse textbooks might represent a greater variety of cultures in the United States, but they might also turn out to reinforce a kind of monoculturalism, not multiculturalism, in the way those cultures are framed or constructed within the text. And an uncritical teacher, thinking that the mere mention of Cabeza de Vaca is enough to make the day's lesson multicultural, perpetuates the monoculturalism lurking in the anthology.

Not all anthologies, however, portray cultures as the Holt text does. McDougal Littell's *The Language of Literature: Grade 11, American Literature* (1997) presents Cabeza de Vaca in quite another context. First, it presents a much larger excerpt (four pages) from Cabeza de Vaca's account, along with the title *La Relación*. Second, the historical background establishes a clearer account of the events, the principal players, and their motivations.

> In 1527, Pánfilo de Narváez, a Spanish conquistador, led a five-ship, 600-man expedition to Florida. His second in command was Álvar Núñez Cabeza de Vaca. The expedition was a disaster from the moment the Spaniards entered the Caribbean. After the loss of two ships in a hurricane and of more than 20 men by drowning and desertion, the Narváez expedition finally made its way to the West Coast of Florida. Against the advice of Cabeza de Vaca, Narváez separated 300 of his men from the ships and marched these forces overland. Narváez intended for the ships to meet the land forces at a Spanish settlement on the coast of central Mexico, but he grossly underestimated the vastness of the territory and the difficulty of crossing it. Eventually, overwhelmed by hunger, disease, and Indian attacks, the land forces decided to build five crude barges to get them to Mexico more quickly. These barges, each carrying about 50 men, soon drifted apart, and the one commanded by Cabeza de Vaca was shipwrecked on Galveston Island, off the coast of what is now Texas.
>
> Ultimately, Cabeza de Vaca and three companions were the only survivors of the Narváez expedition. They wandered for more than eight years before reaching Mexico City, thus becoming the first Europeans to cross North America. After returning to Spain in 1537, Cabeza de Vaca wrote *La Relación*, a report addressed to the king of Spain. (80)

Here the situational context is much clearer. First, Narváez is clearly the captain. Second, Narváez's plan, unrealistic as it may seem to those who understand the geography of North America, is at least clear, and explains the sending of men into the wilderness. Finally, the disagreement between Narváez and Cabeza de Vaca regarding this decision adds a dramatic tension to the narrative which strengthens its claim as a piece of American literature, and not just American history.

McDougal Littell, although it does not frame itself as the paragon of inclusion, is clearly more thorough than Holt in its presentation of the historical context of Cabeza de Vaca's narrative. For reasons of space, I have excerpted a section of the longer four-page excerpt, with the hope that it will, fragmented as it is, illustrate to some degree the merits of the narrative as a piece of American culture and literature. In the following passage, several of the hand-built barges wash ashore at what is now Galveston Island, Texas. There Native Americans feed and befriend Cabeza de Vaca and the rest.

As the sun rose next morning, the Indians appeared as they promised, bringing an abundance of fish and of certain roots which taste like nuts, some bigger than walnuts, some smaller, mostly grubbed from the water with great labor.

That evening they came again with more fish and roots and brought their women and children to look at us. They thought themselves rich with the little bells and beads we gave them, and they repeated their visits on other days.

Being provided with what we needed, we thought to embark again. It was a struggle to dig our barge out of the sand it had sunk in, and another struggle to launch her. For the work in the water while launching, we stripped and stowed our clothes in the craft.

Quickly clambering in and grabbing our oars, we had rowed two crossbow shots from shore when a wave inundated us. Being naked and the cold intense, we let our oars go. The next big wave capsized the barge. The Inspector and two others held fast, but that only carried them more certainly underneath, where they drowned.

A single roll of the sea tossed the rest of the men into the rushing surf and back onto shore half-drowned.

We lost those that the barge took down; but the survivors escaped as naked as they were born, with the loss of everything we had. That was not much, but valuable to us in that bitter November cold, our bodies so emaciated we could easily count every bone and looked the very picture of death. . . .

The Lord willed that we should find embers while searching the remnants of our former fire. We found more wood and soon had big fires raging. Before them, with flowing tears, we prayed for mercy and pardon, each filled with pity not only for himself but for all his wretched fellows. (82–83).

The passage goes on to show how the Indians returned, found the sailors in worse condition than their first encounter, and proceeded to take them to their village to care for them, while the sailors were unsure whether they were being saved or taken to their slaughter. Ironically, despite the assistance from the Karankawa, disease spread until only sixteen sailors and half the tribe were left (83–84).

The first element worthy of note in the account above is the more complex portrayal of the contact zone that occurs when the two cultures meet. Missing is the Eurocentric theme of "Manifest Destiny." The Spaniards, although condescending in their gifts of trinkets, are hapless victims of the powerful sea, desperately praying to their God to be merciful. Meanwhile, the Native Americans appear culturally strong; there is no account of the endlessly poor diet of the local tribe. In this narrative the Native Americans bring adequate, hard-earned food to sustain the sailors. Furthermore, the piece is truthful to what we have come to know of the health consequences of the contact between Europeans and Native Americans; the Karankawa are not invincible, but all too susceptible to European diseases. Finally, Cabeza de Vaca's narrative as portrayed in this textbook appears to have as much cultural and historical value as do the traditionally canonical accounts by John Smith and William Bradford. It is roughly equivalent in length to the Bradford account included in this textbook, explores the similar consequences of the harsh conditions of the New World, and relates the Europeans' encounters with the Native Americans. Smith's account, in fact, is absent from the textbook, apparently replaced by the Cabeza de Vaca account.

Finally, beyond the historical and cultural significance of the narrative in the McDougal Littell textbook, *La Relación* functions as a genuine piece of American literature. The passage is well written, presenting a picture of shipwreck and doom as dramatic as in the *Odyssey* or *Robinson Crusoe*. The narrative has plot, characters, and dramatic tension. Nature plays the antagonist, while the Karankawa serve as benefactors. The scene where the men depart naked on their barges, only to be swept back to shore by the sea, is told in the poetic language of imagery and metaphor—they row "two crossbow shots" from shore, only to be "inundated" by a wave—and the account is intensified by the graphic description of their emaciated condition.

The purpose here has been to show how textbooks construct authorship by the contextual devices they employ. It would be unfair and irresponsible to praise the McDougal Littell textbook as flawless while judging the entire Holt text on the basis of its treatment of one author, without looking to see if the treatment of Cabeza de Vaca represents a consistent pattern in the textbook. A thorough examination of both texts would take greater time and space. However, the point I want to reiterate is that the Cabeza de Vaca portrayed in the McDougal Littell text is a teachable option for classroom teachers; he is an author of a work of cultural, historical, and literary merit. In the Holt text, he is presented as none of these. This difference illustrates the real power that an anthology can have on the construction of authorship in the classroom. Even if a teacher using Holt wanted to discuss Cabeza de Vaca, there is not enough material to do so adequately. For a teacher who has access only to the stunted information presented in the Holt text, the anthology can easily dictate the curriculum.

However, strong confident teachers can create dynamic courses when the anthology serves the curriculum. If, as Tompkins suggests, literature should be studied because it offers "powerful examples of the way a culture thinks about itself" (xi), then the anthology acts as a repository of textual artifacts which serve to illustrate such thinking. Furthermore, the ways in which texts are represented in the anthology also serve to illustrate how the culture thinks about itself—as does what gets excluded from the anthology. Within this framework for thinking about anthologies, teachers and students can use an anthology alongside other texts to explore cultural issues through large- and small-group discussion, writing, and other activities that enable critical thinking. For example, class discussion can serve not only to hold up the anthology's texts as great pieces of literature, but also to open a dialogue regarding their role as literature—operating within a framework of guiding questions, including the age-old student question "Why are we studying this?" As well, composition can easily operate in tandem with such a conception of literary studies, where student writing serves as a medium in which students grapple with cultural issues in response to the literature they have been reading and discussing. Literature class need not be about reading texts in order to have read the great works of Western literature; it can be about interacting with those texts in order to arrive at one's own understandings, interpretations, and constructions—of literature. In the end, despite the influence of publishers, state review boards, special interest groups, and literary critics in the construction of anthologies, it is ultimately students and teachers who make American literature, as they construct for themselves what all of this means to them. But they must enter into the task with a critical eye, ready to question the constructions presented in the anthologies, and ready also to question their own assumptions about literature. In this way, despite the fact that the anthology might seem unsatisfactory, students and teachers can use it effectively as they make American literature in their classrooms.

Works Cited

Apple, Michael. "Textbook publishing: The political and economic influences." *Theory into Practice* 28 (1989): 282–87.

Elements of literature: Fifth course: Literature of the United States with Literature of the Americas. Austin: Holt, 1997.

The Language of literature: Grade 11, American literature. Evanston, IL: McDougal, 1997.

Tompkins, Jane. *Sensational Designs: The Cultural Work of American Fiction, 1790–1860*. New York: Oxford UP, 1985.

Tyson-Bernstein, Harriet. *A Conspiracy of Good Intentions: America's Textbook Fiasco*. Washington, DC: Council for Basic Education, 1988.

5 A Case Study of American Literature Anthologies and Their Role in the Making of American Literature

Dave Winter
Wheeler High School, Marietta, Georgia

I've been an English teacher at Wheeler High School in Marietta, Georgia, for the past nine years. Although I've taught several different English courses at several different levels during that time, I've settled in as a specialist in eleventh-grade American literature. To understand more about the position I occupy, I decided to investigate the history of the American literature course at my school. The premise of my research is that the secondary classroom is a valuable source for historical inquiry, one that has been almost wholly neglected. Literary historians don't think to look there, and secondary teachers don't think to approach the subject of their professional lives as a valuable history.

The goal of my research is to create a case study in the history of American literature as it has been taught at one school. By attempting to encounter the course as individual teachers have taught it over time, I hope to understand better why individual teachers make the decisions they do and how their decisions as teachers interact with national changes in the discipline.

The relationship of an American literature teacher and his or her anthology is one such exchange. After interviewing individual teachers and studying the anthologies from which they taught American literature, I have found that the relationship between a teacher and his or her anthology is complicated. In Wheeler's early years, teachers by and large submitted to the authority of the anthology, for many reasons—among them the teachers' relative inexperience, the paucity of classroom resources, and the authoritarian school and community culture that prevailed at the time. As these conditions changed, so too did the role of the anthology in the classroom. In the 1970s, as teachers became more experienced, as alternative classroom resources became readily available, and as school officials enacted reforms that encouraged teachers to place less emphasis on their anthologies, teachers both welcomed and resisted opportunities to shape, adjust, resist, or subvert the anthology. As demographic, curricular, and institutional changes profoundly altered the role of teachers and anthologies, teachers faced difficult decisions that at times pitted their personal values against their professional ethics.

———————

For teachers and students accustomed to the modern classroom, a tableau of the Wheeler High School cafeteria, circa 1965, might seem like a lunchroom not just from another era but from another planet. Marynell Jacob doesn't believe it herself when she recalls it, and she was there, a first-year teacher in a first-year school populated only with sophomores and juniors.

At 12:30 every afternoon, Jacob would walk without a word to the doorway of the cafeteria, and—just as silently—her junior American literature class would form a single-file line behind her.

"They knew to watch for me when it was our class's turn. Because that was what all the classes did. You'd see Ms. Womack's class over there at 12:20, Ms. Harvey's class over there at 12:25, Ms. Jacob's class over there at 12:30, and they would line up behind us and we would walk back down to the room," Jacob recalled.

No bells rang. Just like the tables and chairs they left behind, the rows of students were aligned perfectly as they marched from the cafeteria and back to the classroom where their textbooks awaited them.

"It was just the authority of the school," Jacob offered as an explanation. "The school still had the last word on how students behaved at the school. It was just the way that it was at that time period."

Just as students obeyed the authority of their teachers, so too did Jacob obey the authority of her anthology. In her first years as an American literature teacher, Jacob would start at the beginning of the textbook, and would march from selection to selection until the semester ended:

"I was still under that authoritarian sort of thing, somebody else knows more than I do, so I have to do what they say do. When they said, 'Start here,' I started here. [When they said,] 'Read this poem,' I read that poem."

Roger Hines, who taught American and British literature at Wheeler for twelve and a half years beginning in 1971, espoused a similar view about the authority of the classroom anthology:

"I mainly followed the book. I chose not to fight the book. I know that the book is just a tool, but—my Lord—we are paying a fortune for those things so we ought to use them or quit buying them, one. So normally if that's the adopted textbook then that's my text, and I do believe in text. The textbook should contain a text, and a text should be taught."

The classroom culture Jacob created in 1965 reflected the values of the community it served: authority figures were obeyed. The first juniors at Wheeler to study American literature encountered it as presented in the 1963 Scott, Foresman edition of *The United States in Literature* (edited by Walter Blair et al.). The school's authoritarian culture wasn't the only reason that teachers placed an unusually complete credence in the anthology. The school's library was so strapped for resources that teachers felt disinclined to venture too far from the textbook.

As Jacob remembered, the school's first library, as it were, was confined to a "little conference room at the end of the guidance office." The library boasted two holdings at the time: "They had a subscription to the Marietta paper, a subscription to *The Atlanta Journal*, and that was it."

The library existed merely so the newly opened Wheeler High School could meet state requirements to stay open. The entire master schedule revolved around the available anthologies. Because they had boíKÕhfor only half the students at the school, Jacob taught literature to half the class, and grammar and composition to the other half, then switched them the next semester. Without a serviceable media center, Jacob did not have much discretion to assign outside reading or independent research. Without a countywide syllabus or instruction plan to assist in such activities, Jacob omitted them from her curriculum and returned to her anthology, the only real source of literature the school had to offer its students. At least for a time, the anthology, for all intents and purposes, *was* American literature.

Unbeknownst to the students, a war over the essence of American literature was being fought in the pages of their textbooks. Was American literature to be organized by theme, chronology, or typology? The eventual victors in that battle would have been clear to anybody who compared the 1963 text to its predecessor, the 1957 edition of *The United States in Literature*. In an apparent effort to appease all parties in the debate over the central organizing principle of the eleventh-grade

American literature survey, the editors of the 1957 edition (Robert C. Pooley et al.) chose three. They organized one-third by theme ("The American Spirit in Literature"), one-third by chronology ("Great American Authors and Their Times") and one-third by literary genre ("The Development of Literary Types"). The hybrid organization schemata would not survive the book's reincarnations in 1963 and 1968.

The revised text offered a seemingly straightforward chronological structure. The book was divided into two main sections: "Three Centuries of American Literature 1607–1900" and "Twentieth Century American Literature." In the first section, the editors grouped the selections chronologically into six time periods, beginning with "Planters and Puritans" and ending with the turn-of-the-century "New Outlooks." As had been the case in the 1957 edition, the editors also identified one author to represent each historical period. Although other authors followed the representative author in the 1963 and 1968 editions, they were not presented with the same rich biographical apparatus that was woven into the presentation of each era's formerly exclusive "representative" author. The result was something of a Literary League of America, a celebration of authorial superheroes, each endowed with his own superpower: Ben Franklin (wisdom), Washington Irving (imagination), Henry David Thoreau (optimism), Walt Whitman (democracy), and Samuel Clemens (yarn spinning). Only the "Planters and Puritans" chapter, a new addition to the 1963 text, broke this pattern by settling for two representative authors: William Byrd and Jonathan Edwards. This sort of Mount Rushmore approach to American literature (with seven White male heads instead of four) was more muted than in the 1957 text, but it remained an integral feature of each chapter representing a historical period.

While the study of literary forms is subordinated to the chronologically ordered main sections, the chronology creates the impression that American literature had evolved over four centuries, culminating in higher aesthetic forms, that is, in the genres of literary art. Understanding this progression, of course, requires getting to the end of the textbook, something that did not happen in Jacob's first American literature class in 1965.

"What I would do is start at the beginning and get as far as I could and then stop," Jacob said. "It didn't occur to me at first to teach from each section in order to be sure that I covered all the time periods."

The manner in which Jacob taught each individual selection also reflected how closely she relied on her textbook. There was no official syllabus to guide her, and of the four English teachers that comprised the first-ever Wheeler High School English Department, two were first-year teachers; the other two had just completed their first year of teaching.

"I was real big, back at that time, on reading stories and answering the questions," said Jacob. I figured if they put the questions in the book, then they were good questions and we should spend time on them."

Jacob was a first-year teacher then, and her personal experience provided yet another reason to stick close to the anthology. Like many of her colleagues, she did not feel prepared to teach American literature out of college, nor did she particularly wish to teach the course. After having completed a university education that compartmentalized every period and genre of British literature into specialized semester courses, Jacob often felt overwhelmed by the American literature course she was assigned to teach.

"It was not a good experience," she said of that first year. "First of all I did not particularly want to teach American literature, and second, I didn't know any. I didn't have the range of knowledge. I didn't have the depth, and it was a pretty frightening experience, and I was much more comfortable the semester when I got into the grammar books because it was, you know, 'Open your books, do the exercise.'"

In pursuing her English degree at Mississippi College in Clinton, Jacob took two American literature courses: a survey based on the Norton anthology and a course in Modern American Poetry. The rest of her coursework consisted of British literature. Jacob laughs now when she remembers leaving college with the assumption that "all the writers in the world were either American or British, preferably British; the best American novels copied British novels."

Her experience is typical of the early teachers at Wheeler. Given their training, the teachers usually taught American literature not because they wanted to but because they were assigned to teach it. Teachers like Jacob, who came to love teaching American literature, ended up educating themselves in the discipline and how to teach it well. Patsy Musgrove, who came to Wheeler in the early 1970s, came to love American literature during the summer prior to her first year of teaching in Miami. In a public library across the street from her home, she read American Nobel Prize winners in chronological order. She hadn't studied them in her literature coursework at Duke. Others, like Roger Hines, pursued American literature as a second passion, deeply felt but clearly secondary to British literature. Still others taught the course without ever warming to it. Marilyn Winter and Jane Frazer taught the course for several years without identifying with the subject as a specialty.

Some aspects of the 1963 edition of *The United States in Literature* were suited to teachers trained (as Wheeler teachers had been) to impart strategies for close reading of literary texts, not for understanding and appreciating the historical context behind them. Not only was the back half of the book devoted to organization by genre, but the book began with a preview entitled "Introducing American Literature," which featured modern short stories amenable to the New Critical approaches Jacob had learned in college. Jacob remembers feeling very comfortable teaching that section in her first year at Wheeler.

"I opened the book and there was Conrad Richter and Karl Shapiro," said Jacob of her first encounter with the text's introductory chapter. The modern short stories—those at the beginning and the end of the text—were early favorites:

"I had a better understanding of those. I didn't need as much historical background, the way I did with the colonial, revolutionary, and Civil War literature, and they were easier for me to understand and to present, so that was my favorite part. And also the students enjoyed it. You didn't have to spend as much time generating interest, doing extra things to get them involved."

As the anthology evolved to emphasize historical context and chronological organization, Jacob's view changed. The introductory section of short stories disappeared from Wheeler High School's American literature textbook in 1975. The introductory section had disappeared from Jacob's American literature course long before: "Gradually it occurred to me that you don't have to use that first chapter. It was kind of an introduction I guess, like reading for entertainment, but then the second chapter started with the colonial American, so I went through it in chronological order, and the only materials we had were the textbook."

And so Jacob taught herself history, so that she could teach her students:

"I read more on my own and learned that American literature is actually very significant in world literature and did come into its own once it quit copying British people."

The "Planters and Puritans" period, which she had dreaded, became her favorite section to teach, partly because she loved the start of the school year, but mainly because she loved teaching Anne Bradstreet and Edward Taylor. Jacob supplemented her anthology by bringing in other poems by Bradstreet and by helping students learn Taylor's difficult poems by teaching the couplets and inversions found in the Bay Psalm Book. "'Who in this Bowling Alley bowled the sun?' That is one of my favorite lines in all of American literature," she said. "I love that line, and I just got more and more excited about the extra things I was reading."

Jacob's self-education forever changed her relationship with her anthology. Instead of the book or its makers assuming authority over her classroom decisions, she became the authority on how to use the text: "At first, you felt like you had to teach every single thing, and the second time around with the book you learned which things you might be able to leave out in order to make room for other things."

The editors of the Scott, Foresman anthology evidently grappled with many of the same questions. Throughout the 1960s, *The United States in Literature* maintained a relatively stable table of contents. While the introductory collection of modern texts departed markedly from the 1957 edition, the authors contained in it were all White, although Pearl Buck, Willa Cather, Amy Lowell, and Esther Forbes made the section disproportionately female in comparison with the rest of the text. Downplaying the literary superhero approach did not significantly alter the background of the authors who represented each historical chapter. The first half of the 1960s text, covering the first three centuries of American literature, included three female authors: Anne Bradstreet (one poem), Sarah Orne Jewett (one short story), and Emily Dickinson (thirteen poems). Bradstreet and Jewett were not in the 1957 text, and Dickinson's place in the secondary canon increased markedly from the two poems found in 1957. Her inclusion in the "New Outlooks" chapter, behind Stephen Crane and Sidney Lanier, however, is telling because, unlike in later textbooks, the editors placed her in the chronology based on the date of her discovery and subsequent publication by Thomas Wentworth Higginson (1890s) rather than when she wrote the poems (the 1850s and 1860s).

Female authors appeared more frequently in the second half of the book, devoted to twentieth-century literature. Katherine Anne Porter and Eudora Welty entered the anthology for the first time, making up 20 percent of the short story section. Women wrote twelve of the fifty-nine poems (again 20 percent) in the modern poetry section, although they were absent from the "First Voices" subsection (nineteen poems) and abundant in the "Swelling Chorus" subsection (seven of seventeen). One female essayist (Nancy Huddleston Packer) entered the text for the first time, while one female biographer (Catherine Drinker Bowen) remained from the 1957 edition. Overall, women authors wrote 19 percent of the selections in the text, but of the thirty-six selections written by women, twenty-six were poems (72 percent), and half of those were by Emily Dickinson.

Minority authors remained negligible as a portion of the whole. There were no Latino authors, and Monica Sone, the lone Asian American author in the 1957 version, vanished from the text. James Weldon Johnson, Gwendolyn Brooks, and Ralph Ellison entered the text, bringing the total number of Black authors to four. Remaining from the previous version were spirituals, which were moved from the thematic "Love and Faith" section to the historical "Conflict" section between Robert E. Lee and Abraham Lincoln. Black poets were absent from the modern short story section and the "First Voices" poetry subsection. Countee Cullen and Johnson appeared in the "Swelling Chorus" subsection, while Brooks appeared in "Newer Voices." Ellison's "Living with Music" was included in the "Article and Essay" section. Of the Black authors included, only Ellison was a nonpoet.

The tendency of anthologies to overrepresent female and minority authors as poets is well chronicled and certainly has outlived the 1960s text analyzed here. Not only are the poems buried in the backs of textbooks, but they also take up less space. The fact that longer works by women and minorities are less likely to be anthologized further reduces the emphasis that American literature teachers place on women and minority authors. The number of pages in the anthology devoted to women and minority authors (or, more to the point, the minutes in the classroom spent studying them) must have been less than the percentage of women and minority authors represented in the text as a whole.

If one were to stop at this point, he or she might conclude that the anthologies were responsible for restricting the secondary American literature curriculum at Wheeler High School. A closer investigation of the American literature curriculum as it developed into the 1970s, however, reveals that the anthology, while certainly a factor in creating the secondary canon, was not the only force shaping what Wheeler students studied and how they studied it.

The anthology may have been less representative of minority authors, but the textbook percentages of minorities in the 1960s editions of *The United States in Literature* exceeded those found in the Wheeler student body. In the 1960s, there was not one student of color at Wheeler High

School. The integration of the school came in 1970 and proceeded without incident (at least without any that the teachers noticed), but the minority student population did not increase substantially during the 1970s. The school's 1982 Southern Association of Colleges and Secondary Schools (SACS) report indicated that the student body was still 96.77 percent "White," 1.13 percent "Hispanic," 1.08 percent "Asian," and 1.02 percent "Black."

While Wheeler High School would become one of the most diverse schools in Georgia over the next two decades, it was the anthology—not the school—that took the first steps toward diversity. You could judge the mission of the 1973 edition of *The United States in Literature* by looking at its cover. In place of the 1968 cover image—Erich Locker's multihued photo collage of skyscraper windows reaching forever upward in the night sky—the 1973 cover displays a representation of Navajo artist Jeff King's sandpainting *Lighting Armor House*. Since King's painting—the sixth of eighteen sandpaintings he performed during the Navajo blessing ceremonial "Where the Two Came to Their Father,"—was an ephemeral performance piece, the 1973 cover image is an illustration, which Maud Oakes "recorded" during the ceremony. The description of the image and its place in Navajo tradition is the first supplement in the teacher resource book that accompanied the edition.

From the very cover, then, the 1973 edition sends the unmistakable message that the editorial team of James E. Miller, Robert Hayden, and Robert O'Neal sought to create a text whose canon included a more diverse group of writers, one that represented all of America. In the "Introducing American Literature" section, the editors replaced Bernard De Voto with N. Scott Momaday, Conrad Richter with Bernard Malamud, Pearl Buck with Ralph Ellison, and Robert Penn Warren with Gwendolyn Brooks. Fewer than half of the selections from the 1968 edition—Karl Shapiro's "Auto Wreck," Willa Cather's "The Sculptor's Funeral," Amy Lowell's "Patterns," and William Saroyan's "The Oyster and The Pearl"—survived in the introductory section of the 1973 edition.

Latino authors, previously noticeable only for their absence, appeared in the twentieth-century portion of the anthology for the first time, as short stories by Prudencio de Pereda and Américo Paredes entered the text, along with poems by Luis Muñoz Marín and Victor Hernández Cruz.

Nowhere was the revision of the text more drastic than in the representation of African American authors. Where there had been four

African American authors in 1968, there were seventeen in 1973. From Phillis Wheatley's inclusion in the "Founders of the Nation" section to Gwendolyn Brooks's inclusion in the book's introduction and in the modern poetry section, and from James Pennington and Frederick Douglass's placement in the "End of an Era" section to the inclusion of Imamu Amiri Baraka and Michael S. Harper, African American authorship more than tripled in the book in just one edition.

Jacob remembers very well her first encounter with the textbook:

"I never heard of Phillis Wheatley until I taught her. It astounded me when I heard myself saying, 'She's our first major African American author.' I never even had heard of her. Frederick Douglass, I guess I knew the name. Certainly, Scott Momaday and some of the Native Americans. No Asians. Absolutely no Asians."

Like Jacob, Musgrove remembered the arrival of the 1973 edition of the Scott, Foresman book as the moment when she encountered many authors for the first time: "Well it [the first consciousness of cultural diversity at Wheeler] must have been when those brown books [copies of the new anthology] came in [during the 1974–75 school year]. I mean that must have been a very conscious awareness that those things were there that hadn't been there before."

The course anthology challenged Jacob and Musgrove to broaden their classroom canon. From the anthology, Musgrove taught the Harlem Renaissance, James Baldwin, and Lorraine Hansberry. While Jacob and Musgrove were receptive to the idea of incorporating a more diverse group of writers into their American literature curriculum, many teachers resisted the idea of including any contemporary authors, regardless of their background. Although Wheatley, Douglass, and Pennington were situated within the historical chronology of the first half of the book, the other minority authors—all of the Latino authors and all but three of the African Americans—were situated in the twentieth-century section. And herein lies a problem: the move to diversify the literary canon became conflated with the move to make the canon more relevant and contemporary.

The movement to stress relevance and the movement to achieve greater diversity clearly were concurrent with the 1973 edition of *The United States in Literature*. While attempting to represent minority populations more substantially, the new editors also sought to make the selections more relevant to their young readers. Leo B. Kneer, the editorial director of the Scott, Foresman 1973 America Reads edition, made that goal clear when he outlined the philosophical principles that "controlled the development of the individual anthologies" in an introductory letter prefacing the *Teacher's Resource Book to Accompany The United States in Literature*:

> Materials studied by students must be relevant to students—selections must be capable of engaging young people of this time and place. But relevance has nothing, necessarily, to do with time. Is anything more "relevant" for example than "Do unto others ...?" There is relevance of manner as well as relevancy of matter. The way a piece is presented—by author, publisher, and teacher— is crucial. (viii)

The way the pieces were presented in the 1973 Scott, Foresman edition certainly reflected this professed emphasis on the relevance of literature to young people. By adding contemporary selections at the end of each historically organized chapter, and by drastically reducing the contextual apparatus preceding each selection in the text, the editors sought to make the text more accessible and more relevant to the students in their own time. As a consequence, the effort to place authors in their own historical context was drastically retrenched.

Roger Hines remembers well his favorite author to teach from his American literature anthology: Robert Frost. He also remembers one of his most memorable teaching moments: the golden spring day in 1973 when he taught his Advanced Placement seniors the Frost poem "Nothing Gold Can Stay."

On that spring day Hines made one of the serendipitous, spontaneous discoveries that teachers remember for the rest of their lives: "It just hit me: 'nothing gold can stay.' As surely as I sit here, on that day, had you gone out and looked around, everything was gold because literally he's right, 'nature's first green is gold,' it's not green. That yellow pollen and those little leaflet tips that come out there are golden as they can be, so we went out to the Wheeler football stadium—it still stands, I guess—and we had our class there that day and stayed there the whole hour and talked about that one poem, 'Nothing Gold Can Stay.'"

"And I told them we were going to come back in two weeks and, 'You are not going to see this gold. You're going to see green.' And let me tell you, [I remember] one person that was in that class, a girl named Debbie Smith . . . just eating that up and helping me teach."

Had he relied on the 1973 edition of *The United States in Literature*, Hines wouldn't have been able to teach "Nothing Gold Can Stay" to his juniors because the poem was not one of the six Frost poems included in the anthology. Luckily for Hines, who came to Wheeler from Mississippi in 1972, Scott, Foresman's days as Wheeler's "official" literature anthology were short-lived. On April 1, 1975, at the conclusion of Cobb County's first language arts textbook adoption process, Hines and the English department heads of the other nine Cobb County high schools voted to make the Harcourt Brace Jovanovich Adventures series the county's official text. The America Reads series by Scott, Foresman, which had provided Wheeler's text throughout the school's history, was out.

Frost appeared far more prominently in the 1973 "Classic Edition" of Harcourt's *Adventures in American Literature*. With eleven selections, among them "Nothing Gold Can Stay," Frost was the most prominent of the poets in the twentieth-century section of the text; Carl Sandburg was a distant second with four selections. The new prominence of Frost, who rejected modern conventions in favor of more traditional poetic modes, aptly illustrates how the anthology differed from the Scott, Foresman text published in the same year.

While not a complete reversion to the contents of the 1963 Scott, Foresman anthology, the Harcourt text bore a striking similarity to it in many respects. When the text arrived at Wheeler in the fall of 1975 after being adopted by countywide vote, the book had to have been seen as a move away from both diversity (in the textbook canon) and immediate relevance (as an instructional strategy in presenting that canon to students). The diversity found throughout the 1973 Scott, Foresman text is noticeably absent in the 1973 Harcourt book. Where there had been eighteen African American authors, there were now four, all in the twentieth-century section and all poets except for James Baldwin. The first half of the book included no minority authors and the entire text featured no Latino authors. The first half of the book featured two female authors, Emily Dickinson (twelve poems) and Willa Cather, whose "The Sculptor's Funeral" had been a staple in all of the Scott, Foresman editions. Five modern authors (two short story authors and three poets) bring the total number of female authors to seven.

Perhaps most telling were two sidebars, "Indian Literature" and "The Literature of Minorities." These summary pieces were included in the text to represent the literature of minority cultures. The "Indian Literature" sidebar, squeezed in on page 17, the final page of an excerpt of William Byrd's *The History of The Dividing Line*, discusses not Native American authors but the gradual increase in anthropological studies of them. The "Literature of Minorities" sidebar, on page 741, follows the final page of James Baldwin's "The Creative Process" and discusses the contribution of all immigrant groups to American literature: German, French, Italian, Polish, Russian, Irish, Jewish, and African. Four modern Black authors are mentioned, but none who wrote before the nineteenth century. Neither Asian American nor Latino culture is listed in the summary; nor are any authors from those cultures discussed.

The racial homogeneity of the authors found in the Harcourt text paralleled the same homogeneity of the Wheeler High School student body at that time. According to one teacher, Mardette Coleman, who lived in the Wheeler district but taught at neighboring Sprayberry High School from the mid-1950s to the mid-1980s, members of the Wheeler community pointed to their racial homogeneity as a source of pride compared to other county schools, such as Sprayberry, which had integrated earlier.

This attitude may have existed in parts of the Wheeler community, but the teachers' personal and professional experiences prove they were not only aware of African American culture but also had taken idealistic steps to combat discrimination in their schools and communities. Before coming to Wheeler, Musgrove attended a National Defense Education Act Institute at Duke University that was intended for and attended by Black teachers from rural North Carolina. After that formative experience, she taught Cuban refugees in Miami, an experience she now recounts as one of her fondest teaching memories.

As a second-year teacher in Meridian, Mississippi, Hines volunteered to switch schools with a Black middle school teacher in a teacher exchange program intended to integrate and balance the schools. Hines left a prestigious, all-White junior high school to join the faculty at an all-Black junior high school. Three years later, Hines found himself at Wheeler. Marynell Jacob's early background in Mississippi was similar. Horrified over the deaths of civil rights workers Chaney, Goodman, and Schwerner, Jacob attended a memorial church service at a Black church where Joan Baez sang "We Shall Overcome." Wishing to escape the cycle of racism that gripped the state, including members of her own family, she decided to leave Mississippi and move to a more urban setting.

The decision to adopt Harcourt's textbook series and reject Scott, Foresman's cannot be explained as a rejection of diversity. In rejecting a textbook whose editors were motivated by diversity and relevance, teachers at Wheeler and in Cobb County faced an insolvable dilemma.

The teachers' clear personal commitment to effect racial progress came into conflict with their professional commitment to a rigorous and demanding education for their students. Ultimately, the desire to reject the relevance movement, which drastically altered Wheeler and the Cobb school system in nearly every conceivable way, was stronger than the desire to integrate the curriculum.

During the mid-1970s, Wheeler, along with the other schools in Cobb County, adopted the open classroom, where teachers teamed together to teach large groupings of twenty-five to thirty students per teacher. The American literature teachers worked together: Jacob teamed with Patti Bledsoe and Hines, and Jane Frazer and Patsy Musgrove worked together. Reformers, aiming to create a more student-centered, interdisciplinary learning environment called the reform "team teaching." Wheeler's American literature teachers derisively called the reform "turn teaching" because that's how the large-group instruction was effected in the school's American literature classrooms.

Beginning in the 1972 school year and for twelve school years afterward, Cobb County schools also adopted a quarter system of instruction, one that divided the regular school year into three periods, each with a discrete course. Under the quarter system, students were required to take three quarter-long classes in English, and the new system also inspired the creation of elective courses, which could replace the American literature survey and count for any of the three required English credits.

"For 12 years," said Hines, "we were on a quarter system, and then [we moved] to the semester system we have now, but during that quarter system, it was the elective courses, and that was a concession to the protest days of making things relevant. . . . Teachers were able to come up with their own courses such as 'The Search for Self in Literature,' and that probably colored the teaching of American literature a little bit. . . . We had so many electives—'The American Novel,' 'The Search for Self in Literature,' thematic titles that teachers made up and gave their courses and were put on the course offering list."

Hines in fact found two benefits in the quarter system: the elective courses did make courses more relevant, and students were required to take one quarter of grammar and composition, which emphasized and therefore improved student writing. These improvements in literature instruction, however, came at a large (and what would later be deemed unacceptable) cost: students were no longer required to complete a full survey course in American literature. Students would and did graduate without studying the whole of American literature.

"We didn't use anthologies as much during that quarter period as we do now," Hines remembered. "We bought 'em, and paid bundles for them, but we didn't use 'em. If you were teaching 'The American Novel,' you'd use paperbacks and you didn't use the textbook even though you had some in the school waiting for you. There was a lot accomplished in that ten-year experiment, and there was a lot wasted."

English teachers could not reject the quarter system, and they could not overthrow team teaching, but they could reject the 1973 Scott, Foresman textbook that so clearly reflected the same principles that were shaping local education reform. Hines put it this way:

"You think you hear the word *diversity* today, you should have heard the word *relevant* in the '70s. . . . The word *relevant,* we got sick and tired of it. There was a musical entitled, *Tell It Like It Is,* and that was a phrase that was too much with us: 'Tell it like it is.' The school systems did try to respond to that age, and they tried to make things relevant. The relevance movement and the war protest movement affected us, and that's why we had elective courses. We were trying to be relevant. We probably went too far, but I learned a lot of things from it."

Hines remembers seeing the move toward relevance in the Scott, Foresman text and not liking it:

"The books started including some of these protests and poems. Sylvia Plath, you never heard of her until the early '70s. Writers like her that showed not the angst but what—suicidal tendencies—what shall I say?"

In the 1973 Harcourt edition, Hines found a text that rejected the move toward relevance. As Wheeler's English department chair in 1975, he cast his vote and influence toward adopting the new text. Hines remembered the switch well, claiming to have been "a Scott, Foresman man" while teaching in Mississippi, only to become a devout Harcourt fan during his tenure at Wheeler.

"I liked it because it was not watered down," he said. "Some of these books want you to beef up Ralph Nader instead of water down Ralph Waldo Emerson. It's easier to take the difficult one and help students with it, than to take these so-very-contemporary ones and try to blow them up. I liked [Harcourt] because it was a challenge. It was a historical approach of course, and it had good, measured historical background essays, and even back before we were accentuating writing so much, it had some good writing activities in it."

In the curricular war of relevance versus traditional rigor, the selection of the Harcourt text signaled a rejection of contemporary relevance in favor of traditional texts that, in the committee's view, stood the test of time. Stella Ross—then the English department chair at Pebblebrook High School and later the county's first secondary language arts coordinator—recalled the selection process as a return to "the tried and true" classicism of years past. She pointed to the committee's decision to adopt the "Classic Edition" of the Harcourt text as evidence of the commitment to restoring the place of canonical texts in the classroom. Prior to the work of this textbook adoption committee, the county did not have an official American literature textbook. Each county school was free to order any literature text that was approved by the Georgia Department of Education. Hines also remembered that the committee was comprised almost wholly of traditionalists. "Selections and authors—that was our concern," he said. "We wanted the students to read the authors they needed to know for college." Hines also felt that the anthology pieces he selected to teach must stand the test of time to be included on his syllabus:

"I believe there is such a thing as literary history, and I'm concerned with the place of this author or the place of this piece in the body of literature. Shakespeare has etched out his place from now until doomsday. So has Mark Twain. Certainly those [authors] who have etched out for themselves a place in English or American lit, they have got to be taught. I think Walt Whitman has got to be taught. I think Mark Twain has got to be taught; whether I like him or not, I've got to teach him. So, it depends on the significance of the writer and his work. I don't just pick those I like. . . . Sometimes I base it on my druthers, but usually I'm thinking of literary history: 'Does this have a secure place in literary history or does it not?' If it does, I make sure I teach it."

What became of the 1973 editions of the Scott, Foresman text, a book that was Wheeler's "official" text for but one year? The visual image of the class set of anthologies in Patsy Musgrove's classroom, with blunted, tattered corners, ratty folded pages, and decades of inappropriate student comments on the spines, tells a story all its own. The inside cover of each textbook in her room has more names on it than the box will allow. Musgrove (along with several of the other literature teachers at Wheeler) continued to issue the text and the 1968 edition that preceded it, until her retirement from teaching in 1999.

It's possible that Wheeler did not have enough copies of the Harcourt anthology to go around in the mid-1970s. The increasing school population, which put a huge strain on all of the school's material resources, even put classroom space at a premium. At times during the 1970s, some classes were conducted in the storage room in the library and on the cramped stage in the gymnasium.

Hines and Ross, however, doubt that scarcity caused teachers to issue the Scott, Foresman textbook instead of the Harcourt book. Although Ross didn't entirely discount the possibility, she distinctly remembered that the committee "adopted one textbook per child" because they did not want teachers to rely on classroom sets to teach their classes.

"I'm satisfied that they did have enough [Harcourt] textbooks," Hines added. "The [Wheeler] community was pretty outspoken and demanding about these things."

Several teachers remembered that it was not uncommon or inappropriate for Cobb teachers to keep old class sets of anthologies. For Musgrove, the climate of teacher autonomy made Cobb County Schools distinct from neighboring school districts in Georgia. "I always felt free to teach whatever I wanted in Cobb County. I always believed that I should have a variety of books to choose from," said Musgrove, who also remembered preferring the Harcourt book to the Scott, Foresman book for the quality of its introductory essays and its illustrations. Despite this preference for the Harcourt book, Musgrove could not part with her class set of the Scott, Foresman text.

Musgrove essentially became her own American literature anthology, choosing the selections she deemed appropriate for her students and relying on three sets of anthologies to do it. In the absence of a clear county curriculum that told them what to teach, teachers were free to create their syllabi as they saw fit. Musgrove is fond of recalling that the teachers who teased her for keeping the old books later requested to borrow them. Her refusal to discard her old anthologies can be characterized in several ways—subversive, resistant, empowering—but no matter how one characterizes her motives, one conclusion is clear: the teachers had more control over the curriculum than did the anthologies they used.

———————

When Patsy Musgrove retired in 1999, I inherited the box of old tattered anthologies with the faded brown covers, and with them, the problems they presented and the lessons they taught. The challenges I face as an American literature teacher in the year 2000 aren't markedly different than those my predecessors grappled with a quarter century ago. Delving into the past at my own school has taught me to avoid simple characterizations of the classroom. What occurs there is far more complex than I had ever considered. No matter how unfair it may be, additions to the established canon send multiple and perhaps conflicting messages when they are incorporated into the secondary canon of American literature.

Perhaps more important, I learned how little I know about the classroom experiences that preceded mine. Any teacher knows how hard it is to find time to talk with present-day colleagues, let alone find time to identify and interview those who came before. But what a shame it is to exist in survival mode as we so often do—young teachers recreating everything, driving without a map—when all that prior experience, all that accumulated wisdom goes untapped. To make American literature in the present and future, teachers must first discover how it was made in the past.

Acknowledgments

A heartfelt thanks to the following Wheeler High School and Cobb County educators for sharing with me the stories of their professional and personal lives: Mardette Coleman, Jane Frazer, Connie Heyward, Roger Hines, Marynell Jacob, Patsy Musgrove, Faye Rivers, Stella Ross, and Marilyn Winter. Thanks also to the members of the 1999 Kennesaw Mountain Writing Project Advanced Summer Writing Institute: Mimi Dyer, Patsy Hamby, Bernadette Lambert, Man Martin, and Leslie Walker. As colleagues in every sense of the word, they helped me conceive, organize, and revise this piece, but most of all, they motivated me to write, because I did not want to let them down. I also would like to thank Dr. Sarah Robbins of Kennesaw State University, Dr. Anne Ruggles Gere of the University of Michigan, and Dr. Clifford Kuhn and Dr. Ronald Zboray of Georgia State University for guiding me to focus my research and to sharpen my writing.

Works Cited

Blair, Walter, et al., eds. *The United States in Literature*. Chicago: Scott, 1963.

Blair, Walter, et al., eds. *The United States in Literature*. Chicago: Scott, 1968.

Early, James, et al., eds. *Adventures in American Literature*. Classic ed. New York: Harcourt, 1973.

Miller, James E., Robert Hayden, and Robert O'Neal. *The United States in Literature*. Chicago: Scott, 1973.

————. *Teacher's Resource Book to Accompany The United States in Literature.* Glenview, IL: Scott, 1973.

Pooley, Robert C., et al., eds. *The United States in Literature.* Chicago: Scott, 1957.

II Learning about American Literature from Students and Learning about Students from American Literature

Peter Shaheen
Seaholm High School, Birmingham, Michigan

Every student comes to class with a suitcase full of issues that impinge on the teaching and learning that goes on there. My friend Paul reminds me that since students have lives outside the classroom, teachers ought to be shaping instruction to address at least some aspects of these lives. Teachers need to make sure that connections get made between the curriculum and the day-to-day affairs of students outside the classroom. "How can we talk about Daisy and Gatsby," Paul asks, "without talking about love to students who are just beginning to experience the agony and ecstasy of its emotions?"

This section of the book acknowledges and affirms the teacher's role in planning instruction with the student in mind. At the same time, this project recognizes that the teacher who closes the door and attempts to mind his or her own business will soon feel isolated—and with that isolation comes stagnation. Acting in isolation also means that a teacher must face the slings and arrows alone. It means there are no other teachers to help one devise ways to improve one's practice.

The chapters in this section emphasize teamwork, showing how teachers can join forces, often across levels and institutions, to improve their practice. Drawing on the expert opinion of teachers in a variety of classrooms across the country, the authors included here show how they determine what will work best in their individual classrooms. Thus while the authors in this section teach in very different contexts from each other, and perhaps from any given reader, their reflections—such as Kara Kuuttila Shuell's suggestions about reorganizing and refocusing the American literature curriculum, or Ann-Marie Harvey's discussion of how to help White students become more aware of their own ethnicity—can be taken up by teachers in varied situations. In other words, these chapters suggest that we can share teaching ideas across school and regional boundaries. Many of our concerns have both local and universal dimensions, and we can benefit from one another's insights. We all know that there is a great difference between a first-hour class and a class that meets during the last hour of the school day. Similarly, students in adjacent districts often have very different needs. The professional teacher is responsible for shaping instruction that best meets the needs of students in specific classrooms, and an individual teacher's reflective practice can and should be shared with other teachers.

What unites all of the selections in this section is the conviction that teachers can be most effective by foregrounding the needs of their students. This doesn't mean simply listening to what they say. It also means actively reflecting on their concerns and, often, changing one's practice in response. Each of the teachers included in this section recounts how he or she paid attention to what students were saying about American literature. And each narrates significant instructional changes made in response to what students said. In other words, each of the selections included here shows how teachers learned from their students and, in the process, learned about their students as well as about American literature.

When one of Kara Kuuttila Shuell's students complained, "The Puritans have nothing to do with my life," Shuell could not ignore the comment and simply move on. She was troubled by her immediate reactions. First, she thought about a detention for insubordination, and then she responded, "Please trust me. There are some really interesting things we'll study as the semester goes on. We just have to get through this time period first." Rather than simply "just get through," however, Shuell directly confronted the question "What do Puritans have to do with my life?" This chapter tells of her efforts to bridge the gap between the curriculum and the needs of her students. She turned the question into a way of shaping her entire course. With a little help from her friends, Shuell abandoned the chronology she had used in teaching American literature in previous years. After much planning and discussion, she decided on the theme "Passages" as a way of connecting the Puritans' voyage to her students' lives. After a series of lessons, Shuell and her students learned that the passages made by diverse people to get to America are both similar and dissimilar, and that by studying our own unique voyages, we can learn more not only about ourselves but about each other as well.

"Students, American Identities, and Whiteness" by Anne-Marie Harvey is another exploration of students' needs. Harvey uses the tried-and-true theme of what it means to be an American and spins it as only a teacher can by listening to what her students had to say. Even though she included Whiteness in her approach to complicating her students' understanding of American identity, Harvey found that her White students felt they possessed no culture. Through a close reading of her students' writing and careful examination of what literary texts like *The Great Gatsby* tell us about Whiteness, Harvey shows how teachers of American literature can help students rethink American identity in self-empowering ways.

It may come as no surprise that many of Harvey's students felt devoid of a literature about themselves. The twist, however, is that the students were White. One of her students explains the predicament: "Certainly, one cannot expect me to identify with the whole of Caucasian America simply because we share the same skin color." Feeling a nudge from her students, Harvey found herself moving in new directions. By using Du Bois's *The Souls of Black Folk*, she challenged the notion of a standard norm for American culture.

Harvey also noticed that elements of consumer commercialism were influencing some of her students' inability to identify a culture to call their own. Through a series of reflective practices, she and her students finally came to the conclusion that grappling with one's identity can be a productive exercise no matter how mysterious that identity may turn out to be, and no matter how difficult the struggle might become.

David Anthony likewise shows how he learned from his students. He begins by describing a course he had taught before he participated in a summer workshop. It was a reasonably successful course, but in reading student evaluations, thinking about the patterns of class participation, and, especially, looking at writing produced by students in the class, Anthony realized that students were not truly engaging with the literature he was teaching. They were waiting for him to feed them the "right" answers so they could give them back to him. When he faulted students for failing to be original in their thinking, they were distressed and perplexed.

After working with other teachers in the NEH-funded Making American Literatures project (see the foreword), Anthony began to think about writing assignments in more complicated ways. He realized that students could engage with literary texts by writing in genres other than standard literary essays. In his chapter, Anthony details the assignments he gave in his revised course. The very moving student texts he includes demonstrate how effectively he achieved his goal of fostering student engagement in the work of the course. He shows convincingly that his students learned a great deal about American literature and about themselves as Americans.

My own chapter focuses on teaching the novel *The Education of Little Tree: A True Story.* It explains how my students informed and improved my practice. This book had all the makings of a classic that was sure to be taught alongside *To Kill A Mockingbird* in high schools across the country. When the author, Forrest Carter, was discovered to be a fraud, the fortunes of his "autobiography" suddenly took a turn for the worse. I thought I could take advantage of the controversy and teach the book anyway.

My plan was to use the text as a way to illustrate the notion that all writing is autobiographical because it is tied to a specific political and social context. I withheld my knowledge about the controversy surrounding the text itself as I picked out some of the more obvious themes that the story addressed. In effect, I set a trap for students. I was going to trick them into liking a book and then tell them everything that the story advocated was a pretense for some malevolent political ideology. When I was sure I had them, I would spring the trap and let them know the truth.

I did just that, but the reaction I received from my students was not what I had expected, and it led me to rethink and revise my teaching. This experience suggested that there was much for me to learn about teaching even after twenty years in the classroom. I learned more about what my role is as a teacher—promoting democratic communities, particularly when American literature is the subject. And I learned how to go about achieving that goal—asking better questions. Most of all, I learned—again—that I can learn from my students.

6 The Puritans Have Nothing to Do with My Life

Kara Kuuttila Shuell
Southfield High School, Southfield, Michigan

Please trust me. There are some really interesting things we'll study as the semester goes on. We just have to get through this time period first." I was trying to explain. Rather than issuing a detention, I had chosen to engage in a discussion with the student whose dissonance had become a behavior problem in my classroom. While he and I sat in conference in the computer lab across the hall, his classmates, the other twenty-nine juniors and seniors back in the classroom, were supposed to read about Jonathan Edwards. In reality, they were probably speculating about our conversation. I lamented; I just hoped there was *some* learning going on somewhere.

"*No.*" He shook his head in one decisive and forceful nod. "The Puritans have nothing to do with my life."

To Sean, that was the end of the discussion. No explanation from me would convince this seventeen-year-old African American growing up in the 1990s in Southfield, Michigan, that there was any need to study those who landed on Plymouth Rock nearly three hundred years before. Sean's world didn't include patience with a teacher who begged for his trust. He was growing up in a middle-class environment with nice parents who were college educated and professionals in their fields. His parents provided all the modern comforts a teen could desire—clothes, vacations, computers, and so on. But more than that, I think they instilled in their son a desire to really use his brain. He was an "A" student and a good writer. But Sean didn't passively accept what was put before him; he had to shape new learning into his own worldview. And the Puritans didn't fit. I admired the way his refusal to participate was a part of his character. He reminded me a little bit of myself; I was always one for a good protest. His statement pounded in my head again. "The Puritans have nothing to do with my life."

As I sighed, I couldn't help but wonder about his argument. What *did* the Puritans have to do with his life?

Until I met Sean, I taught American literature chronologically. I started with the Puritans and continued on through time until the semester ended. This maybe got the class to the 1950s if we hurried through the 1800s. It's the way I was taught, and it was the only way I knew. I never considered anything else. But then I had to remind myself of a time when I was the student challenging the status quo. *The Catcher in the Rye* had been banned from the high school classrooms in the small town where I grew up, but I defiantly read the novel and confidently quoted from it in a speech to the school and the community. Just because that's the way it's been done before doesn't mean it's the best way. It may be the *easiest* way, but Sean forced me to ask another question: *For whom* was it easy?

It certainly wasn't easy for Sean to sit through what he saw as a torturous journey through American literature. We were in the first unit, and already he saw my class as disconnected from his life. If I lost Sean now, would I ever get him back?

We didn't reach any decision that day, but Sean and I came to the only agreement immediately possible. At least he would try to keep his contempt to himself so as to not cause general chaos and disharmony throughout the whole class. But then, I had to ask myself the question I had been avoiding all through my discussion with Sean. He just happened to be the one who complained. How many others felt that the Puritans had nothing to do with their lives? Heck, what could *I* say that the Puritans had to do with *my* life?

As a teacher I've learned that students often ask hard questions that have no ready answers. I knew that something had to change. What good was I doing in my classroom if no one really cared? But what was I going to do differently? And the bigger question: How was I going to do it? Just like the Puritans, I put myself in a new territory by asking these questions, and I sure hoped I wouldn't starve to death before the first winter snow melted.

The first European settlers in what is now the United States were fortunate to meet Native Americans who taught them how to hunt and fish. As I began to really make some concrete changes, I sought out my own colleagues. My discussion with Sean occurred in early September, and I spent the rest of that school year thinking about changing my American literature class. Change is hard. It takes time and effort. It was summer before I could realistically expect to work on revisiting such a huge issue as curriculum. I was thankful to have colleagues with whom to work.

The summer after my class with Sean, I was involved in a workshop with the NEH-funded Making American Literatures project (see the foreword for more about this project), along with Rita Teague, one of my colleagues at Southfield High School. For two weeks, we went to our sessions during the day and stayed in a University of Michigan dorm at night. It was one such night while Rita and I were drinking diet soda and sitting on our dorm beds with our spiral notebooks in hand that we came up with ways to alter the American literature curriculum at our school.

The first thing we did was to list and examine our units from the past. We acknowledged that we had used the traditional approach: We'd started with page one of the textbook and continued onward, turning the pages and gliding through the centuries. The content had integrity, but what I learned from Sean was that this approach wasn't reaching everyone. Rita and I weren't going to throw out everything we had covered in the previous curriculum, but simply using the chronological approach and working forward through time wasn't engaging kids. How could we hook kids into these texts that were seemingly so far removed from their lives? How could we connect the Puritans to the lives of today's students?

The Puritans left England to embark on a new adventure. They were excited about venturing out to a new land. The New World meant liberty. However, Sean was quick to point out that wasn't the case with all those who boarded large ships to sail the rugged waters to America.

"Not everyone was happy to come here."

He was a young man of few words; those he uttered were significant. Sean was right. How could we portray the relative freedom on the Puritans' ships without the contrast of the imprisonment on the slave ships?

We decided that we would take a thematic approach rather than a chronological one. We put the Puritans, slave ship narratives, and several other perspectives on coming to America into a unit entitled Passages. We would work with the texts we already had and supplement with articles, poems, essays, and other texts about more current situations of peoples making a passage to America. Why did they come to America? How was their search similar to or different from students' diverse life dreams today? We weren't looking to exclude the Puritans, we just decided to contextualize the Puritans as one group of many throughout history who have made the journey (whether willingly or not) to America.

Like all schools, we had our limitations: a lack of newer books, insufficient cultural diversity in the books we did have, and of course our budget constraints. What we *could* do was to become more deliberate with what we already had. Our greatest strength was our capacity to work together with the students and with one another.

The next school year I felt like a Puritan who had survived a year in the New World. Just like our ancestors, I approached life with a new confidence. Armed with a thoughtfully reorganized curriculum, I walked into my classroom renewed. I started the Passages unit with a wonderful brainstorming exercise: On the board, I drew a map of what is now the United States. (My students told me all my drawings looked like pork chops, but we persevered anyway.) They drew maps in their journals, too. Once we had our maps, we began to place peoples on them. Who came to America? That led us to begin exploring the question we would look at in more depth through literature: How and why did these "Americans" come to America?

We began to look at this question with lots of brainstorming, drawing, and furious note taking. There were, of course, many answers. And our answers crossed time periods, modes of transportation, and ethnicities. I used this brainstorming session to bring in literature involving all the peoples we put on the map. Many texts were carried over from the previous year, and I added some new ones to align with our brainstorming. This opened the door to literature from a variety of cultures. For example, we studied the Asians who came to America through Angel Island. We read the perceptions of the Native Americans who already were in America before anyone else arrived. We thought about Hispanic Americans who entered the United States from Mexico. We read about the African slaves who were forced to come to America against their will. We discussed babies from Russia and Romania who are being adopted by U.S. families today. We studied the Haitians who risk their lives floating on makeshift rafts, just for a chance to reach the United States.

And the best thing was—we even got to the Puritans! During the brainstorming, a student in the class offered the Puritans as one people who came to America. I couldn't resist a smile as I drew the Puritans landing at Plymouth Rock. I'll admit that my drawing had them somewhere nearer to Maine, but it was the generating of ideas that was important, not the accuracy of the teacher's map. And by working together, my students and I discovered that the study of the Puritans as one group among many who left their original country to come to America was an exciting study. Who would have thought?

As I took materials to the library for copying, I met with Sean again. As it turned out, he was a library assistant during my prep hour. The previous year, he had been a junior in a junior/senior class. He and I had many discussions about the curriculum, including my report to him about his prompting my hard look at the curriculum. I told him his voice had been heard. Sean took a copy of each addition to the curriculum. He said he wished he could take the class over again.

The newly revamped curriculum also had to be reflected in the assessment tasks. These tasks started with collective journaling and led to literary analysis, poetry, and, for the final assessment task, letters written from the perspective of five of the different groups studied. Each student had to draw together his or her learning from the unit, either by using characters from literature or by creating new ones. The letters were powerful and showed that the students really understood the goal of seeing other points of view. In fact, this unit, like all in our curriculum, was intended to last for one six-week marking period. Instead, it continued throughout the semester. As we went on to the American Dream, Struggles and Conflicts, and American Cultures units, my students were still drawing on their knowledge and ideas from the Passages unit. When given a choice for their final exam essay, most went back to Passages.

Revisiting existing curriculum isn't an easy task. But it's an honest one when we really consider the students and their needs. Listening to students like Sean is important if we really want our kids' learning to be meaningful to them. I learned that we had to work from our strengths and stick together. Having a colleague like Rita with whom to work made an enormous task possible. Like the Puritans making their way in the New World, we had to create new directions for ourselves because the old ways just weren't working any longer.

7 Students, American Identities, and Whiteness

Anne-Marie Harvey
University of California, Berkeley

I am jealous of those who have their own distinct culture apart from being American, even though they may sometimes feel left out or at a disadvantage in English-dominated "white America." Myself, I am hopelessly searching for some fascinating background or culture which, even if I found it, would never be truly mine because a background would have to be just that—back, in my past.

Mary Brater

It's hard to explain what it feels like to have no culture at all, to have no history to be proud of, to have no national origin to look to, to belong to no one. . . . Certainly, one cannot expect me to relate to the whole of Caucasian America simply because we share the same color of skin.

Louise Cardwell

My students have never failed to nudge me in new directions. For instance, years ago, I included W. E. B. Du Bois's *The Souls of Black Folk* midway down a syllabus and expected the book to offer one in an array of versions of American identity. The class characteristically and fruitfully ignored my intentions, quickly making Du Bois, with his complex and revealing articulation of "double-consciousness," the central text of the course. As surely as Du Bois unfolds a central vision of American identity, students of various racial and cultural identities (often various within each student) used his book as a lens for reading other literature, including the "White" and the canonical, and for reading their own lives.

Subsequently, *The Souls of Black Folk* has become an important part of my ongoing efforts to contest that version of American culture in which there is a central norm—White, privileged, male, straight (and, in the context of the literature classroom, canonical)—from which everything else differs. Too often, efforts to represent various identities in American literature classrooms array "different" voices around "standard" ones, placing the already marginalized in the margins one more time.

As I try to help my students reconfigure the traditional landscapes of American literature and culture, I have also tried to make my classroom a place where authors, texts, and students are not asked, explicitly or implicitly, to represent entire groups in American culture at all. One of the ways in which I have attempted to achieve this effect—and here Du Bois comes into the picture again—is to invite discussion of the mixed, conflicted, and multiple character of *all* American identities. None of us, and no text, is exclusively shaped by one group or identity; no group or identity is uniform. Certainly no one, inside or outside a literature classroom, should be expected to speak for an entire group—cultural, gendered, racial, or otherwise.

One of the most challenging aspects of encouraging students to reconceive American literature and identity in these ways has been to rethink how I treat Whiteness in my classroom. In the past, my main approach to Whiteness has been to offer representations of Whites as belonging to specific cultural groups. For instance, we would read Denise Giardina's *Storming Heaven*, a novel about Appalachian coal miners who possess a distinct culture: dialect, music, cooking, religious practices, modes of family, connections to the land, and so on. Or I would incidentally-on-purpose offer myself as an example: my family is from northern Florida, Alabama, and Texas—a background which similarly entails possessing regional cultures, some of whose features I can identify. In fact, I have made a practice of opening all of my UC Berkeley courses with a getting-to-know you exercise in which my students interview one another about where their parents or grandparents lived and then introduce one another to the class. Everybody, including the White students (and the adopted students) has a family history, and therefore a cultural history.

I have tried to demonstrate that Whiteness doesn't entail a cultural blankness, as well as to point out that the uniformity Whites do possess is often the result of a calculated forgetting. This spring, I read aloud to my students this paragraph from an article by Senator Tom Hayden of California:

> I was raised in an Irish-American home in Detroit where assimilation was the uppermost priority. The price of assimilation was amnesia. Although my great-grandparents were victims of the Great Hunger of the 1840s, even though I was named Thomas Emmet Hayden IV after the radical Irish nationalist exile Thomas Emmet, my inheritance was to be disinherited. My parents know nothing of this past or nothing worth passing on. (When I asked my mother, "If I'm the fourth, who were the others?" she answered, "The first, the second, and the third.") (20–21)

A number of heads in the classroom nodded in recognition. As my students have noticed, depictions of such forgetting of a cultural past are readily available in American literature: consider, for instance, that Midwestern son of German stock James Gatz's arduous self-remaking into the fabricated, fabulous, and rootless Jay Gatsby.

Among the principles at stake here is demonstrating that the perfectly mainstream White American doesn't exist; as soon as you think you've found him, he turns out to be ethnically distinctive, behind his masks. Once the masks are removed, the forgetting reversed, the "norm" turns out not to be actually embodied anywhere. The center or "standard" of American culture and literature loses some of its monolithic weight.

I still think this general approach to Whiteness is productive in my classes. Yet I have learned that it's not enough. At the end of a course in which my students and I explored the cultural specificity contained in White identities, I read intelligent, honest essays by Mary Brater and Louise Cardwell in which each describes a sense of possessing no culture at all. Mary writes:

> This class, my reactions to the experiences of people here, and college as a whole have made me realize that I have been wanting to borrow, or take on, an interesting heritage because I feel I do not have one at all. The influences of my family, who seem to be uninterested in their own heritage, as well as my own somewhat pessimistic views on America have led me to think of "white Americans" like myself as culture-less.

Mary makes clear that, for those without ready access to a cultural past outside of the recognized mainstream, the search for cultural identity can end up in culture envy. Louise sums it up in a phrase: "In short, I was ashamed and envious"—ashamed, that is, of membership in a group "associated with oppression and enslavement" and envious of those whom she perceives as possessing culture.

Such shame and envy are a personal and intellectual cul-de-sac. The sense that White Americans or, in Louise's phrase, "European mutts" possess no culture reinscribes a featureless, normative center in American culture. At their worst, attempts by Whites to self-identify as "ethnic" by pointing to cultural roots outside the mainstream can culminate in denial of privilege (as in, "Sure, I'm White, but my ancestors were colonized by the British or exploited by the ruling class") or cynical appropriation of "otherness." Louise and Mary, however, being both sensitive to their own privilege and savvy about the long history of cultural appropriation, do not make such moves.

These student essays have made clear to me that it's not enough to demonstrate that Whites belong to distinctive and sometimes marginalized cultural groups. I don't want my (few) White, Anglo-Saxon, Protestant students walking out of my classes thinking that they haven't any cultural or racial identity—at least none that they want to own and live in—or that they must scrounge up some Irish-Americanness or gay-Latvian-Americanness or whatever supposedly exotic otherness they still have access to. I don't want students of color and immigrants in my classes to feel "othered" or exoticized by anyone's belief in a blank, White American norm, or by anyone's difference envy. Instead, I want my classroom to be a place where students feel empowered to bring all of themselves to the table, as they are, and where we productively put identity itself, not people, on the spot.

In keeping with my students' focus on cultural identity, one important possibility for pushing in these directions presents itself readily. What would happen if my students and I really bore down on describing the specific features of contemporary, mainstream, or dominant American culture—that accepted norm that is so hard to define because so many Americans are trained to breathe it like air, not to taste its flavors but rather just to absorb it?

In her essay, Mary first suggests that "much of the problem" in gaining a sense of her own cultural identity has been that she "[does] not believe Americans have a distinct culture of their own." Yet she then suggests: "There must be, of course, an American culture—one that goes beyond television and advertising and 'pop culture'—though I admit that right now I have no idea what that culture consists of."

In that same course, when I asked my students to describe a widely held, mainstream American culture, they frequently began to talk about the mass media and American consumer culture—and they frequently dismissed them as empty or false, as a cultural vacuum. One road, then, would be to pursue that discussion further, to ask students to take a hard look at some portion of "television and advertising and 'pop culture'" to see if, as a group, we might define some of American mass culture's distinctive features, as well as its connections to American culture more broadly considered. I am engaged in just such a project now, in a course about American literature, advertising, and consumer culture. We'll see how it goes, whether studying mass culture renders it any more a "real culture," and whether students' relation to it—however complex and resisting that relation may be—seems any more admissible as partly defining their own identities.

Several students have implicitly suggested to me another way to discern the features of American mainstream culture, including and going beyond the mass media. In his essay "What Constitutes Being 'American'?" Ibrahim Madany writes:

> The only time I feel like a complete American occurs when I travel to foreign countries and the people around me instantly label me as such, mostly because of my "American" way of dressing and speaking. In Europe, for example, I have encountered people . . . who assume that I am an American and pursue me to ask me questions about the United States and my life there. This assumption and questioning, in a sense, transforms me into a representative of America; my actions and behavior are automatically labeled as American.

What would happen if I pursued such thinking further, with a whole class? Seen through "foreign" eyes, what constitutes an "'American' way of dressing and speaking"? What "actions and behavior" does someone outside the U.S. perceive as peculiarly American?

Another student, Erica Rose, pursued a similar line of thinking and, working both from her own experiences in Italy and from a reading of *The Great Gatsby*, arrived at a striking observation about American culture.

> It has been two years since the summer I spent with an Italian family, and in the time that has passed I have realized that the understandings I have developed about the Italian culture can offer me valuable insights into my own. As a white, middle-class American, I had never had the experience of balancing two cultures. I had never been able to form a definition of an American. . . . In the absence of anything else to be I have always felt that I'm an American, but what exactly does that mean; what characteristics is that conclusion drawn from?

As she spent time in Italy, Erica grew disturbed by her Italian family's apparent complacency in a circumscribed life on a small farm, their lack of interest in progress or expanding horizons. Getting past her initial shock, she developed the observation that many Italians appear to "exist fully and happily in the present."

This observation, together with Judith Fetterley's writing about *The Great Gatsby*, led Erica to an insight into American culture. She quotes Fetterley on Gatsby: "[This story's] concern is with the experience of longing and the sense of loss—a romantic readiness for the future and a romantic nostalgia for the past" (79). Erica concludes that, in contrast to Italian culture, one cultural strand that connects Americans involves

> the way that our beings are divided between the past and the future, always remembering, always planning, always dreaming.

> . . . Happiness is conjured up from memories of the past, in which
> we lived in an imaginary golden age, and our goals for the future
> are often goals for a re-creation of that former joy.

Erica's thought rings true for me: in large part, Americans are dissatisfied with the present, and restlessly long for idealized pasts and the futures we plan to re-create from those pasts. (Already, here is a connection to American consumer culture, with its uses of an idealized past and its offers of an idealized, never-quite-attained future.) This kind of observation about American culture—subtle, convincing, crossing many lines of identity—has the potential to undo a mainstream sense, like Louise's, of having "no culture . . . no history . . . no national origin." To foster this sort of insight, I can imagine asking students to interview someone who has undertaken such travel, or someone from another culture (including one another), about what seems strikingly "different" about mainstream American culture.

In order to more fully contest a notion of mainstream, dominant, White American identity as a lack of identity, I suspect that it is also important to move beyond articulating culture and to begin treating the specificity of Whiteness itself, imagined as race. Louise suggests that, "certainly, one cannot expect me to relate to all of Caucasian America simply because we share the same color of skin." Certainly not, especially since all of "Caucasian America" doesn't even share a color of skin. (Asserting his Iranian American identity, Ibrahim Madany writes, "Having a light skin doesn't constitute a race or an identity; yet I have noticed that all those of light skin color get grouped together into the 'White' category.") Similarly, consider the absurdity of asking another person to relate to all Asian Americans because of her facial features, or asking another to relate to all African Americans because of the quality of her hair. Like "Caucasian America," such categories encompass more difference—genetic and cultural— within themselves than they do between one another. Race itself is patently absurd, a collective fantasy, a device, a hoax. Yet it does exist. If our understanding of American identity still includes racial identity for people of color, than aren't we letting Whiteness off the hook again, reinscribing it as the blank norm, if we never examine its features?

In an article entitled "White Privilege: Unpacking the Invisible Knapsack," Peggy McIntosh lists elements of White privilege. These include items such as

> 5. I can turn on the television or open to the front page of the
> paper and see people of my race widely represented.

6. When I am told about our national heritage or about "civilization," I am shown that people of my color made it what it is.

7. I can be sure that my children will be given curricular materials that testify to the existence of their race. . . .

12. I can swear, dress in second hand clothes, or not answer letters, without having people attribute these choices to the bad morals, the poverty, or the illiteracy of my race. . . .

14. I can do well in a challenging situation without being called a credit to my race.

15. I am never asked to speak for all the people of my racial group.

McIntosh writes, "I repeatedly forgot each of the realizations on this list until I wrote it down. For me, White privilege has turned out to be an elusive and fugitive subject" (11). As its title suggests, McIntosh's article breaks through a barrier of unknowability, or invisibility; it succeeds in articulating specific features of White privilege. I would be curious to see what might happen if I shared this article with all of my students and asked them to extend its list.

But I wonder if the features of White privilege adequately describe Whiteness—and I suspect that they tell only part of the story. What about Whiteness in an even broader sense, including but going beyond privilege? How do any of us in American culture represent Whiteness to ourselves? What metaphors for and associations with Whiteness circulate in American literature and language?

One starting place, as both Louise and Mary implicitly suggest, is the sense of lack itself—absence as a metaphor for American Whiteness. Color has a presence that Whiteness envies and longs to appropriate and absorb. In *Playing in the Dark: Whiteness and the Literary Imagination*, beyond offering the insight that Whiteness in American literature and culture consists largely of its uses of Blackness, Toni Morrison also identifies a number of metaphors for Whiteness, including that of lack. Referring to characters in Hemingway's *The Garden of Eden*, Morrison writes that "blackness is something one can 'have' or appropriate; it's the one thing they lack, she tells him. Whiteness here is a deficiency" (87). Elsewhere, having addressed Twain, Poe, and Faulkner, among others, Morrison writes: "Whiteness, alone, is mute, meaningless, unfathomable, pointless, frozen, veiled, curtained, dreaded, senseless, implacable" (59). The metaphor of a veil connects this description of race to Du Bois's in *The Souls of Black Folk*. While, in his terms, the veil limits, hides, mystifies, and exoticizes Blackness, it also blocks and mystifies Whiteness, rendering it hidden even for those who live inside of it. The veil over Whiteness hides a "dreaded" power, yet it is at the same time like the curtain that hides the Wizard of Oz: It suggests a supreme magical power that turns out to be a trick—in this case, a really dirty trick.

Morrison's language helps me to spell out my own imaginings of Whiteness, acknowledging the importance of metaphors of absence, yet also pushing toward the *presence* of Whiteness. Just as privilege is not the whole story, neither is lack or concealment. I have begun my own list of associations with American Whiteness: a list which, like any formulation of racial attributes, necessarily consists of "lies," impossible generalizations, many of them connected to Protestants and to my own family. Some of what Whiteness calls to mind for me:

> Individualism, solitude.
>
> In seeming contradiction, conformity and mass culture: each person alone yet conforming.
>
> Inability to confront suffering.
>
> Self-discipline and order.
>
> Close ties to immediate family, strong connections little spoken of directly.
>
> Correspondingly, lack of strong interdependence with an extended family or community: self-reliance.
>
> Quietness, the importance of the unspoken. Dry humor.
>
> Quiet menace: power so omnipresent it needn't be spoken, but only exercised.

I'll extend this list with a similar one by Diane Glancy, who writes about the White part of her that coexists with her Native American identity:

> I can look at the Whiteness in my mother's family and say there was a determination, a punctuality, a dependability. There was a sense of Manifest Destiny, which was another tool for dominance. There was a need for maintenance and responsibility. A sense of a Judeo-Christian God. A holding to one's own. There was a need to be goal-oriented. To make use of resources. There was also opportunity to do all these things. (7)

These lists of associations remind me of an exercise suggested by Bernadette Lambert, a colleague in the NEH-funded Making American Literatures project (see the foreword for more about this project). She writes the words "white" and "black" on the chalkboard and then asks her middle school students to make lists of words they associate with each term. This exercise makes a starting point for taking apart racial stereotypes—including those associated with Whiteness.

In a college classroom, I can imagine productively addressing Whiteness by inviting students to examine, as Morrison does, the language surrounding White characters in literature. For example, how does F. Scott Fitzgerald represent Jay Gatsby as a White man? In what sense do Fitzgerald's (that is, Nick Carraway's) descriptions of Gatsby reveal his, and American culture's, imaginings of Whiteness? One point of interest might be Gatsby's ethereality. In contrast to characters such as Meyer Wolfsheim, described with grotesquely physical and racialized characteristics, Gatsby "[drifts] coolly out of nowhere (54)." He is restless, "never quite still," and rootless: "A dim background started to take shape behind him but at her next remark it faded away" (68, 53). He seems at some points to be more an empty suit than a fleshly man: "I could think of nothing except the luminosity of his pink suit under the moon" (150). Gatsby is also characterized by solitude, repeatedly described as "standing alone" (57).

Rather than attempt a reading of Gatsby's Whiteness here, I'll pose some questions: What do Nick's descriptions of Gatsby have to do with American representations of Whiteness? Does Tom Buchanan's brute physicality make him, in Nick's or Fitzgerald's view, less White? Does that possibility have anything to do with Tom's feeble pronunciations of White supremacy, or with Jordan Baker's remark that "We're all White here" (137)? What about other White characters such as Daisy, Jordan, Myrtle, and Wilson? How are Fitzgerald's representations of Whiteness inflected by gender, class, and ethnicity?

More important, how can examining American representations of Whiteness—literary or otherwise—help achieve the goal I described at the opening of this essay: helping students to rethink the landscape of American identity in self-empowering ways? Can a careful look at representations of Whiteness help students to consider which aspects of it they want to change, which they recognize and embrace, and how they want to define and use their own racial and cultural identities? I'll conclude by quoting one more student, Kara Lee Smith, who insists on the integrity of her identity, and on including Whiteness as a part of that whole identity: "I am Creole; we have our own food, music and language. By only claiming my blackness, I felt that I was denying a whole part of my ancestry that continues to remain a mystery today." I would like to create a classroom in which Kara, and all of my students, can grapple productively with all of the identities that define them, how-ever mysterious and difficult they may be.

Works Cited

Du Bois, W. E. B. *The Souls of Black Folk: Authoritative Text, Contexts, Criticism.* 1903. Ed. Henry Louis Gates Jr. and Terri Hume Oliver. New York: Norton, 1999.

Fetterley, Judith. *The Resisting Reader: A Feminist Approach to American Fiction.* Bloomington: Indiana UP, 1978.

Fitzgerald, F. Scott. *The Great Gatsby.* New York: MacMillan, 1992.

Giardina, Denise. *Storming Heaven: A Novel.* New York: Ballantine, 1999.

Glancy, Diane. "When the Boats Arrived." *Hungry Mind Review* 45 (Spring 1998): 7.

Hayden, Tom. "Notes of an Irish-American Son: History, Amnesia and Northern Ireland." *The Nation* 266.18 (May 1998): 20–22.

McIntosh, Peggy. "White Privilege: Unpacking the Invisible Knapsack." *Peace and Freedom* (July/August 1989): 10–12.

Morrison, Toni. *Playing in the Dark: Whiteness and the Literary Imagination.* New York: Vintage, 1993.

8 Students, Narrative, Historical Longing: The Stories We (Americans) Tell about Ourselves

David Anthony
Southern Illinois University

Several years ago while teaching a course entitled Introduction to American Literature, I decided to organize the syllabus around the related issues of historical narrative and national identity. My goal in this class was to offer students a chance to see how various contemporary American authors were both enacting and critiquing (often simultaneously) the ways in which the notion of American identity, broadly configured, depends upon the act of storytelling—upon the stories we tell others and hear from others, as well as the stories we tell ourselves about ourselves. I saw this as a variation on the more familiar "American Dream" framework and felt that students would respond to it eagerly.

The opening page from one of the texts I used during that term, Michael Ondaatje's *The Collected Works of Billy the Kid*, exemplifies much of what I was aiming for. Occupying the top two-thirds of the page is an empty box, apparently the frame for a photograph, below which is a fragment from a correspondence between two unknown people about the (missing) image. "I send you a picture of Billy made with the Perry shutter as quick as it can be worked—Pyro and soda developer," the first sentence tells us. Immediately we're made to see that Ondaatje is putting considerable interpretive pressure on the reader, who in the absence of an actual image of Billy the Kid, American legend, is forced to conjure up such an image for him or herself. Ondaatje continues this narrative imperative throughout the text, piling up a composite of various narrative perspectives on Billy (excerpts from letters, newspaper articles, poems both by and about the notorious gunslinger, uncaptioned nineteenth-century photos from the American "West") that, taken as whole, do as much to unravel the notion of a single identifiable "history" of Billy the Kid (or of an "American" legend) as they do to provide one.

This version of an American history was one of many acutely self-aware texts I chose for my class, much as Tom Romano, I later learned, used in his classroom. Offering students a fairly comprehensible (if somewhat abstract) model for thinking about the relationships between narrative, national historical myths, and national identity, such texts would, I hoped, eventually help students to see that the narrative process Ondaatje was commenting on was one in which they themselves were deeply enmeshed as "Americans" inhabiting various identities with various histories—socioeconomic, racial, ethnic, regional, and otherwise. Indeed, as Anne-Marie Harvey makes abundantly clear in Chapter 7 of this volume, one of the greatest challenges facing an instructor is that of convincing students who see themselves as simply normal, average, or just inherently "American" (often middle-class White suburbanites) that they too have a relationship to the nation that can be told *and* untold in various ways.

My class, however, never really seemed to get off the ground. Students were initially taken by the self-reflexive and nontraditional nature of texts such as *Billy the Kid*, and class discussions were usually fairly active, with students (albeit usually the same half dozen or so) often raising their hands, and sometimes even arguing certain points. Something was lacking, though—not just during class discussions, but also in the papers they were writing. Simply put, students seemed either unable or unwilling to see the relationship between the characters they were reading about (Nick Carraway in F. Scott Fitzgerald's *The Great Gatsby*, Lupe Arredondo in Sandra Cisneros's "Bien Pretty" from *Woman Hollering Creek*) and themselves. For a while this left me frustrated, but eventually I began to suspect that the problem lay with the paper topics I was assigning. Most of my prompts resulted in papers that were flat and predictable. Worse, they tended to leave many students unable to get outside of the discussions we'd had in class (especially my comments during these discussions). The result was that I frequently had to give low grades to students who were saying all the "right" things. At the end of the term I found myself reading a handful of evaluations that made my mistakes embarrassingly clear. "This class was okay, but the teacher seemed to grade our papers down whenever our ideas didn't match up with his," read one comment. I don't think this was entirely accurate, but it wasn't entirely wrong, either. Why was it so difficult to provide assignments that allowed students the freedom and the motivation to engage with the course material in ways they were actually invested in?

Part of the problem, I had to admit while reading over my student evaluations, is that graduate students (as I then was) at research universities don't receive the sort of training that might help in creating paper assignments for students. Nor do we put much time into talking with one another about how to do this effectively. Indeed, this trouble communicating about topics such as paper assignments is something I noted numerous times during my two-year involvement in the Making American Literatures project (see the foreword for a project description). Whereas from day one the main interest for the participating secondary school teachers was classroom methodology ("How can I turn this issue into the various stages of an assignment that will lead to a full-length paper?"), many university participants tended to focus on issues and concepts ("How are categories of race and gender being constructed here? What does this text have to say about nationhood and otherness?"). This was especially true during our 1997 summer workshop in Berkeley. Almost every day, we listened to guest speakers, many of them nationally recognized experts in nineteenth- and twentieth-century American literature, who spoke on a text we were reading, or an issue related to the text. At the beginning of the seminar I assumed that these presentations would be the raw material for discussions or follow-up group work about how to read (or reread) texts such as Nella Larsen's *Passing*, N. Scott Momaday's *The Way to Rainy Mountain*, and others on our syllabus. What I found, however, was that these presentations were routinely missing the point: "How do I teach this text?"

As a member of the project's leadership team, I helped to redesign the 1998 workshop in Ann Arbor so that pedagogy was more fully integrated into our study of literary texts. In the pages that follow, I want to describe an assignment which I put together with several of my secondary school colleagues, and which I tried out the next semester in a revised version of the course I describe above. Our goal was to come up with a group of texts and a paper assignment that put students— either high school seniors or first-year college students—in the position of having to grapple with fairly complex issues of form and narrative, while at the same time seeking to understand these issues in terms of history and national identity. After much debate, we decided that the best way around the pitfalls I had encountered in my earlier version of the course was to allow students to avoid straightforward textual analysis, forcing them instead to utilize the texts as *models* and *examples* for engaging with the broader issues of narrative, history, and national identity. In other words, rather than writing *about* a text such as *Billy the Kid*, we wanted students to perform the techniques Ondaatje employed while writing his book. We decided that this difference was crucial, as it would allow students to create and "own" a document that wasn't automatically overshadowed by literary "masterpieces" such as *The Great Gatsby* or *Huckleberry Finn*. Just as important, we felt that this move would help students avoid the pitfall of repeating ideas already hashed out during class discussions (something that, to my mind at least, would make teaching more liberating—no more worrying about giving away all the "answers"!). The result of all this, we felt, would be that students would learn far more about the *processes* involved in creating literary texts than they might otherwise have been able to learn. And this lesson, we hoped, would extend into the reading and criticism of future texts.

A set of panels from *Maus II*, Art Spiegelman's comic book history of his father's experiences in Auschwitz, provides an example of some of the issues we wanted students to engage with, as well as examples of the kind of narrative techniques we hoped they might use in their own papers. Driving with his wife Francoise, Spiegelman (having depicted himself, Francoise, and all the other Jews in the text as mice, and all the Germans as cats) reflects on his efforts to render his subject in cartoon form: "I feel so inadequate trying to reconstruct a reality that was worse than my darkest dreams," he says. "And trying to do it in a comic strip! . . . There's so much I'll never be able to understand or visualize. I mean, reality is too complex for comics. . . . So much has to be left out or distorted" (16). Radically self-reflexive, Spiegelman emphasizes that his text almost necessarily fails to provide an objective picture of the past. In doing so, he highlights some of the most basic of "American" truths: that his relationship to himself (as individual and as second-generation American citizen) is painfully contingent upon the history of his own fractured and traumatized family. The problem for Spiegelman, as for many Americans, is that writing is inadequate to the task of composing or providing this history, a point he emphasizes in his reflections on using a comic book form for his novel. Much like Ondaatje in the opening of *Billy the Kid*, Spiegelman is telling us that the historical narratives we rely on to anchor us in our understanding of ourselves (as the children of immigrants, as "Americans," and so on) are subjective and often decidedly unstable.

N. Scott Momaday makes a similar point throughout *The Way to Rainy Mountain*. Seeking to provide a "history" of the Kiowa Indians,

Momaday juxtaposes on each page of his text three separate narrative perspectives: a mythic voice relating the origins of the Kiowa and the world; a clinical voice relating an official, documented "history" of the Kiowa past; and a nostalgic voice recalling moments from a Kiowa childhood. In doing this, Momaday emphasizes that no single historical voice or perspective does justice to the history of a person or people. Instead, his readers are forced to juggle the three perspectives he provides, an activity that puts them in a position similar to that experienced by readers of texts by Ondaatje and Spiegelman.

In order to help our students create similarly challenging texts, we decided on the following criteria for the books we wanted them to read: first, they must be relatively short and straightforward (no *Absalom, Absalom!* here); second, they must have been written within the past thirty years (this because recent "postmodern" texts tend to be more self-reflexive about the role of writing); and third, they must work fairly overtly to link the issues of narrative form with national identity. The texts we selected were Ondaatje's *The Collected Works of Billy the Kid*, Spiegelman's *Maus II*, N. Scott Momaday's *The Way to Rainy Mountain*, Sandra Cisneros's *Woman Hollering Creek*, Maxine Hong Kingston's *The Woman Warrior*, and a long essay by ethnographer James Clifford entitled "Identity in Mashpee," from his book *The Predicament of Culture*. The assignment we came up with was one we each modified to suit the demands of our own institutions and courses, but we shared its core concept. My version of the assignment provides a sense of what we were after:

> Many authors attempt to write narratives about American identity by integrating various narrative forms (alternate forms of prose; poetry; images; etc.). By way of demonstrating your understanding of this method of storytelling, you will accomplish two tasks in this assignment. First, construct a 5- to 7-page history of an individual living in the United States since 1776, one which utilizes various narrative forms (your own prose, the prose of materials you've researched, photos, drawings, etc.). This history needn't end with the date of the person's death; for example, a history of Elvis Presley could easily include his role within culture today. Second, write a 3- to 4-page rationale for the various decisions you made in terms of form and content while writing this history.

As the discerning reader will note, the key to the assignment is the "rationale" portion. Here, students are asked to state precisely *why* they have made the various decisions they have made in composing their history (the inclusion of photos, excerpts, interviews, bits of newspaper articles, and so on). Further, students are asked to explain the intended *effect* of such moves on their imagined readership. The intent here is to keep this from being the "creative" assignment which many students may at first mistake it for being, one in which the narrative they create simply flows out of their sense of how things "ought" to be, aesthetically. Instead, this section forces them to think about both *what* they're saying and *how* they're saying it. Indeed, the key is to get students to see the relationship between the "what" and the "how"—the form and the content—of their own work, just as they might be asked to see and discuss this relationship in an essay about Spiegelman's use of the comic book form, or Ondaatje's use of photos, poetry, and imagined letters to and from Billy the Kid. The other key aspect of this assignment is that we decided to give it to students at the *beginning* of the unit on narrative and national identity, so that they could be formulating their paper ideas not after but *as they read* the texts.

A good example of the type of work this assignment elicited is a paper by Joe Lee, who narrates the history of his relationship with his father, a first-generation immigrant from Korea. The history is a composite of various short narratives, all having primarily to do with Mr. Lee, who owns a convenience store outside of Detroit, Michigan. Included are excerpts from phone conversations between Joe and his father about his poor grades in school (tellingly punctuated by bursts of Korean that are unintelligible to Joe, who does not speak Korean); short narratives about Mr. Lee from his mostly Korean American employees, all of whom seem to revere him for helping them obtain U.S. citizenship; excerpts from journal entries by Joe about his frustrations with his father, especially his lack of understanding about teenagers in America; and reproductions of letters between Joe and his older brother and sister about their father. Each of these separate documents provides an affecting snapshot of a strained relationship between father and son; more significantly, they outline the tensions between first- and second-generation immigrants in America. Like many other narratives of Asian immigration such as Hisaye Yamamoto's "Seventeen Syllables" or Kingston's *The Woman Warrior*, Joe's paper shows how nuanced these tensions can be, affecting everything from language to one's choice of clothing and leisure activities.

Joe's depiction of these tensions is perhaps best exemplified by the computer graphics Joe employs at various points in his paper. Repeatedly referring to Mr. Lee as "the head of the Korean Mafia," Joe visually represents his father as either Marlon Brando or Al Pacino from the Godfather films, and himself as Jason Lee from *Mallrats*, Kevin

Smith's 1995 film depicting the lifestyle of what Joe describes as "Generation X slackers". This juxtaposition is wonderfully sharpened by Joe's decision to superimpose these images on the Korean flag and the American flag, respectively. The pairing is humorous, but it is also revelatory. As Joe explains in the rationale for his history, "At first I thought that using these two images would just be funny. But what I didn't realize until later is that my decision to show my dad as someone out of *The Godfather* also shows how "American" *I've* become: I can't seem to imagine my dad without thinking first of Academy Award–winning movies and actors. This makes me want to work harder at bridging the gap between us, before it's too late."

Joe might have added that his choice of the Godfather films carries a double irony, in that the films themselves treat the vicissitudes of American identity as experienced by immigrant families. But the key here is that rather than talking about cultural conflicts as played out in a text such as Yamamoto's, Joe is able to construct a multifaceted narrative about the ways in which he *lives* these issues, and then write critically about his own performance. I think that this exercise made his paper more meaningful for him to write (and certainly more interesting for me to read), but it also provided him with a set of critical skills that I later saw him bring to texts such as Anzia Yezierska's *Bread Givers* and Fitzgerald's *The Great Gatsby*, both of which are novels narrating early-century struggles (of characters such as Sara Smolinksy and James Gatz) to assimilate into an American future free from the constraints of the past. Joe's paper on these two novels was particularly memorable to me because he (unlike many others in the class) was able to see and articulate the fact that the process of assimilation is one that requires telling yourself a new story about yourself in the present—an act of self-narration that, as he put it, "means losing a part of yourself and your past in the process."

The second student example I want to provide here is in many ways the most poignant essay I received in response to this assignment. A student named Anna Grand wrote a history of her grandmother's experiences growing up on a farm in Kansas during the Great Depression and World War II. Building the majority of her history around excerpts from several taped interviews with her grandmother, Anna focuses on her grandmother's memories of living with fifteen siblings, and her recollections of being hungry almost constantly throughout her youth. Placed on the page alongside advertisements from *Life* and *Look* magazine for food rationing, and newspaper clippings from these periods about the struggling economy and the War, these excerpts are powerful. But they are doubly so because Anna parallels this narrative with her own reflections about her continuing struggles with an eating disorder. Juxtaposed with her grandmother's tales of extreme poverty and hunger, Anna's confessions provide a startling image of what she herself terms "guilty American citizenship." As an identity built up in negative relation to the past as experienced by both her grandmother and the nation, this conception of citizenship seemed to emerge over the course of Anna's various revisions.

Hence the pathos of the opening image which Anna uses for her paper (Figure 1). A clipping from a recent grocery store advertisement in a local newspaper, it is a photo of her grandmother standing in a fully stocked bread aisle and holding two loaves of bread. In the photo her grandmother wears a wide grin, one that in the context of Anna's paper seems to suggest that she has come a long way since her days of childhood hunger. But the image also captures the sad irony of Anna's position: plagued by guilt over her own troubled relationship to food and to her own body, Anna is in a sense trapped by the past that her grandmother apparently put behind her long ago. As she herself puts it in the rationale section of her paper: "I chose this picture not only because it represents my grandmother as I see her, but also because it shows her in front of an aisle of bread. During the Great Depression, many families could scarcely afford bread, and during World War II, there were rations on the amount of bread a family could have. Now, in 1997, people can buy and eat as much as they want. I think this is also why I have chosen this image: because it makes me see how disappointed my grandmother would be if my mother ever told her about my eating disorder. She would think me unworthy of being an American."

It's difficult to be analytical about a statement like this, but by way of concluding I want to make two brief points in relation to Anna's reflections on this photograph of her grandmother. First, it's worth pointing out how strongly such a moment echoes the painful reflections offered in *Maus II* by Art Spiegelman, for whom the past possesses a validity that his American present simply lacks. But it's also worth pointing out how an assignment such as the one I've tried to describe here allowed a student like Anna to analyze and then make use of the narrative techniques deployed by the likes of Spiegelman, Ondaatje, and Momaday, to name just three such authors. That Anna seems here to have finished her paper in a state of confusion is of course sad, but it strikes me that her dilemma is less a contradiction than a fitting commentary on the vexed nature of what it means to be an American at the current historical moment. Seeking to tell stories about Americans and

Figure 1. Photo from grocery ad featuring Anna's grandmother

the American past, we instead find ourselves providing unsatisfying and often irresolvable tales about ourselves in the present. This is the sort of a lesson I feel my students can benefit from learning.

Works Cited

Cisneros, Sandra. *Woman Hollering Creek and Other Stories*. New York: Vintage, 1992.

Clifford, James. *The Predicament of Culture: Twentieth-Century Ethnography, Literature, and Art*. Cambridge: Harvard UP, 1988.

Fitzgerald, F. Scott. *The Great Gatsby*. New York: Scribner, 1992.

Kingston, Maxine Hong. *The Woman Warrior: Memoirs of a Girlhood Among Ghosts*. New York: Vintage, 1989.

Momaday, N. Scott. *The Way to Rainy Mountain*. Albuquerque: U of New Mexico P, 1969.

Ondaatje, Michael. *The Collected Works of Billy the Kid*. New York: Vintage, 1970.

Romano, Tom. *Writing with Passion: Life Stories, Multiple Genres*. Portsmouth, NH: Boynton/Cook, 1995.

Spiegelman, Art. *Maus II: A Survivor's Tale: And Here My Troubles Began*. New York: Pantheon Books, 1991.

Yamamoto, Hisaye. "Seventeen Syllables." *Seventeen Syllables and Other Stories*. Latham, NY: Kitchen Table—Woman of Color Press, 1988.

Yezierska, Anzia. *Bread Givers: A Novel: A Struggle Between a Father of the Old World and a Daughter of the New*. New York: Persea Books, 1975.

9 *The Education of Little Tree:* A Real True Story

Peter Shaheen
Seaholm High School, Birmingham, Michigan

Gramma said when you come on something good, first thing to do is share it with whoever you can find; that way, the good spreads out no telling where it will go. Which is right.

Forrest Carter, *The Education of Little Tree: A True Story*

In 1991, on my urging, the language arts department bought a hundred or so copies of the best-selling book *The Education of Little Tree: A True Story*, and I passed them out to the ninth-grade honors students. The book had recently won a prize at some big publishing convention in New York, and accolades were being showered on it as the hottest new text since *To Kill A Mockingbird*. Our school made the purchase before any of the hubbub hit the streets in the fall. We got in on the ground floor, so to speak. Newspapers started printing stories about the rise of a new literary star, as librarians began to sing the praises of a great new manuscript and television started promoting *Little Tree* as the natural successor to *Dances with Wolves*. For a brief fifteen minutes, I enjoyed celebrity for picking an up-and-coming classic. Then, all very suddenly, word about *Little Tree's* author being a racist, a member of the KKK, a former speech writer for Alabama governor George Wallace, promoting segregation forever, put egg on the collective face of many book lovers, publishers—and me.

The "folksy wisdom" of a simple Native American text suddenly got very complicated. I was one of those teachers with egg on my face, but the great thing about literature is that even the lowest life-forms are able to redeem themselves and resurface as heroes. After much reflection and some discussion with colleagues, I decided to teach *Little Tree* again, two years after the fraud was revealed, with the intention of at least redeeming myself if not metamorphosing into a hero.

The key ingredient in my planning centered on illustrating to my students that insofar as all writing is tied to political and social contexts, all writing is autobiographical. I'd fixed on this notion in the summer of 1997 during the first year of the Making American Literatures project (see this book's foreword). We had looked at a variety of texts, and they all seemed closely connected to the authors: Gatsby's issues were Fitzgerald's, and Cisneros's *House on Mango Street*, Petry's *Tituba: Witch of Salem*, and Larson's *Passing* all included elements of autobiography.

The idea for this particular unit came from discussions with Native American studies scholar Gerald Vizenor. I asked Vizenor what he thought about Carter's fraud, and his reaction had a big impact on me. He spoke about how the history of Indians (Vizenor uses the term interchangeably with Native Americans) is written by White America. Much of what White Americans "know" about Indians is a simulation— a collection of stereotypes that define our perceptions but that have little basis in truth. Vizenor also said that Native American culture valued the role of the trickster. *Little Tree* is the best-selling Native American text for the University of New Mexico Press, easily beating out N. Scott Momaday's *The Way to Rainy Mountain*. Vizenor acknowledges the trickster at work here, and he convinced me that *Little Tree* is a complicated piece. What better way to teach my students about complex social and political contexts?

Antigovernment bigots are happiest when left to their own devices, and the themes that weave *Little Tree* together also support the racist ideology of people like Carter. Students could benefit from understanding the political perspective from which Carter wrote.

My plan was to use the *Little Tree* controversy as a way to help students strengthen their reading strategies, and, specifically, to help them develop a more "scholarly" set of reading strategies for engaging a text. My intention was to enrich my students' ability to engage a text by calling on them to place the text in a social and political context. I would exploit their sense of justice to motivate them into developing these sophisticated strategies.

Before handing out the books, I asked my students the following questions:

- Do the author's intentions matter to the reader?
- Is it important to know about the author's political or philosophical perspectives before reading?
- Can an author feel vehemently about a subject and still write a book taking a different stance altogether?
- Can a reader divorce the author from the text?

With books in hand, we read the first chapter together and pointed out that Grandpa was out of his element when he was forced to go into the city. Kids also knew right away that, during an incident on a bus, the driver and one of the riders were just plain rude to Little Tree's new family. Students understood too that Grandpa slowed his gait to make Little Tree more comfortable during a walk home. In short, the students pretty much got all the subtleties they were supposed to get. They were encouraged to find passages that would help them celebrate the diversity of Native Americans and write them in a homework log. We created a list of cultural differences that we could respect even if we didn't quite share in them, and then I forged a consensus with students that these differences were worth valuing. I took notes during class about student reactions, had the students write responses in journals and asked students to answer a post-study evaluation to monitor the results of the study.

Ah, the best laid plans of mice and English teachers. . . . The deeper we got into the text, and the more I was able to help students recognize what I determined to be the hidden agenda of Forrest Carter, the bigger the boomerang effect grew to be. As our class discussions evolved over the four classes reserved for discussion of the novel, certain themes began to surface repeatedly:

- Little Tree and his family were better off left alone.
- Little Tree and his family would have been perfectly content to be left alone by the outside world.
- There was a special code or "way" in which Little Tree lived that Whites—especially Whites from the North—were incapable of learning, understanding, or even respecting.
- Little Tree and his family did not live well in the world of Whites.
- The government was always interfering with Little Tree and his people.
- People from Washington in particular were bad news.

It was clear to me that if you buy into all of the subtleties as they are presented above, it would be easy to make the transfer from *Little Tree* to the racist South during the tumultuous times of desegregation: Leave the South alone to settle its own problems. These damn Northerners come down to places like Alabama sticking their noses where they don't belong and making trouble for everyone else who is perfectly content to live by themselves and not mix with anyone too different from themselves.

From this perspective, Eisenhower, and later Kennedy and Johnson, mobilized federal troops to go down South and stir up a mess of trouble. If you buy into the thesis of *Little Tree*, you would have to agree that these great American presidents were the culpable parties in spoiling the peculiar institution that was the Old South. Southerners would have been better off without the morally corrupt Catholic-hating politician at the trading store who was full of contempt for just about everyone, including Grandpa and Little Tree.

Little Tree was a manifesto for the message of states' rights, and students were buying into it without even questioning it. So much for those sophisticated reading strategies I was teaching.

Finally, I sprang the trap: I told my students about the controversy surrounding the author. I pulled out a picture clipped from *Time* magazine showing then-Governor George Wallace spewing his fiery White supremacist rhetoric, and I read from the article about how Wallace's infamous speech on the steps of the Alabama Capitol building was written by an anonymous face in the background of the picture. Of course, that face belonged to *Little Tree* author Forrest Carter.

"How does this Wallace speech line up with the language of *Little Tree*?" I asked. Then, for the first time, I read aloud the complete title and the name of the author: *The Education of Little Tree: A True Story* by Forrest Carter. Next, I opened up to the introduction and read the part by Rennard Strickland claiming that the book contains "autobiographical remembrances." Feeling a lot like Spencer Tracy in his portrayal of Clarence Darrow (the model for Tracy's character Henry Drummond), I went for the jugular: "Could it be that Forrest Carter created *The Education of Little Tree* to promote his White supremacist teachings?"

The groundwork had been laid as perfectly as I could imagine. The message had been deconstructed before their very eyes. All that remained for my students was to experience the moment of "aha!" that I had intended for them.

Immediately after I "revealed" the truth about Carter's malevolent past, the class was in an uproar. They were engaged in energetic, emotional discussions. My little soldiers of learning were taking up sides. Everyone had an opinion about the revelations. Some had more than one.

"How can you not see the truth? Look at the guy's picture!"

"Good writers always layer their message like an onion." This last comment must have been modeled on something I'd said.

And, of course, the uncommitted third regiment also weighed in:

"Can we see the movie?"

"Why does everything have to mean something?"

"Even Freud says sometimes a cigar is just a cigar."

"My friends always say one thing and mean another."

"Shut up and let him teach."

And if I remember right, the bell rang at the fury's zenith. I like it when class ends in a tempest. It makes me think that there's learning going on, but something was different in this case. There was a bit of a hangover to deal with all right, only this time it didn't involve the students but rather their teacher.

I could feel my colleague Deborah Juarez's knowing glare. I had set my students up. She would have told me in no uncertain terms that my plan backfired because I actually ended up telling my students they were incapable of accurately negotiating meaning when they read. Worse, I was in danger of rewarding those who sided with my official interpretation more heavily than those contrarians who insisted on being allowed to interpret the text absent of history. How did that constitute teaching sophisticated reading strategies?

At first glance, this inner turmoil may seem obtuse and self-serving to some extent, but for me it speaks to the essence of my teaching. Here's the rub: Given that I believe it is my duty to promote a marketplace of ideas in order to preserve democracy, how does tricking my students promote this value? How does pronouncing the truth help students debate ideas and determine the value of those ideas through a democratic process? After years of criticizing the formalist approach in the high school classroom, was I pronouncing myself the expert on the text?

About one-third of the class was fully on board. They bought the arguments hook, line, and sinker. They were willing to believe anything I told them. Megan epitomizes those who were on board with me. She is an honors student who has always enjoyed success in school and the praise of her teachers. Before we read *Little Tree*, we read *Fools Crow* by James Welch. We talked about the variety of characters and personality types in this novel. Our conclusion (mine too) was that *Fools Crow* did a wonderful job of establishing that a variety of peoples—all with complex personalities—exist within the pages of the novel. Megan did what many honors students do who are used to being praised for their schoolwork. She accepted the teacher's ideas and refined them with her own special perspectives. She wrote, "Looking at the contrasts between *Little Tree* and *Fools Crow*, Grandpa and Mik-Api, Mr. Chunk and Mr. Slick, and the Napikwan, it becomes apparent that the characters in *Little Tree* are a simple caricature of the tragic, majestic, and antagonistic figures portrayed in *Fools Crow*. The main characters in each novel, *Little Tree* and *Fools Crow*, are both young men faced with a challenge. . . . However Little Tree seems too successful. He comes to the mountains almost literally a baby. It seems odd that a five year old would master such tasks that it takes an adult years to learn."

Another third of the class was ambivalent. They could see no relation between what I was saying and what the book had to do with their lives, nor were they willing to look for a connection. A pessimist might comment, "Welcome to American high schools."

The other third failed to buy into the hidden message. Their overall position in capsule form was, "It's just a book; it doesn't have to be about anything other than what it's about."

I had begun to make several realizations about my lesson. I was left wondering why some students were reluctant to give more careful consideration to what I saw as an obvious position. After all, it is clear that Carter was a racist, so why is it so difficult to see his book as an instrument he uses to promote that philosophy?

There may be two positions which can explain what happened. The first is that most of the students are not sophisticated enough in their reading strategies to make these kinds of difficult connections. They may in fact believe that sometimes a cigar is a cigar and Freud is damned. While I tend to doubt this position because I have seen students readily employ a variety of sophisticated strategies in the past, I cannot rule out this option as a possibility.

My hunch, however, tends toward a different position. Since these youngsters are on a college-bound honors track where virtually every student goes on to college, these students tend to succeed because they do what their teacher expects of them. If I were to simply have said at the beginning that Carter's purpose in penning this quaint tale of the Native American was to promote racist ideologies, students would have taken notes and would have been prepared to recite that factoid back in some test at a future date. I know this is true because in the past I have convinced students that Edgar Allen Poe wrote the first poem and, as a result, we now call the genre poetry after the founder of the form. Despite my best (or worst) attempts at humor, students many times sit through the lecture straight-faced and without questions, accepting me as the literary critic in the class and mindlessly taking notes.

The worst-case scenario contends that I gave students license to read the story in any way they wanted. Some may have been testing out reading wings to see if I would validate their own interpretations. In that sense, their reactions were more of a test for me. Students were hypothesizing about whether or not I was willing to live up to my end of the bargain by allowing them to have a position antithetical to mine.

After catching my reflection in the window, I realized that, in fact, I had only partially granted students permission to engage the text freely. I learned that giving permission means that those students who read the text differently need to be acknowledged, valued, and encouraged.

Diverse interpretations make life hectic and frequently disorganized. We are uncomfortable with the notion that students can read and get whatever they want out of a text because we fear that they will leave more behind than they bother to pick up on. It is counterintuitive for teachers to work so hard and then be so nonchalant about meaning.

Some students were trying to let me know that they felt they'd been had. They insisted that a cigar is sometimes a cigar even while we all know that it is never just a cigar because they were calling me out. Later, when I unburdened my soul with one of my colleagues, Jim White, he agreed with my students.

"They're right," he said, "you set them up big-time; at least let them own their response if you tell them they are permitted to have one."

It is important that students learn to engage a text for themselves on their own terms, and, since I believe formalist thinking inhibits this growth, I see it as a not-so-effective teaching strategy. Nonetheless, with the help of my friends, I recognized that I was guilty of being overly formalist in the teaching of *Little Tree*.

The handling of these diverse opinions is the essential component in teaching reading. The negotiation of meaning in the face of diverse interpretations is the most essential step in the reading process because it models the way in which conflict should be resolved in a democratic society. If we allow our students to engage in free debates in an open market of ideas where those ideas with intellectual capital become valued, then we can better become what we envision our future to be. Reading is democracy. Students will make mistakes, and the teacher can be there to ask good questions.

In fact, questions that call for students to understand the purposes of authors and the purposes of audiences in reading a text are essential ones for teachers to ask. My students taught me that there is an art to asking those questions. My friends and colleagues will continue to help me learn that art.

When Gerald Vizenor talks about Native American tricksters, he gets this tie-your-shoelaces-together gleam in his eye. He is a trickster and appreciates a good prank. It isn't unreasonable to assume that I had fallen victim to the coyote, a traditional Indian trickster. Here I was spending lots of time and energy preparing a teaching sleight of hand that would dazzle and amaze my students by leaving them with egg on their face. Not only was I wrong, but my strategies had the opposite effect. The funny thing is, when all is said and done, I don't feel bad about the experience. My colleagues and my students ended up teaching me more about reading than I had planned on teaching my students.

Works Cited

Carter, Forrest. *The Education of Little Tree: A True Story.* New York: Delacorte, 1976.

Welch, James. *Fools Crow.* New York: Viking, 1986.

III Location, Location, Location

Sarah Robbins
Kennesaw State University

Teaching American literature leads inevitably to questions about *place* and *space*. Scholarship in feminist epistemology and postcolonial studies has been emphasizing how the social positions of people examining any question—and certainly such issues as what a national literature should be—shape their possible answers in distinctive ways. What, then, are the instructional implications of such theories? A teacher preparing a syllabus for an "American literature" course in a classroom on a Caribbean island would probably have a very different map of the discipline in mind than would an instructor situated in, say, Oklahoma, despite the longstanding tendencies of many textbooks and curricular descriptions to narrow the term *American* to equate it with the United States. How does living in different parts of the United States and the world lead us to "see" American literature differently? How, for example, might a teacher who has grown up in Canada respond to traditions of North American writing that are often ignored in conceptualizing "American literature," as they are ignored in anthologies that are labeled as "North American Literature" books but contain maps that literally erase Canada.

And what about teachers whose first learning about "American literatures" occurred in other countries, say, India or Macedonia? This was one of the questions we asked in workshops conducted as part of the Making American Literatures (MAL) project (see the foreword for a description of the project), and we found that such teachers were shaped as much by their original home cultures as by immigration to the United States, and their personal perspectives on the discipline often encouraged us to expand boundaries, question assumptions, and think intertextually. During a workshop exploring "Southern" literature's representations of religion, our own memoir writing—along with teacher-participant Milka's piece on her youthful experiences of Christian holidays in Communist Yugoslavia, compared with her current family celebrations in Cherokee County, Georgia—played in productive ways with our spatial, temporal, and sociopolitical conceptions of regionalized American literatures.

Talking with teachers from different parts of the United States shows that regionalism wields complex influence on teachers' decision making, on students' perceptions of the discipline, and on community values about American literatures. When, as part of the MAL project, we asked teachers from Michigan, California, and Georgia to share several examples of literary texts that they felt best represented their respective regions, we were surprised by each others' individual choices of texts (What? No Faulkner?), but the related follow-up conversation about the varying impact of area school boards' unique expectations, state standards, and even particular school departments' differing ideas about curricular needs was equally instructive. This kind of discussion inevitably underscored ways in which some assumptions we have about American literature are more locally based than we realize, while others really do represent national trends.

The shifting demographics so obvious in public school classrooms—many of which might have been relatively homogeneous a few decades ago but are now experiencing a massive influx of new students from all over the world into "American" schools—offer challenges. We want to find ways for our instruction to affirm such students' visions of themselves and of what it might mean to be "Americanized" at the turn into the twenty-first century. And we understand our responsibility to examine related questions of language differences in our schools and universities. To what extent should the American literatures we teach be multilingual and multiethnic? How can we carry out the study needed to teach unfamiliar texts from "new" multicultural traditions, and still have time for the pressing duties of everyday teaching? And how can we best provide English language learners with effective access to the European American texts that will probably still dominate much curriculum in the early twenty-first century?

Answers to these questions are generally tentative, distinctively local, and dependent upon particular students' needs and interests, as well as their special talents. In Georgia, for instance, some of our initial examination of language-related and border-crossing issues can benefit from the work of colleagues in California, who welcomed many Spanish-speaking students to their state's schools long before the current wave of immigrants from Mexico and South America now challenging metro Atlanta teachers. In the end, the most powerful voice we heard on this subject in the MAL project was a student author's, when Georgia teacher Diane Shearer brought José Reyes to one of our school-year sessions to describe his reading of Richard Rodriguez's *Hunger of Memory.* José shared some of his own poignant writing about multiple physical and psychic border crossings between Mexico and the United States. For us, José was certainly "making American literatures," both in his studies within Diane's classroom and in this writing about his experiences of a hybrid cultural space. Another student, Jolynn Khamky, was guided by José's authorship when writing a feature for her school newspaper on recent immigrants learning to speak English while attending Wheeler High in suburban Cobb County. Jolynn's piece eventually won first place in the state-level journalism contest, thereby reconfirming for all of us a commitment to encouraging students to "make" American literature in their own regions.

All of our efforts in the MAL project to examine the implications of "location" for the study of American literatures were not so immediately rewarding, of course, and most of our questions are still far from resolved. As a result, the essays in this section show teachers at work on these issues—sometimes through the informal teacher research that all reflective practitioners do, sometimes through more formal and sustained curricular reformation, and sometimes through creatively dialogic interaction with student texts.

Emanuel Martin's "Popular Culture in the American Literature Class" recounts his efforts to identify an appropriate place for contemporary texts from a range of media in the literature curriculum of his ninth-grade classroom. Committed to cultivating his students' appreciation of the Great Books tradition he himself dearly loves, Martin shares the story of his increasing awareness of the power that popular culture texts like film, song lyrics, and television shows can exert in his instructional program. As a former syndicated cartoonist who is well aware of the appeal of contemporary visual imagery, and as the author of a creative Web site integrating appreciation for Shakespeare with twenty-first-century graphic design and contemporary word play, Martin admits his continued confusion over the responsibility of the teacher to transmit high culture to students, especially in light of their clearer enthusiasm for material from their everyday experience. Drawing upon his study of Twain as well as his own experiences in the classroom, Martin celebrates his students' influence on his teaching while explaining why and how he has gradually expanded his conception of the rightful position of American popular culture in schools and, in turn, changed both the content and the pedagogy in his classroom.

In "Making American Literatures in Middle School," Laura Schiller shifts our attention from high school learners to sixth graders, even as she invites us to see the productive possibilities associated with integrating literary and historical study. An equally important "locational" dimension to Schiller's work, however, is the particular community where she teaches—a suburb of Detroit which has shifted from an overwhelmingly European American population to one that is primarily African American and Chaldean. Building upon conceptions of alternative history writing and "survivance," Schiller has sought ways to have her middle school students explore the available official and unofficial histories of their community, identify gaps in those histories, and write themselves into the story of Southfield, Michigan, through a series of collaborative examinations of archives, public history sites, oral histories, and interactions with various local residents (including parents). Schiller's revisiting of location themes from the Making American Literatures project is embedded in an activist *doing* of theoretically informed learning—a reflective practice self-consciously situating her particular instructional strategies within the local space of her teaching. Seeing her community as an interactive resource, she draws upon key concepts learned through the MAL project but adapts them to her own dynamic teaching location.

Jim White's "Literature of Place and Place in Literature: Orienting Our Maps" expands our sense of place in American literatures beyond the geographic and social to the natural/environmental and the cultural domains. Revisiting a number of generative questions about the "location" of writers, readers, and communities in the study of literature, White describes how he has invited his students to identify and critique the unique positions of published authors such as Henry David Thoreau, N. Scott Momaday, and William Least Heat-Moon as a step toward focusing on links between literature making and specific landscapes. To illustrate how the MAL project pushed him to rethink the complicated relationships between place and power, White explains how his teaching of *To Kill a Mockingbird* was redirected to emphasize issues of social position and race.

Typical "location" constraints of space and time can be undone via technological tools such as listservs and Web sites, and Peter Shaheen's "The Good, the Bad, and the Ugly: Technology in the Classroom" discusses both the challenges and the opportunities of incorporating listservs and Web sites into the teaching of American Literature. Shaheen talks about his love/hate relationship with technology through his experiences in the MAL project, and he looks at three specific ways in which technology has entered into his teaching and professional development. Shaheen starts his narrative with an acknowledgement that the lives of teachers are often cluttered with detail. So why would anyone want to complicate the picture by adding more to an already full day? Giles Corey in *The Crucible* might simply answer, "More weight," but teaching can be more complicated than witch hunting.

Technology continues to inform Shaheen's teaching in ways he never anticipated. He talks about his experiences in three areas: the Making American Literatures listserv, the development of a Web site for the community in which he teaches (Birmingham, Michigan), and the development of a Web site for the particular program in which he teaches (the Flexible Scheduling Project [Flex for short] at Seaholm High School). As a result of these projects, Shaheen has come to realize that technology is revolutionary because it does change the world. Technology has helped him and his students realize that they can have active voices in their communities and can redefine their relationships with institutions that have previously seemed dispassionate. Shaheen also realizes that technology is not a panacea. In many instances, Murphy's Law applies: Everything that can go wrong will. In the end, however, Shaheen sees educational potential in the computer revolution.

10 Popular Culture in the American Literature Class

Emanuel Martin
Stephenson High School, Stone Mountain, Georgia

I think every teacher has had this experience: From time to time when I introduced a literary term to my class—and in order to "connect" with my students, show how "hip," "with it," and "down" I am—I used an example from a popular TV show. Then suddenly I would feel as if I were driving a car when the steering went out; the class veered out of control. Instead of discussing something important and meaningful, like, say, the influence of Emerson on Thoreau, the whole class started talking about *The Simpsons*. What's worse, they were discussing it with more animation, enthusiasm, and genuine curiosity than they ever seemed to feel in approaching the Transcendentalists. I'd shake my head and, with the patience of Job, drag the class back onto the subject. The real subject, remember? What I came to teach. I would vow never to mention that TV show in class again; heaven forbid any student of mine should ever get that excited in English class.

That was when I was a novice teacher, but I had already learned to talk a good show about activating prior learning and teaching at the proximal zone. I had learned from education courses that my mission was to ignite students' interests and passion for learning. I believed this. Yet, at the first sign of actual ignition, I mentally screamed, "Fire!" and beat a hasty retreat to the safety of the teacher's edition. Before I even got my first paycheck as a teacher, I had drawn, as if with a heavy black marker, a thick line between subjects fit to discuss in a literature class and subjects not fit. In moments of daring I would make brief forays into the forbidden zone, illustrating a point here and there with something "the kids are familiar with," always making sure it was bland enough and general enough not to arouse any interest for its own sake. The boundary had never been directly articulated to me, but it had been ubiquitously acted out in every classroom I'd been in from kindergarten on. Everyone I knew had unconsciously learned this distinction and applied it in their own lives.

"A classic is something everybody praises but nobody reads," said Mark Twain, showing that even before the turn of the century this dichotomy was well known. "Popular culture" and "high culture" are two different animals—descended from a common ancestor, perhaps, but accustomed to different environments and unable to mate; all the great works belong in high culture, and everything else, the trash, belongs in popular culture. Popular culture is that part of culture which is widely enjoyed, and high culture is that part which is enjoyed only by the elite. Therefore, the less you like something, the more likely it is to be great. And the more you like something, the more likely it is to be trash.

This definition is perverse and doubly debilitating. It intimidates people in the presence of established great works and inhibits their genuine enjoyment. Finding fault with a Jane Austen novel may be more of a negative reflection on the reader than on the novel. Such a polarized definition of culture also precludes turning serious critical attention to literature, music, and art in popular culture. Any time someone dares to look below the most superficial level of a popular work, he or she is likely to be greeted with, "You're reading too much into that," or "Don't think about it so much, you'll spoil it."

This is not to say that the unspoken ban against popular culture in the classroom arose without any justification. And the justification goes deeper than the comfort zone of teachers or questions of classroom management. Traditional works of high culture have demonstrated that they are able to withstand and reward sustained intellectual scrutiny. Works of popular culture suffer from their own proximity to us in time; they are illuminated by the haze of glamorous currency, making it hard to determine whether they will be able to shine on their own. Moreover, there is the dread of cultural relativism; do we really want to send the message that *Archie Comics* is as worthwhile as *Othello*? Literature teachers love literature and rightly feel a desire to pass on an enriching appreciation of it to their students.

These are no small objections, and they need to be dealt with seriously. If popular culture is included in the curriculum as a way to pander to student tastes, then we are shortchanging our students. If our intent is to conceal the truth that, in the eyes of many observers, some works have more merit than others, then we will stunt the critical facility we want to instill. Yet to continue replicating the enervating chasm between popular culture and works that people read only if they have to is clearly unsatisfactory.

It took time to overcome my own objections to bringing popular culture into the classroom. After all, not only had I experienced years of subtle instruction telling me that this was not something teachers were supposed to teach, but also I had accumulated my own empirical experience of discussion breaking out every time I made the slightest reference to anything currently in the theaters or on TV.

Even in my first year of teaching, though, while I didn't admit it to myself, or think about it very deeply, popular culture came in, not only as an invited guest, but an assistant teacher. When teaching my poetry unit to a primarily Black class of ninth graders, I felt stymied by the weak, uninteresting selections included in the text. I asked students to bring in lyrics of music videos, subject to the proviso they all be G-rated. I picked the ones I found most interesting and projected them on the overhead so that we could study them for content and for the use of poetic devices. The students and I were both intrigued to find unsuspected levels of meaning and craft in some of their favorite songs. Moreover, traditional texts became more meaningful. Students who earlier might have felt alienated by Emily Dickinson or Edgar Lee Masters now saw them as poets—different from, yet akin to, their personal idols. The unit was a hit with the students, and although each year I seem to change everything I do in my classroom, that's one activity I always do.

I should have seen from this experience that including pop culture in the curriculum can awaken students' critical facility on both ends: making them more receptive to traditional works and more richly conscious of familiar ones. For many of my students, this poetry unit has also helped correct the misapprehension that thinking about something spoils the pleasure of it. On the contrary, many students have enjoyed probing deeply into lyrics they had listened to only casually before; others relished the chance to share insights they'd gained while listening to songs that other people had taken for granted.

A breakthrough for me came in the fall of 1997, when my students and I studied *Pudd'nhead Wilson*, a novel that had been assigned for summer reading. This was a fortuitous coincidence because, during the summer before, I had studied original typescripts of *Pudd'nhead Wilson* and *Huckleberry Finn*. What I had seen there was the tug-of-war over creative control between Twain and his publishers. Twain's texts are still in dispute because of the difficulty in sorting out the author's intent from the incidental, coincidental, and deliberate alterations made by the typist, publisher, and printer. This confusion is compounded in the case of *Pudd'nhead Wilson* because it was originally written as a longer novel that included *The Comedy of Those Extraordinary Twins*, the unlikely saga of a pair of Siamese twins who are put on trial for murder. Twain performed a sort of authorial surgery separating *Twins* from *Pudd'nhead*, but he didn't make a very thorough job of it. Remnants of each novel remain in the other; there are scenes in *Pudd'nhead* that aren't funny and scarcely even make sense unless you realize the Capelli twins in *Pudd'nhead* were originally meant to be joined at the hip. I shared the problematic nature of Twain's texts with my class, and we realized that, before it had been canonized, *Pudd'nhead* had been a *popular* novel, the work of a man dealing with economic and personal pressures similar to those a writer might face today.

Because of my experience with Twain, I began to stress the historical environments that gave rise to other works we read. I did this in the most traditional way imaginable, in the form of lectures, class discussions, and essay assignments. Together we tried to untangle very complex riddles about why great works were passed down to us in the forms they were. For example, why does Ben Franklin cut such a mythic figure in his autobiography? According to his own version of events, when the most prominent man in Philadelphia arrived in that city he could barely afford the two fluffy rolls for his only meal. True or not, what image of himself and of opportunities in the colonies was Franklin trying to construct for the readers of his time? Let me stress that my students are ninth graders of mixed abilities, and I was asking them to grapple with questions of serious scholarship. Asking students to write an essay in which they separate probable fact from probable fiction in *The Autobiography of Benjamin Franklin* calls for thinking skills of a very high order.

At first blush all of this may seem to have nothing to do with using pop culture in the classroom, and at the time I didn't see the connection myself. The point was, though, I was treating the great works as having been originally *popular* works. It was the other side of the coin from examining, say, *Cinderella* as a literary work. This not only allowed me to present high school students with intellectually challenging issues; it also liberated the students from treating everything in the county-issued textbook as sacred writing, immune to criticism from mere readers. Not that uninformed criticism, the kind that prevents people from trying new things with an open mind, does any good. "I don't like all that Shakespeare stuff" is not an outlook likely to be productive. Of course, one way for teachers to get around this objection is not to ask students to *like* anything—only to *appreciate* it. Maybe the word "appreciate" is meant to imply that not even the teacher really likes this stuff. There's plenty of time to like things when you watch TV and get to see all the things never allowed in English class.

I am no longer content to trot out some hoary old tome, saying reverently, "Here it is. Appreciate it." I want my students to enjoy what we read, because I enjoy it. I'm convinced, and my students' reactions have helped convince me, that an enlightened critical outlook enriches any text. The critical outlook should contain the explicit recognition that almost without exception, every canonized text was once a popular text, and I would submit that no work can long survive in the academic environment unless it has at some point enjoyed popular success also.

So, is that when I opened the floodgates to let in sitcoms and funny papers? No. I'm cautious by nature and uninclined to leap from high dives before I've thoroughly satisfied myself regarding the depth of the water. I persisted in drawing the rare example from a contemporary work to illustrate a point in lectures, and in allowing students to bring in favorite lyrics during the poetry unit. The results of the latter were marvelous; the results of the former were as likely to be distracting as illuminating.

I decided that by degrees I would turn my students loose into the world of popular culture. At the time, I was teaching four ninth-grade classes, one of which was advanced. In conjunction with reading Daphne du Maurier's "The Birds," I like to show Hitchcock's film version of the same story. (As an aside, "The Birds," including Hitchcock's film version, is a case study of a work in transition from pop culture to high culture.) In preparation for having my students write a film review of "The Birds," each day I showed them a brief video clip from a different film for class discussion. The idea came from Alan Teasley's and Ann Wilder's marvelous book, *Reel Conversations* (1997), which encourages teachers and students to consider films from three different angles: literary, dramatic, and cinematic. Following the advice of this book, I showed clips from *Popeye*, *Boyz N the Hood*, and *Stand by Me*. Students howled each time I stopped the video because invariably the chosen clip ended at the most exciting point, but they brought more energy to examining metaphors, symbolism, and tone than I had seen before.

This was pretty daring stuff. I was showing my classes movies, or parts of movies anyway, that weren't even in the county curriculum. Yet I was very confident about what I was doing. I knew that if my department head walked into the room, far from being dismayed at what she found us doing, she would be excited. I began bragging on my class and telling other teachers what I was doing.

Pop culture had entered my classroom in a big way. As the second semester neared an end, I decided to take a bigger leap. While reading Hal Borland's *When the Legends Die* with my advanced class, I introduced some ideas of Carl Jung and Joseph Campbell—specifically, the shadow, the trickster, and the hero's journey. Since these patterns and character types occur in almost all stories in our culture, it was easy to find examples of them in cartoons, sitcoms, and even video games. When we finished reading the novel, I gave my advanced class an assignment to write a literary analysis of a work from popular culture. I told my students to write about any work they chose; they could use a movie, a TV show, a book, whatever. I made only two stipulations: as always, it had to be something I could share with their parents without blushing, and it could not be anything we had studied as a class, anything they had studied with another class, or anything they thought they were ever likely to study in a class. Since this was new ground for all of us, I continued to hold pretty tight reins on the project; I gave my students very specific instructions on my expectations for the papers and provided a model paper that I encouraged them to follow as closely as they wished.

The success of the project can be measured not just in the final product but also in the interest students showed toward it outside of class. Each day between the time I gave the assignment and the time it came due, students stayed behind after class to ask me about their projects and fill me in on their progress. Did I think Scar from *The Lion King* was more of a trickster or a shadow? Would Eddie Murphy's *The Nutty Professor* make a good topic? Would it be better to write about Disney's version of *Cinderella* or a more recent one starring Whitney Houston? The students experienced the delicious thrill of being the supreme authority on one subject.

The resulting papers were very strong, but one in particular stands out for me. Latoya is a bright, energetic student who wrote uniformly excellent papers, meticulous in their content and execution. The rub here is the adverb "uniformly." She was so consistently good, whether writing to persuade, entertain, explain, or describe, that I could never quite overcome the nagging feeling that she wrote not so much from the well of desire within her, but in order to please me, her teacher. That's not all bad, of course; I like being pleased. For her pop culture piece, though, she showed me a side of herself I hadn't suspected.

Latoya chose to write about a children's book written in second person so the reader is the hero. Here Latoya made an absolutely daring and brilliant move because I had specifically told my class that when writing this sort of literary analysis, they were to avoid using first person. Latoya had deliberately chosen a work that required her to write in first person. "*I* am the hero." This is resistance in its most fertile and productive form. I tell my students two things about writing: that what makes great writing is learning to break a rule for a clever reason, and that if anyone asks, Mr. Martin taught you everything you know about writing.

I don't know if Latoya will follow the second piece of advice, but she'd found an ingenious way to apply the first. Am I going too far in suggesting that, in foraging on the far side of that heavy black line that I used to draw between "high culture" and "popular culture," Latoya also began to question other artificial divisions set up in English class, such as which pronouns go in which papers? OK, I'm going too far. Latoya had a spark of intellectual mischief in her to start with, or she never would have chosen that work, but certainly she would not have been able to choose such a work in the first place had not the assignment given her license.

I have discovered that I can use pop culture less as a means of introducing the study of traditional literature than as the culmination of the literary study. "OK, class, you've acquired some tools and concepts, let's see you apply them in the broader world." The heavy black line is beginning to turn from vertical to horizontal—not separating dusty works from breathing ones, but connecting them.

As I've written, I never seem to teach a class the same way twice, so I've already started thinking about an assignment for next year. If students can deconstruct Ben Franklin, why can't they do the same with, say, *The Fresh Prince of Bel-Air*? What social and political environment made this story take the form it did? What improbabilities were introduced to gratify a modern audience?

I approach this latest idea with trepidation, however. Time and distance make *The Autobiography of Benjamin Franklin* easier to deconstruct. It's harder to see the strings animating a work when those strings are also attached to your own arms and legs. How can I prepare my students for the intimidating task of analyzing the sort of person that *Fresh Prince* is constructing for its viewers? I'd have to lay the groundwork carefully, help them establish their comfort and confidence before I hit them with such a difficult assignment. I'll start with something easy to grasp that the students can connect to. Something simple. Maybe *Moby-Dick*.

Work Cited

Teasley, Alan B., and Ann Wilder. *Reel Conversations: Reading Films with Young Adults.* Portsmouth: Heinemann, 1997.

11 Making American Literatures in Middle School

Laura Schiller
Birney Middle School, Southfield, Michigan

I taped a cartoon to my classroom door showing a student raising his hand in class and asking the teacher, "May I be excused? My brain is full." That's how I felt after two weeks of a summer workshop. By the time I'd listened to speaker after speaker, engaged in discussion day after day, and read late into the night, my notions of text and teaching took on new layers.

We explored issues of authorship, wondering where the writer's work leaves off and the editor's work begins. We reconstructed history from original archival documents, historicized texts to deepen our understandings, and studied anthologies to determine what works are included and whose voices are not represented. We paired novels, poems, and films to reconsider treatment, theme, and point of view. We further complicated the notion of text by looking at advertisements, film, music, and art as ways of reading—even shopping malls could be "read" for all they said about our society, all in the context of coming to terms with who's doing the Making, what is American, and what constitutes Literature.

I was particularly influenced by Gerald Vizenor, scholar and author, who presented the idea that absence is presence when speaking of Native Americans. So little remains of Native American history that is authentic, and the Native American perspective is so often left out of officially sanctioned histories and anthologies, that their obvious absence is a reminder of their presence. The idea that absence is presence applies to other marginalized peoples as well. I think about African Americans and Hispanics, who, until recently, were seldom found in history textbooks and literature anthologies.

Vizenor spoke of the myths that fit a dominant society's view of the savage American and of the fact that much of what passes for truth regarding Native Americans is, instead, simulation. Later, I would use

Vizenor's term *survivance* to shape my choice of literature for the classroom. Works that left the reader with a sense of pity for helpless victims were bypassed in favor of literature that focused on the strength of a people to survive and rise above adversity.

The issues we studied seemed particularly relevant to my setting, an urban/suburban middle school in Southfield, Michigan, made up mostly of African Americans and a significant number of Chaldean students, Christians from Northern Iraq. Issues of voice and representation, it seems to me, are critical to my nonmainstream English-speaking students. Do they see themselves in our history books and literature anthologies? What can I do to ensure that my students will feel connected to school and learning?

Archival Research

My exposure to archival documents at a workshop led me to imagine that there might be archives in my city. In recent years, Southfield's population has shifted as Whites have moved to outer-ring suburbs and African Americans and Chaldeans have moved into the city. As a resident and teacher in the city, I was well aware of the changing demographics and wondered just who would be represented if we did have local archives.

Archival research could integrate social studies and language arts, the subjects I teach. Reading archival collections could engage my students as interpreters and makers of history and literature. I wondered if they would see themselves in the city's history, given the recent demographic shift? If not, could we contribute to the archives so that my students and their families would be represented?

I thought about my nonmainstream English-speaking students and the notion of cultural responsiveness and what it means to construct knowledge. I want my students to value literacy and see connections to their lives. I want my students to see themselves in many of the texts we read. But what happens if there are no texts for my students to identify with? It has been difficult to find stories that reflect the culture and language of my Chaldean students who come from an oral tradition. My guess was we might not find many artifacts or documents in Southfield's archives that would reflect my African American students either. Could this absence still lead to engagement in literacy if the students created their own texts, texts of their lives?

Calls to the city and the library led me to a historic section of the city and the original town hall, now used as a local museum. It took me three months of unreturned phone calls and no-show appointments before I was able to gain entry, at which point issues of access had become a real concern for me. What I finally discovered was a treasure trove of original documents, unprotected, sitting in a back closet, dating as far back as the early 1800s.

I begged for permission to bring my students to the museum so they, too, could access these original documents: school board records indicating dimensions for a privy and the price of a cord of wood for the school house; city ordinances and tax rolls over a century old; early Sears, Roebuck catalogs; primers and science textbooks from the 1800s; and medical books with dubious cures for a range of female maladies.

Our public library held a book written by Southfield School's director of information, Dr. Kenson Siver. It was his doctoral dissertation, entitled *Southfield Faces the Crucial Decades: The Development of a Suburb and Its School System in the Years Following World War II* (Siver, 1987). The cover was a photograph of a 1950s Southfield School elementary class. I put it on a transparency and made another transparency of last year's class. Side by side, the two photographs, one all White, the other mostly African American, made for interesting reading.

Field Trips and Follow-up: Complicating Notions of Reading

It turned out that Dr. Siver was the current president of the Southfield Historical Society. He generously allowed me to make copies of his own collection of archival documents, and he arranged and acted as docent for over a week of field trips for our entire sixth grade, by then in freezing November temperatures and snow.

I've visited historic sites before—museums, restored farm houses, cemeteries— but never with an eye to reading them as texts. Carved on tombstones in Southfield's first cemetery were, in effect, histories of demographics, disease, migration, religion, and economics. Coupled with local lore that outlived those buried, these sources allowed us to begin reconstructing history.

My hypothesis regarding representation in the museum was right on. Though early Southfield was populated by the Potawatomi and Ojibwa (Chippewa) tribes, who settled along the banks of the Rouge River, the only evidence that Native Americans ever lived in the region came in the form of a single arrowhead and a one-line mention in a textbook. This omission reminded me of Vizenor's maxim: absence is presence.

A history of Southfield written in the 1960s noted the birth date of "the first white child born in Southfield," whereas the only mention of an African American presence came in the city ordinances for slaves written in the mid-1800s.

Back in the classroom, we continued to layer our learning. We read and collected artifacts connected to our field trip. One student brought in a local newspaper article about how his father was spearheading a petition drive to turn Southfield's Code House, once part of the Underground Railroad, into a historic landmark. Describing himself as an activist, the student's father came to class and told of ways to act on issues one cares deeply about, which made for a memorable civics lesson.

We read sections of a local newspaper from 1934, especially the advertisements. Clothing and food prices led to discussions of inflation. We studied the pictures and the language of the ads themselves, such as one favorite showing an angry man wearing an apron and washing dishes, with the caption "Try it yourself, Mr. Husband! You try doing the housework with a lot of cold, clammy water." It was an ad for a hot water heater, but the clearly defined gender roles were eye-opening for the students.

Melanie brought in her grandmother's math book from the Southfield school district dating back to the 1930s. Narrowly defined gender roles were unmistakable in the story problems. Women and girls cooked, sewed, and raised children; men and boys did carpentry and worked outside the home in building, banking, and business. By pairing a math text with advertisements from the same period, we were able to reconstruct history from gender and economic perspectives.

The Community as Museum

Repeatedly I asked myself how I could scaffold concepts as sophisticated as simulation, representation, archival research, and regionalism for sixth graders in ways that would enable them to build their critical thinking skills and allow them to try on the roles of historian and author. Since, as our museum findings clearly indicated, the students were not represented in Southfield's history, it seemed logical for them to preserve their own histories, and the class set out to create personal archival collections.

Containers of all sizes overflowed our classroom for most of the year. Photographs, obituaries, deeds, baby clothing, audio and video interviews, stories, and family heirlooms brought histories to life. I, too, created a personal archival collection: a treasured videotape of Great-Grandma, my mediocre Birney middle school report card (I attended school where I now teach), a photo of my first class as teacher, and other artifacts I value so much that I put the box away for safekeeping.

We videotaped our presentations to preserve them for posterity. We wrote poetry about our most cherished possessions and laughed and tried to guess what that green box was that Dion brought in: truly ancient, a small portable record player that could adjust for 45s or 78s. No one knew what it was.

We invited grandparents to come to class to relate their various experiences of growing up. The stories ranged from confronting Jim Crow laws in the South to buying ice from the "ice man," and from shoveling coal into the furnace to picking up bits of road tar for chewing gum—and all led to further ideas for inquiry.

Preserving our own histories and viewing history through our grandparents' eyes set the stage for us to go beyond our stories and into the broader community. In social studies, we were learning about the Bill of Rights, governments, and immigration. Keeping in mind the concept of community as museum, we organized a field trip to Freedom House.

Several years ago, parents introduced me to Freedom House, a refuge for illegal aliens located across from the Ambassador Bridge between the United States and Canada. Housed in what was once a convent next to St. Anne's, the oldest Catholic church in the city of Detroit, Freedom House provides shelter, medical care, and legal aid to those seeking asylum from all over the world.

For several years I've arranged for field trips to Freedom House wherein we bring an ethnic lunch and much-needed basic supplies; it takes a donation of a four-pack of toilet paper to participate in the trip. There, thanks to the kindness of the volunteers at Freedom House, we divide up into small groups and, with the aid of interpreters, interview families from all over the world who are seeking asylum in the United States and Canada. At tables with refugees from the Middle East, Chaldean parents, acting as chaperones and interpreters, translate from Arabic to English. My bilingual parents and students were respected for the important role they played. This year, three classes visited Freedom House, and twenty-nine parents took a day off work to join us. Several parents over the years have continued to support the shelter, with one even teaching weekly English classes. When we ask the question "Who and what is American?" a look at the issues surrounding refugees and immigration offers insight.

Our primary research allowed us to become historians. We were living and recording history, gathering stories and points of view that might otherwise go unheard. Long after our visit, we sent clothing and raised money to help Freedom House, thereby taking action to make a difference in the world. By unpacking the history represented in our archives, field trips, and interviews, we generated long lists of topics for further inquiry. Teacher and student collections of videos, novels, poems, music, children's books, posters, and a wide selection of non-fiction texts filled crates and extra tables set up to hold our museum. Sentence strips posted on the bulletin board reminded us of overriding focus questions to guide our inquiries: How is history made? Who is telling the story? Whose voices are heard? Whose voices are silenced?

New Definitions of Text: Reading Critically in Social Studies and Language Arts

For several years, I'd been trying to integrate my social studies and language arts curricula with limited success. To deepen my students' understanding of content, I wanted them to make connections across disciplines in several authentic ways. I learned to pair texts, layer perspectives by rereading from multiple points of view, and expand my definition of what constitutes "text" to include artifacts, the community, and photographs and other media.

As we read about the European conquest, or the exploration of the New World, depending on one's point of view, I collected over a dozen different pictures purported to show Columbus. We looked in our social studies textbook for images of Columbus and wondered why they all looked different. Our question led us to discover that no one ever painted a portrait of Columbus in his lifetime; therefore, all of the pictures were simulations.

We also read Jane Yolen's *Encounter*, illustrated by David Shannon. Yolen and Shannon researched Columbus's first known landing in the New World and tried to recreate the experience from a Taino boy's point of view.

Once again, paired texts deepened our understanding. After reading *Encounter*, we pulled out our social studies book and looked at the painting that depicted Columbus landing in the Caribbean. We read the painting for point of view and historical accuracy. Above the caption, "What might Columbus have said on these occasions?" was a simulation showing native people, draped in cloth, seated before a standing Columbus who is flanked by crosses, the Spanish flag, and plumed soldiers. We wondered what the natives might have said on such an occasion.

Our study of Columbus led to a study of slavery from an economic and historic perspective. *Amistad* was out in movie theaters, adding further timeliness to our studies. We were becoming purposeful makers and consumers of American literatures.

Amy brought sugar cane and sugar beets to school so we could imagine the labor required in order to cut the thick cane and, in turn, see how the change to growing beets for sugar lessened the need for the backbreaking labor that had been forced onto slaves and, as a result, brought important changes in both human and economic terms.

Jerry brought in a book filled with simulations of artifacts from slavery. *Lest We Forget: The Passage from Africa to Slavery and Emancipation*, by Velma Maia Thomas, was a gift to Jerry from his parents. In this way, our lives, our studies, our families, and our literatures were interwoven. There was a sense of purpose and community that extended far beyond the classroom.

Our link to language arts consisted not only of what we were reading—textbooks, children's books, pictures, films, artifacts—but also of *how* we were reading, always mindful of the source, the stance, the times, and the omissions.

If Not the Canon, Then What? American Literature in Middle School

Choosing literature for my middle school program is one of the most important curricular decisions I make. While high school colleagues struggle with augmenting or supplanting the traditional canon of American literature, I am fortunate to be free to base my decisions on other criteria. Over the course of a school year, I think about balance: balance among various long and short forms, including novels, short stories, picture books, and poetry; balance between classic and contemporary writings; the need to include multiple perspectives; the need to provide for a range of reading and interest levels; and a concern that my students see themselves reflected in nonstereotypical ways. Survivance is now an organizing principle for me. Are victims of discrimination helpless, to be pitied, or do they muster the will to overcome adversity and survive? I've accepted or rejected books on this basis.

I also think about other categories of genre in that balance: It's important that students read widely in both narrative and expository texts. And I think about the thematic instruction that drives my teaching and the need to fill the room with related readings. I've become a young adult book connoisseur.

American literature lives in middle school. It's just not the canon. Our American literatures included provocative children's books as appropriate for adults as for adolescents. Often told from a child's perspective, with illustrations that add meaning to the text, children's books can be read aloud in one sitting, emotionally engage listeners, build community, and clarify complex events across time. The power of story for learning is well documented and the children's books I read were carefully selected to stimulate critical thinking and further inquiry related to issues generated through our archival research.

Our touchstone texts, the ones we often referred back to, the ones that anchored our studies, included Eve Bunting's *Cheyenne Again*, which treats Indian schools from a Native American child's point of view and offers an accurate simulation of a ledger book used by children placed in Indian schools—schools designed to "civilize" Native Americans by replacing their language and culture with European American ways (Grutman and Matthaei).

We also read Evelyn Coleman's *White Socks Only*, which framed issues of racial segregation as we tried to imagine living in the South under Jim Crow laws. In the book, a sign on a water fountain reads "whites only," so an African American child removes her shoes and drinks from the fountain in her lacy white socks.

Our inquiry broadened when we read *Passage to Freedom: The Sugihara Story* by Ken Mochizuki. In 1940, Jews fleeing the Nazis begged the Japanese Consul to Lithuania for visas to allow them to travel by way of Japan to safety. This true story, retold to the author by the ambassador's son, with illustrations that extend the understated text, leaves readers emotionally drained.

We also read Yoshiko Uchida's "Letter from a Concentration Camp" (Durell and Sachs), which led to further inquiry into the Japanese internment in the United States during World War II. Ken Mochizuki, influenced by his father's internment in Idaho, wrote *Baseball Saved Us*, which allowed students a glimpse into an internment camp from a Japanese perspective. Yukio Tsuchiya's *Faithful Elephants: A True Story of Animals, People and War* added yet another perspective to our inquiry into World War II. During the bombing of Tokyo, the Japanese army ordered all the wild animals in the zoo to be put to sleep so they wouldn't run wild if the zoo was bombed. This is the story of how the performing elephants died and how they are remembered.

The book begins with a message, "To the Readers," from Chiekio Akiyama, a radio and television commentator from Tokyo. Akiyama tells how he has read this story over television and radio every year since it was published to remind viewers and listeners of the senselessness of war and the need to work for peace.

At the same time that I read aloud powerful texts that connected and extended our studies, students in both my social studies classes and my language arts class pursued their own related reading and viewing during workshop time. The wide array of materials, from picture books to novels to films, made it possible for every child to find an entry point into our studies. The opportunity for students to read individually or collaboratively was another way I scaffolded reading for all students. Equally important was the fact that students could pursue issues that grew out of their own histories. Relevance and personal connections lead to student engagement.

In my mind, I had a big picture of where we were going and ultimately where we'd end up. But I'd built in lots of room for student ownership along the way so that our studies both related to and made sense to each of us. Rather than doing isolated reading about World War II, the study evolved from a grandparent's experience. Rather than starting an isolated unit on slavery, we pursued these readings because of the stories contained in our personal archives relating to discrimination and prejudice. Then we traced the history to understand how we came to this juncture in time.

The largest segment of my language arts curriculum is devoted to expository text. For years I've teamed up with my colleague Rita Teague's high school senior honors students in English, who became mentors and co-researchers with my sixth graders on self-selected topics relating to various issues in society. Leading up to our inquiries, we share several common readings and meet for discussion.

This year both sixth graders and their high school mentors read Sandra Cisneros's "Hairs" and "Four Skinny Trees" from *The House on Mango Street*; an excerpt from Melba Pattillo Beals's memoir *Warriors Don't Cry*; Henry Louis Gates Jr.'s chapter "In the Kitchen" from *Colored People: A Memoir*; and the Palestinian story "If You Were a Horse . . ." from *Men in the Sun* by Ghassan Kanafani.

These are sophisticated readings for sixth graders. Some I read aloud, and then we reflected on them in our notebooks. We tried reader's theater with *Warriors Don't Cry*, read Cisneros in literature circles, and compared her version of "Hairs" with Henry Louis Gates Jr.'s "In the Kitchen," also about hair. By the time we met for discussion with the high school students, the sixth graders could comfortably contribute to the conversation.

Our focus questions were the subtext for all we read, wrote, and discussed, deepening our thinking, layering our reading. How is history made? Who's telling the story? Whose voices are heard? Whose voices are silenced? With these overarching thematic questions driving the curriculum, I was able to integrate social studies with language arts.

As we began our extended study of expository text it was clear that students had moved from simplistic readings of the world toward a more critical stance. Noelle researched and took a position on affirmative action. Jerry addressed the present state of race relations and implications for the future. B. J. stood out as a vivid example of what can happen when a student is engaged in critical thinking and reading and writing from multiple perspectives throughout the school year.

B. J. spent all of his elementary school years in special education. Sixth grade was his first year without special services or a "special ed" designation. His first draft of a poem, written in October, began as follows:

> The guy who has no clue
> he does anything for a girl
> even fight a bull.
>
> Will never stay away from you
> even if you're cruel . . .

I asked B. J., "What are you really trying to say?" We co-wrote his first published piece, discussing, writing, and revising together. By the time memoir came around, B. J. was a more experienced writer.

> My bag is coming apart like Mr. Potato Head. In fact,
> I have to attach the tongue of the bag to the arm of it leaving
> a huge knot with threads jutting out like the quills of a
> porcupine . . .

Near the end of the school year, having decided to research NASA and its role as we head into the new millennium, B. J. was reading *National Geographic* for information and wrote, "What draws us to the unknown? How can we quench this thirst of conquest, building vehicles to the stars?"

B.J.'s transformation was no accident. Asked to focus on meaning, historicize texts, think critically about point of view and representation, and use writer's craft—and encouraged to take ownership of his own ideas, readings, and writings—B. J. grew into the conversation around him. My critical stance made it possible to promote conversations that were more likely to be found in college classrooms than in middle schools.

Works Cited

Beals, Melba. *Warriors Don't Cry: A Searing Memoir of the Battle to Integrate Little Rock's Central High.* New York: Pocket, 1994.

Bunting, Eve. *Cheyenne Again.* New York: Clarion, 1995.

Cisneros, Sandra. *The House on Mango Street.* New York: Vintage, 1991.

Coleman, Evelyn. *White Socks Only.* Morton Grove, IL: Whitman, 1996.

Gates, Henry Louis, Jr. *Colored People: A Memoir.* New York: Knopf, 1994.

Grutman, Jewel H., and Gay Matthaei. *The Ledgerbook of Thomas Blue Eagle.* Charlottesville: Thomasson-Grant, 1994.

Kanafani, Ghassan. *Men in the Sun: And Other Palestinian Stories.* Washington, D.C.: Three Continents, 1983.

Mochizuki, Ken. *Baseball Saved Us.* New York: Lee, 1993.

———. *Passage to Freedom: The Sugihara Story.* New York: Lee, 1997.

Siver, Kenson J. *Southfield Faces the Crucial Decades: The Development of a Suburb and Its School System in the Years Following World War II.* Southfield, MI: K. J. Siver, 1987.

Thomas, Velma Maia. *Lest We Forget: The Passage from Africa to Slavery and Emancipation.* New York: Crown, 1997.

Tsuchiya, Yukio. *Faithful Elephants: A True Story of Animals, People and War.* Boston: Houghton, 1988.

Uchida, Yoshiko. "Letter from a Concentration Camp." *The Big Book for Peace.* Ed. Ann Durell and Marilyn Sachs. New York: Dutton, 1990. 57–61.

Yolen, Jane. *Encounter.* San Diego: Harcourt, 1992.

12 Literature of Place and Place in Literature: Orienting Our Maps

Jim White
Farmington High School, Farmington, Michigan

I saw the movie *Diner* when I was in high school. At one point, a woman refers to the Chisholm Trail as if the two main characters she is speaking to should definitely know about it. When she leaves, they turn to each other and one says, "Do you ever get the idea there's something going on that we don't know about?" As one who has often felt this way—that perhaps I would understand more if I just moved over the next hill or around the next corner or if I had only stood on *this* spot *yesterday*—I guess I should not be surprised that the language of geographers has shaped the way I think. Reading is exploration, and writing is a search for understanding. A writer's point of view is a point in space, that place she works from, that one point where the writer engages the world around her and attempts to make sense of it. In experimenting over the last five years with workshop models of reading and writing, I have kept one overarching goal in mind: I try somehow to help make that writer's point of view seem not so far away from the student's own. Writers do not have some magical understanding of the world that is impossible for the rest of us to attain, and, if there are things going on that we don't know about, that place where it's all happening probably is not as far from us as we might believe. To understand is to shorten the distance, and, as a result, learning to me often becomes an effort to find a path across that distance. Our own writing generated in this effort becomes part of our map.

I was in the earliest stages of this thinking in the fall of 1994 as I faced my tenth graders, with a whole month of teaching experience under my belt, and we were bogged down in reading passages from *Walden*. How, I desperately wondered, could I help them connect? I finally asked students to think like Thoreau. "Take fifteen to twenty minutes each day, over the course of a week or two," I said, "and return to a place of your choosing, preferably outside. Just sit down there and open your senses." They were not to talk, but to note observations of what went on around them and of their feelings. I simply hoped to encourage students to become keener observers of life, a skill crucial to writers, but another benefit that I did not expect was that some students actually thanked me for the assignment. Without it, Jennifer said, she would never have taken the time simply to sit and think about her day.

This was an encouraging start, and, while other attempts have flopped or worked to varying degrees with various students over the years, I have hung on to the idea that the writer as observer could be introduced as an archetype. If Thoreau could slow down and truly see his world at Walden, then so could we. Soon, we were looking at others' efforts. Can you appreciate Annie Dillard's detail, I'd ask, or Barry Lopez's imagery, or Walt Whitman's vision? Want to know what's going on here from a writer's point of view? Put yourself at that point. Try it yourself. Start by going out into the world and *noticing* the space around you.

We read those writers who try particularly to set a scene—Joan Didion, Wendell Berry, Aldo Leopold—writers for whom a place becomes a fully developed character. We read excerpts from the man who covers both halves of the depth versus breadth conversation, William Least Heat-Moon. He described a journey around the United States in 427 pages in *Blue Highways* and then settled down to create a 622-page "deep map" of Chase County, Kansas, in *PrairyErth*. We also took observation walks at school, and these slowly expanded into the community. How do we define this place we inhabit, I wanted to know. How did our corner of the world come to be here, to look this way? Who has been here before, felt the air and seen the light at this spot, and what stories could they have told? What about this place gives it its unique character? Many students, of course, think it has none. "Farmington is boring," they say. They let me know that the questions were my own, and they did not necessarily share my desire to know.

Since I am talking about place, perhaps I should quickly sketch this one. Farmington, Michigan, is a suburb about fifteen miles northwest of Detroit. There is a small downtown—furniture stores, shoe stores, banks, a skater apparel shop, a movie theater, and a used book store—which has grown from the first European settlement of 1824. This area is surrounded by the larger, newer city of Farmington Hills, which has no downtown center, but, instead, subdivision, strip-shopping, industrial park, and office development built mostly after 1950. Grand River, the old Detroit-to-Lansing plank road, cuts right through downtown

Farmington. Now, however, most of the traffic whizzes to someplace else along the interstate. While their parents may drive to work in Detroit, it is possible that some of my students have never been there. It is also true, I know now, that several students had another hometown before they moved to Farmington; their roots are elsewhere. In fact, it is becoming almost common to have a student whose roots are in another country, such as Iraq or India or Russia or Albania. I understand; I did not grow up here, either, but moved here after my marriage. Perhaps the reason I keep asking the questions about this place is because I am trying to make it my home.

I think of Sherwood Anderson helping William Faulkner to understand that he had more than enough material for his fiction on his own "little postage stamp of soil" around Oxford, Mississippi. All of my students have some story to tell about living here, even if it's the story of how they came here. "Start with what you know," we are fond of telling fledgling writers. The trick is to find out what you know.

Talking about our own neighborhoods led to taking journals in hand to go watch and record. But later, back in class, explaining why, say, Denise Gundle and Francie Thompson were standing on opposite sides of the street glaring at each other demanded that our listeners have some context for the present. Soon, like Heat-Moon, we were deep-mapping, filling in the recent history of our neighborhoods, and having a pretty good time, too—until someone had to kill it by stepping in as the teacher and saying, "Gosh, it seems to me like the places we all know best have become our texts. It feels like we are *reading* our streets!" Well, I meant well. (It turns out I was not too far off. Gretel Ehrlich says, "To see and know a place is a contemplative act. It means emptying our minds and letting what is there, in all its multiplicity and endless variety, come in" [qtd. in Heat-Moon, *PrairyErth* 5].)

An idea first introduced to me at the Oakland (Michigan) Writing Project is that of creating a memory map. For example, students can draw a map of the neighborhood they lived in when they were six or seven, then make a legend for the map: A is one place on the map where they felt happy, B is a place where they felt sad, C is the nicest person on the map, D is the meanest, and so on. We have made lists of possibilities for the legend. The map becomes the keeper of memories, the document that students return to again and again to search for material for their own writing. It tells who we are and where we are, and how those ideas intersect. *My Map Book*, a children's picture book by Sara Fanelli, gives ideas for several other maps.

One of our inspirations for mapping our home places is N. Scott Momaday's *The Way to Rainy Mountain*, in which he writes:

> Once in his life a man ought to concentrate his mind upon the remembered earth, I believe. He ought to give himself up to a particular landscape in his experience, to look at it from as many angles as he can, to wonder about it, to dwell upon it. He ought to imagine that he touches it with his hands at every season and listens to the sounds that are made upon it. He ought to imagine the creatures there and all the faintest motions of the wind. He ought to recollect the glare of noon and all the colors of dawn and dusk. (83)

We hadn't delved too deeply beneath the pavement and the lawns to the land itself, but we started to look at the place shaped by people. In this part of the country, the most obvious impact on the land is the grid of roads that grew out of the Northwest Ordinance surveying directions. We noticed the names on street signs and saw them again on tombstones. We looked at the architecture of houses of different eras. We wondered not only about the men whose names are on the veterans' memorial but also about the people who erected the memorial. We considered gathering places—parks, restaurants, and places of worship. That I have not spent as much time with students explicitly investigating the natural world around us probably reveals my own suburban upbringing. Yet we realized that before people could shape the place, the land itself provided only certain options. Detroit was established because of a river, and then became an important trading post. Arthur Power passed through Detroit and stopped his wagon here in 1824 because the water supply and soil and climate were all conducive to growing crops.

In talking and writing about how place affected us, we were locating ourselves in a long tradition. Barry Lopez says:

> The European writing I know rarely recognizes a power in the land that corresponds to a power of being, while one of the things that distinguishes American literature, especially in the West, is that you expect to see the land turn up in a powerful or a mysterious or an affecting way. (qtd. in Heat-Moon, *PrairyErth* 8)

Much of American literature seems to describe the process of Americanization, that is, the grinding down and smoothing of differences of a minority culture until a member of that culture seems to function in the mainstream, the process of adapting to this place and seeking a place in this culture. This process only began in what is now North America with the first European settlements on the continent and could not have continued except that the land was taken from its native inhabitants and, where possible, cleared and built upon. Whatever it means to be American, whether for the first inhabitants or the Europeans who came after, a relationship with this place is part of the definition.

It has occurred to me that our maps overlap with each other's and with the maps of people who have lived here before us. I've played with the idea of building a regional anthology of such works as Harriet Arnow's *The Dollmaker*, Philip Levine's poetry about growing up working in Detroit, and Michael Moore's "Roger and Me." Local landmarks are named in them; perhaps students would enjoy finding that published authors have cared about the same streets and paths that they walk on. The land has layers and layers of history upon it. Henry Ford once owned an inn two miles from school; a major intersection of Potawatomi trails—later an intersection of interurban rail lines—is less than half a mile from our classroom. Stories abound here if we will only allow them time to reveal themselves.

Thinking about this place led me to start asking questions: What does it mean to say we are from Detroit, or Michigan, or the Midwest? How do we define our region? Are we a former major industrial center, now deserving of the Rust Belt tag, plagued by the boom and bust of linking fortunes with one industry? Plagued by a shift of population away from the urban core out across the green fields now laced with sewers and subdivision streets, awaiting the new homes and manicured lawns? Plagued by the negative images across the country of crime and strained race relations in a worn-out city struggling to survive? Is any part of this description accurate, and can it fully communicate the experiences of people of all colors and ethnicities who have shaped Detroit? Would African Americans living next to Mexican Americans living next to Irish Americans on the same street in southwest Detroit describe the same "regional" experiences? If a place is defined by what work is done there or by what its people produce, then what about describing Michigan as a farming region, as a former timber producer, as a center of maritime trade plied on the Great Lakes whose shores define the state's boundaries? To those in the Upper Peninsula—we are, after all, the only state with two halves—we are simply labeled "downstate." The copper country of the Keewanau Peninsula is no closer to Detroit than is Montreal or St. Louis, or the hills of Tennessee.

I wondered: Is any of this relevant to my fourteen-year-olds? Do they see themselves as part of the region described as Detroit? If not, how do they describe themselves? As residents of a "boring" small town? As mall-rat suburbanites?

What we have are several different "regions," many of which converge and overlap at the same points in space. No matter where we came from or which cultures we identify with or what work we do, what we certainly have in common is a place on this planet, a place that we need to understand and nurture if only for our own good. At the very least we are all affected by natural laws.

Scott Russell Sanders, who writes and teaches at the University of Indiana, suggests that we look at these laws as we consider what it means to have a sense of place at the end of the twentieth century, when we are told that technology makes our world smaller every day. He does not believe that the "global village" metaphor works, because we are too free to tune in or tune out of it, whereas "in a real village you are answerable to your neighbors" (16). Nor, he argues, can we define regions based on some ethnic or racial or cultural identity—these divisions tear apart a community more often than they bring it together. What he decides we need, as have Thoreau or Didion or Berry, are fewer people passing through and more that will stop, get to know, and inhabit the earth:

> I suggest we begin our search for a new sense of place not by tuning in to the global village, nor by tracing our ancestry, nor by studying our own remarkable works, but by learning all we can about the land. What soils surround our houses or apartments and what rocks underlie them? How did these soils and bedrocks form, how have they been wrenched and rumpled by the sliding of the earth's plates, how have they been shaped by the long strokes of weather, perhaps by glaciers or volcanoes, and how do they hold and channel water? As for water, we need to know how much of it falls each year in the neighborhood, and where the rain goes after it slides off the roof, into what sewers or creeks, what aquifers, what rivers and lakes, what bay, what sea. Where does the sun rise and set throughout the year, how does the light change, and how do the shadows play? We should observe the seasonal drama of the air, its heat and cold, its moisture and color, its fragrances. We need to know which way the winds blow, and what dust or pollen or pollution they carry. What birds, beasts, insects, and wild plants are native to the area? What crops thrive there? What bushes and flowers and trees blossom in that place, and when? What creatures sing?
>
> The answers to such questions help reveal where we actually live. They point to durable realities that have shaped human existence for millions of years, and that will continue to shape our existence so long as we dwell on this planet. (16)

Seeking these answers makes more sense than knowing the abstract boundaries of townships or counties or states, which the earth ignores. Even Heat-Moon chose Chase County specifically because, traveling from east to west along the waist of the nation (U.S. Route 50), Chase County is the designation given to the piece of earth where the eastern woodlands end and the tall grass prairie begins.

A sense of place affected my initial thinking about what it means to make American literatures. I had tried to help students understand what it is to *make* literature by locating themselves at the points of view of writers. I realized that part of being *American* means having a connection with and being affected by this land. And I thought about *literature* in terms of almost any genre that is rooted in place; for example, I brought folk ballads into class and we compared their ability to carry news of local events to that of newspapers. I was hypersensitive to the idea of place. Suddenly, I found myself looking at it from a different angle, a new point of view.

During a Making American Literatures workshop (see the foreword for more description of the MAL project), literary scholar Genaro Padilla talked to us about his work with primary documents left by Mexicans who had immigrated to California in the nineteenth century. His own interest had begun early, with the books and magazines he had read and the adult conversations he had listened to in his mother's house. "This is *where* the desire [to understand] begins for me, a voyeur's interest in the stories people tell about themselves," he said, and he concluded his own story by saying, "I would like to recover the genealogy of *my place* in the context of the culture" (emphases added). He was doing his research to discover his own location, not on Earth, but within a culture, and he was telling us his story to take us to the point where his interest began. His story was our map, and X marked the spot where we who were following could see how his desire to know became a life work. How many other stories, I began to wonder, were also maps, told so that listeners could be aided as they traveled, attempting to reach their destination, which was a new understanding? Thus the term "location" took on new meanings for me. I could describe my geographical location, but also my location or place in time, in my family, in a cultural tradition, within a group or in juxtaposition with one, such as my location with respect to my students. Again I immediately thought, Where would they place themselves? Thinking this way gave a whole new meaning to the idea of being "lost."

Another time, English professor Mitch Breitweiser sat down to talk with us about *The Great Gatsby*. In the ritual that I was beginning to enjoy as much as hearing any thinking about the literature itself, he began by briefly describing the path that had led him to his seat with us. As an aside, he threw out the observation that "if you feel like you're on the edge, then there must be a center someplace else. You feel like you are missing something; the essence of things is elsewhere." Though it wasn't one of his main points, it sure helped many of my circling thoughts fall into place. Hadn't I always felt that there was something going on just a little out of my sight that it seemed I was supposed to know about, but did not, just like the characters in *Diner*? The fiction we had talked about over that past week was all about characters that were either comfortably at some center or out on the unsettling edge—in either case, positioning was key: Momaday's *The Way to Rainy Mountain* describes not only the way the Kiowa people flowed out onto the plains to find the center of their own tradition, but also the way Momaday traveled to reclaim that center in his own life, after a separation among White people. In *The House on Mango Street*, by Sandra Cisneros, Esperanza, who feels very much on the edge of mainstream culture, dreams of one day owning a house that she is not ashamed of, that she, not a man, will run, and that is big enough so that she can invite "bums" (her term) to come in and sleep in her attic (87). That house will serve as her center, providing safety and respectability. Nella Larsen's *Passing* describes the act of passing for White because that is the perceived center in our national culture, where there is power.

The center is all of these things: a place of comfort, safety, respectability, and power. Where is it? Different characters—even different characters in the same book—may describe different centers, and they may feel that they are at varying distances from their center. Again, much of American literature seems to be at least in part about the process of Americanization, or about its cost, and the idea of the center affords another way to think about this: Americanization may be a matter of finding a secure place at the center, or it may be what happens *to* someone on the edge of the mainstream who cannot get out of the way of the steamroller. Jay Gatsby may initiate this process, whereas others, such as the Ojibwas of Louise Erdrich's *Love Medicine,* are caught up in it more or less against their will, and still others, such as Huck Finn, seek to avoid it altogether and to find a center someplace else. However they personalize it, the center/edge metaphor seems to work in the lives of many, if not most, fictional characters—and for many of us as well. In fact, in the previous spring, I had come across a particularly powerful nonfiction book that dealt, I realized now, with centers and edges—Dale Maharidge's and Michael Williamson's *Journey to Nowhere.*

My ninth-grade students helped me put this thinking together during the following school year. In August 1997, I wanted to approach the year making sure that, no matter what else, the students had plenty of chances to discover their own voices, as writers and also as people. I wanted them to be able to tell their own stories, to feel like their voices were heard. This seemed to me the most important lesson of my summer work; if I listened to my students, then they would go and listen to others, and we all needed this listening if we were to begin truly to celebrate our diversity. I was not sure how to start this, but on my way to school on the third day, a question popped into my head. So in class everyone pulled out a sheet of paper and a pen, and we wrote for ten minutes on this question: Where in your life (even without thinking, I was asking about special places again) do you feel you have power? Then we shared. I let students define "power" any way they wanted to, and Matt said he had power at home, because he could tell his little sister what to do. In fact, all of those who said they had power described this condition of having power "over" someone. Most, though—and I don't know now why this surprised me—said that they did not feel they had power anywhere. Not at home, and definitely not at school.

This writing colored our conversation for the rest of the year. When we were reading *To Kill A Mockingbird*, for example, students were in their literature circles and I was floating around. Nick's group was talking about the scene where Calpurnia takes Scout and Jem Finch to church with her and Miss Lulu gets angry with Calpurnia for bringing those White children. "What's the big deal?" they asked me.

"Well, I don't know," I said. "Do you think if Miss Lulu goes to town, she will be able to go in any front doors?"

"Nope." (We had talked about this already.)

"Do you think Miss Lulu has a lot of power when she is in town?"

"Not really."

"What would happen if she tried to go to the church that Atticus normally takes his children to?"

"They might not let her in."

"They might not," I said. "In any case, would she feel very comfortable there?"

"No way."

"Okay. So Miss Lulu is at her own church, where she is comfortable. She's safe. Does she have power at her church?"

"Yeah, it seems like she does," said Nick.

"I don't know," said Amy. "Nobody else seems to agree with her that the kids shouldn't be there."

"Yeah, but at least she is speaking her own opinion. She couldn't do that in town."

"Okay," I said. "So she can at least talk here. Now, do Scout and Jem have to come in the back door of Miss Lulu's church?"

"No," said Amy.

"So in other words," I said, "Scout and Jem have power anywhere? Is that right?"

"Yeah," said Amy and Nick.

"Okay. Remember how you said that you guys didn't feel like you had power in school? Teachers made all the decisions, right? But if you were with your friends, you felt like you had more of a say in what went on. What if you were hanging out with your friends and I showed up and said, 'All right, let's sit down and hold a lit circle!' How would you feel?"

Amy and Rachel laughed. "No way," said Nick.

"There you go," I said. "And by the way, Nick, I'll be over tonight around 7:30, so have your book."

"Hey, I don't know," I continued. "Miss Lulu might not like Calpurnia, she might just be mean, who knows? But she's in the one place where Black people have power in Maycomb, away from Whites, and then Scout and Jem show up. Does that make sense?"

"Yeah, it does" they nodded.

I had not thought about the scene like this before. If I was one step ahead of Nick and Amy in our conversation it was because, when we started talking, I suddenly was seeing the whole picture in terms of centers and edges. Miss Lulu had a very small center where she felt safe; most of her day was spent on the uncomfortable edge, where she knew she did not fully belong to the community. Scout and Jem, whose centers stretched over Maycomb and beyond, were now violating her space. For a moment, they felt uneasy and would have turned for home, but Calpurnia reassured them and they quickly fit in.

I talked to students about what I was thinking. It gave all of us a new way to read, and a new way to respond to reading. Suddenly kids with strong spatial intelligence could help us imagine stories in new ways. Those with strong kinesthetic intelligence could represent centers, edges, and overlap through movement. It made more sense now to try to see from various characters' points of view. And again, a map— a depiction of the location of these centers—was a handy metaphor.

Like any explorer, I cannot quite resist making another voyage if there is more to discover. I started to think more about where my students felt their own centers were. I was not surprised this time when I met Chris in the fall of 1998 and he said that school was an edge for him and that his center was in the activities he chose after school. I am still pursuing this idea, because I feel it is important to understand my students' sense of place. Ideally, I want the work we do together to be a center in their lives, but I realize that they also must want it for that to happen.

"I like to think of landscape not as a fixed place but as a path that is unwinding before my eyes, under my feet," says Gretel Ehrlich (qtd. in Heat-Moon, *PrairyErth* 5). I think of teaching in the same way. Even when I walk over familiar ground each year in the classroom, there is another layer to find, or a different angle from which to look. My pack is much fuller than when I set out for Walden with my tenth graders that first year. I've got my maps, the stars, a compass, bread crumbs. Even better, as long as we maintain the conversation in class, I have a human lifeline on my expedition. With that in mind, I'm as ready to go as I'll ever be.

Works Cited

Cisneros, Sandra. *The House on Mango Street*. New York: Vintage, 1984.

Ehrlich, Gretel. *Legacy of Light*. Ed. Constance Sullivan. New York: Knopf, 1987.

Ehrlich, Gretel. *The Solace of Open Spaces*. New York: Viking, 1985.

Fanelli, Sara. *My Map Book*. New York: HarperCollins, 1995.

Heat-Moon, William Least. *Blue Highways: A Journey into America*. Boston: Little, 1982.

————. *PrairyErth: (A Deep Map)*. Boston: Houghton, 1991.

Larson, Nella. *Passing*. New York: Knopf, 1929.

Lee, Harper. *To Kill a Mockingbird*. Philadelphia: Lippincott, 1960.

Leopold, Aldo. *A Sand County Almanac, and Sketches Here and There*. New York: Oxford UP, 1968.

Lopez, Barry. *Desert Notes: Reflections in the Eye of a Raven; River Notes: The Dance of Herons*. New York: Avon, 1990.

Maharidge, Dale, and Michael Williamson. *Journey to Nowhere: The Saga of the New Underclass*. Garden City: Dial, 1985.

Momaday, N. Scott. *The Way to Rainy Mountain*. Albuquerque: U of New Mexico P, 1969.

Sanders, Scott Russell. *Writing from the Center*. Bloomington: Indiana UP, 1995.

Thoreau, Henry David. *Walden and Civil Disobedience*. Ed. Paul Lauter. Boston: Houghton, 2000.

13 The Good, the Bad, and the Ugly: Technology in the Classroom

Peter Shaheen
Seaholm High School, Birmingham, Michigan

Recently, my tolerance for including technology in my teaching was tested. Revlon Consumer Products Corporation sent a letter claiming that it held patent rights to the name "Flex" and that our school's Flex program (short for "Flexible Scheduling") was in violation of the Anti-Cybersquatting Act. Apparently, Revlon has a cosmetic line called Flex. News of "flex.org" (our program's Web site) had sparked the attention of Revlon's legal counsel and was now fraying nerves in our Flex program. Revlon's concern over the supposed misuse of its trademark created an anxiety in me about using technology: While Revlon may be a Goliath, I am no David. Besides, as an English teacher, I am well acquainted with the theme of technology as a negative force.

Obviously, technology has far-reaching implications for education. Teachers who understand the power of technology can use that power in their classroom. Teachers who do not understand how technology can change their teaching are certainly missing out on an opportunity, but for them, it is entirely possible that ignorance is bliss. In the following narrative, both the potential of technology and the notion of ignorance as bliss are portrayed as true. Certainly it is reasonable to assume that many great teachers have not made the technology plunge. What follows here is a description of three ways in which technology *has* been included in the classrooms of teachers I know. It is an attempt to suggest ways in which technology is beginning to shape and inform our teaching. For many, this report will appear mundane, nothing out of the ordinary; yet the picture created here may be useful because it serves as a narrative that can help locate the position of technology in our classrooms.

The Listserv

For those of us who have resisted the ever creeping encroachment of computer technology on our everyday lives, the listserv is like a conference call for keyboards (only better). It works something like this. Dave Winters, a teacher from Georgia, reads *Passing* and decides he needs to make a comment and maybe ask a question or two. He goes to his computer and writes a message to the listserv, and a message is delivered to all twenty-five or so participants on the listserv. When Steve Pohling in California opens his e-mail, there is Dave's message. When Jim or Anne Marie open their mail, they too find Dave's message, and all can respond directly to Dave or to all of the other members of the listserv, as they choose.

This method is better than a conference call in that the reader does not have to be available at a specific time in order to get the message. The reader opens the message at leisure. The listserv is also better than a chat room in that, with a chat room, anyone can participate. The listserv controls who is allowed in on the conversation. It is by invitation only. The second advantage over a chat room is that a listserv allows for a more reflective discourse. Anne Marie, sitting at her computer, has time to fashion her response to Dave without pressure to say something immediately—a constant tension in chat room environments.

The listserv, while a valuable idea, is not and never will be a panacea. Not all teachers embrace the listserv with the same degree of enthusiasm. Some teachers would have to be classified as reluctant at best. Without speaking for them, I would suggest that perhaps they are overwhelmed with all the other aspects of teaching, or perhaps they are unimpressed with what technology can do for their practice. If there is a limited number of skills a teacher can teach in the classroom, then perhaps technology is not a priority. And then again, the reason may be even more basic. It may be a matter of expertise and availability. Some teachers may fear technology, some may be unconvinced that it is necessary, and some may not have the time to invest in learning about it.

What is worth noting is that there has to be a substantial commitment for a long-term project like a listserv to succeed. It would be wonderful if a grassroots group of teachers sprang up, and one particularly dedicated computer wizard agreed to set up the listserv and the rest of the teachers were dedicated enough to move it forward, but this sequence is unlikely for several reasons: The group must share a purpose and be working toward a goal. The group must be so focused on the goal that three or four other goals can't suddenly assume a higher priority. And, ultimately, each member of the group must get something from participation in the group. A more realistic way to make technologies like the listserv work is to incorporate them into the scheme of a greater project, so that people have a reason (beyond the technology itself) to take on technology.

The Twenty-Four-Hour Short Story Contest: Looking for the Literary in Student Work

While researching on the Internet, David Winters found a vanity press that was willing to donate funds to have an anthology of student work collected. David sent out a listserv message asking for people to participate. Students had twenty-four hours to write a short story and turn it in to be evaluated. The directions were really that simple. Students had a variety of options to choose from and all they had to do was bring their paper in the following morning. The idea is interesting because what David managed to accomplish was amazing.

His anthology gathered pieces from across the country and allowed for those pieces to be laid side by side for comparison. How did kids in my school write compared with the kids in David's school? Without David's personal genius, the assignment would never have been conceived, but without the infrastructure set up by the listserv, David would have had no way to implement his idea.

The end result of this technological collaboration was an old-fashioned student anthology published as a paperback book that included contributions from across the country. My student got in on being published thanks to David's generosity.

A fair criticism might attack the concept of a twenty-four-hour short story contest as devaluing revision. What are we really teaching when we ask kids just to knock something off? That concern is reasonable, but the concept of a cross-country collaboration on a grassroots level is an intriguing one.

It is also a revealing way to compare student writing from various parts of the country. There is much to learn on that level. What I discovered is that there were similarities between the craft of David's students and that of my own students. The implications of this observation are open to your judgment. It may mean that writing instruction has little impact on the quality of student writing, or it may mean that David's students and mine receive similar instruction.

Another value of this assignment is that technology and collaboration have the potential to help teachers transform the classroom. Currently, politicians and private concerns alike are advocating for educational reform. The listserv seems like a practical way to bring together a cross section of views in a marketplace of ideas. Some of the monies being allocated by universities, private concerns, and government agencies to institute meaningful educational reform might be better spent if teachers were brought in on the ground floor of the planning, particularly where technology is concerned.

As with the zombies that come out of alien pods in a B movie, teachers' eyes roll to the back of their heads when administrators come in and inform them that a new assessment has been designed and they are responsible for implementing a plan devised by someone whom those teachers consider to be a faceless bureaucrat. Or, even worse, some of these reforms were wrought by a few teachers who did all the work while the others commented about how nice they were for jumping through the hoops to make the county or district or principal or whoever happy about whatever measurement we were supposed to be conjuring so we could eventually put it into an impressive binder and ignore it. If it was a really important reform, then a week before the test we would teach to the test and, after the kids were all coached up and reached their proficiency (or not), we would close the door and teach until the county or the district or the principal came back and said it's time to make another test.

So what does this detour have to do with technology? Technology in conjunction with institutional support holds promise. Used effectively, it can unite and "professionalize" teachers, inviting them to make choices that shape their students' learning. More attention, not less, ought to be given to ways in which technologies can connect classrooms and not only reform instruction but improve it as well.

The City of Birmingham Web Site

When I began teaching at Seaholm High School, students had begun a project that was to bring the city of Birmingham a Web site. The city did not have one in the fall of 1997, but that would change by the following spring. My role as designated adult in the project was really that of an editor. I organized students in the processes of developing, writing, designing, negotiating, refereeing—you name it, and I did it. Yet as far as the teaching goes, writing and designing the city's Web page gave students the most authentic literary experience of their four years at Seaholm. They saw themselves not only as part of the Flexible Scheduling program at Seaholm but also as part of the city of Birmingham. They had a real audience. They felt pressure to produce a quality product and to produce it against a real deadline. They had conversations about pragmatic and aesthetic features of the site. They were engaging in the same reflective practices that define not only writing but scholarship as well.

Some of my doubts about my jurisdiction as a language arts teacher becoming involved in this sort of activity started to resolve themselves. What is literary, and what constitutes a text? How do we expand old notions of texts and define the literary? Certainly, the notion of a Web site as text is one worth exploring more and more every day, as the Internet becomes increasingly involved in our daily toils. Questions about what is literary—are we seeing, for example, the emergence of new genres (which might be called "literary") in this new technological space?—may have to be reexamined in light of new computer technologies and in new contexts. This project reified for my students such ideas about the literary and about texts, and it helped them to recognize differences and similarities between the two.

The city's Web site was also a difficult project to manage. Problems with students doing group work are magnified when the stakes are so high. The personality conflicts are compounded when the city manager is added to the mix, because it is the manager's duty to make sure that the site is functional. Deadlines are suddenly more real. Quality means more than a grade. While these high-stakes publication efforts are valuable, it is hard to escape the feeling that you as teacher are being assessed more than your students are. It wasn't always comfortable. There were times when students failed to live up to expectations and I felt more accountable than students appeared to feel. There were times when the students felt exploited and I felt culpable for that. Negotiating around those delicate corners is fatiguing, especially since there are other hats to wear and classes to prepare while the project is in full swing.

While the Birmingham project may be considered glamorous, few projects are that high profile. One example is the Flexible Scheduling program's Web site, located at www.flex.org. It has a lot of potential but too much of it is under construction. Technology tends to drain one's time and energy so that while teachers and students may start off enthusiastically, it is difficult to finish that way. Frankly, I could not persevere and could not get students to maintain the site over time. Even though there are obvious benefits to technology, I am not willing to give anything up for it.

Maybe there are other parts of the curriculum that override the Web site. Maybe the plain truth is that while a Web site is a new, sexy feature of the progressive classroom, it isn't at the point where it is necessarily a useful strategy for the curriculum. These are open questions. And we can, in any case, learn from the Internet without having our own Web pages.

Using technology is like dancing the bunny hop. It is not always the fastest way to move forward, but it is possible to make progress and enjoy yourself. If you can handle an occasional setback and enjoy technology, you will find it easy to use in the classroom. But there is always something . . .

IV New Lives for Old Texts: Literary Pairings

Peter Shaheen
Seaholm High School, Birmingham, Michigan

"The way we understand this," said the high school teacher, holding up her right hand, "is by comparing it with this," as she lifted up her left hand. With that simple two-handed gesture, her students began to understand a fundamental principle of learning: comparisons deepen our understanding. Poets have always known this, as their frequent use of metaphor demonstrates, so it only makes sense that we as teachers learn to master comparison, placing different texts side by side and observing the resulting tension.

An intimation of the value of pairing literary texts might come by teaching *West Side Story* next to *Romeo and Juliet*. Students who resist Shakespeare's language, dismiss the Montague-Capulet feud as implausible, and view the death-filled conclusion of the play as melodramatic became engaged and insightful readers when presented with Maria and Tony. One text can make another more accessible. Of course there are other ways in which paired texts can work to promote learning.

Consider pairing *Wide Sargasso Sea* by Jean Rhys with Charlotte Brontë's *Jane Eyre,* and Brontë's classic begins to take on a new aspect. Rhys offers another version of the *Jane Eyre* story by focusing on the perspective of Bertha, the woman confined in Rochester's attic. In the Rhys version, Bertha's real name is Antoinette, whereas Bertha is the name Rochester imposes on her. A second son with no inheritance, Rochester goes to the Caribbean to make his fortune by marrying an heiress. Once Antoinette's fortune is safely in his hands, he can return to England, dispatch his exotic wife to the attic, and claim that she is mad. Rereading *Jane Eyre* after reading *Sargasso,* we can see issues of colonialism, race, and gender (in particular, patriarchal society) that had remained below the surface in earlier readings. We realize that one text can illuminate another by bringing suppressed voices like Bertha's to the surface. The chapters in this section illustrate a number of methods and purposes for pairing texts.

Colleen Claudia O'Brien and Rita Teague show how suppressed voices and issues can be illuminated by pairing Fitzgerald's *The Great Gatsby* with Nella Larsen's *Passing*. These two novels, written at nearly the same time—*Gatsby* was published in 1925 and *Passing* in 1929—are both set in the New York metropolitan area, and both deal with, among other things, race, class, and identity. Although they present it in different terms, both books are concerned with the issue of passing, the process by which an individual obscures some aspect of his or her identity in order to identify with another group. For Fitzgerald, passing centers on class, while for Larsen it focuses on race.

Despite their similarities, these two books have had very different publishing histories. *Gatsby* has long belonged to the teaching canon in both high school and college, while *Passing* dropped out of print as Nella Larsen herself faded into obscurity. This novel was republished in 1986 as part of the recovery project focused on African American women writers. O'Brien and Teague show how one student's complaint about the negative portrayal of African American males in much of the fiction read in class led to a productive pairing of Larsen's recently recovered book with the more familiar *Gatsby*. The racist statements in *Gatsby*, the concerns with class position, and, most of all, the sexuality suffused throughout it all take on new resonance when considered in light of *Passing*. And together, the two novels complicate the meaning of the label "American." As O'Brien and Teague write, "*Gatsby* and *Passing* both reflect circumstances where a character enacts complex social and political ideas that have evolved in the history of making an American identity."

Barbara Brown's pairing of William Faulkner's *Light in August* with Art Spiegelman's two-volume graphic novel *Maus* offers a similar yet different perspective on the value of pairing texts. Like O'Brien and Teague, Brown is interested in bringing more voices into the American literature classroom. At first glance, these two texts appear to have little in common. One is set in the American south while the other moves from Nazi Germany to contemporary New York. The lengthy and complex sentences of *Light* contrast sharply with the syntax of *Maus*. Faulkner represents a canonical voice, while Spiegelman, who uses a comic book format to deal with the deadly serious topic of the Holocaust, appears much less frequently in the classroom. As Brown shows, however, pairing *Maus* and *Light* illuminates themes in both novels.

Brown's students identified many common themes, including racism, the quest for personhood, the importance of memory, the search for a place in a given community, and the resurfacing of an unmastered past. In addition to common themes, her students found a number of similarities in technique, despite the differences between the two texts. For example, both use interviews, remembrances of specific characters, and conversational style. And, as Brown's students observed, both portray a difficult time in American history.

Alisa Braun and Tracy Cummings introduce another dimension of paired texts in their discussion of translation. As they observe, discussions of multiculturalism rarely include attention to linguistic diversity, even though, both now and in the past, American literatures have been written in languages other than English. Braun and Cummings argue that it is important to acknowledge the existence of the translator and the whole process of translation if we want to promote a truly multicultural literature. Students need to be aware of a text's original language and understand that the English version is necessarily a secondary representation.

To illustrate their point, Braun and Cummings offer a "pedagogy of translation" that emphasizes confluence between distinct cultures. Using Yiddish and Native American texts to demonstrate their pedagogy, Braun and Cummings explain how teachers can use different translations of the same text, use multimedia approaches to presenting texts, consider the audience and purposes of the translator, examine stereotypes assigned to specific populations, and consider the presentation and production of specific texts. As Braun and Cummings assert, this pedagogy can lead to a more self-conscious and complex classroom for students of American literature.

Anne Ruggles Gere suggests still another way to think of paired texts. Examining multiple variations of John Steinbeck's *The Grapes of Wrath*, she shows how multiple authors tell the same story, often using a variety of media and approaches. Gere begins from a concern about students who become discouraged as writers when they read canonical authors because it seems impossible to emulate their work. Pairing less polished versions of a given narrative can help students see that highly effective prose often results from multiple iterations.

Beginning with the work of Depression-era photographer Dorothea Lange, Gere shows how *Grapes* evolved from stories of migrant workers told by photographers like Lange and Horace Bristol, from government reports and interviews, from Steinbeck's newspaper articles, and from documentary films. Gere goes on to demonstrate how the plight of homeless and jobless people continued to be told by singer Woody Guthrie, John Ford's film version of *Grapes*, contemporary journalist Dale Maharidge, and singer Bruce Springsteen.

As these chapters make clear, literary pairings do indeed give new life to texts that have long been part of the American literature curriculum, as well as works that are now gaining notice for the first time—or gaining notice again after a period of being ignored or less attended to. At the same time, such pairings also offer a rich array of new pedagogies for teachers of American literature.

14 Looking for the Other Side: Pairing *Gatsby* and *Passing*

Rita Teague
Southfield High School, Southfield, Michigan

Colleen Claudia O'Brien
University of Michigan

"Why do we keep reading books that show the Black man as a depressed, angry, and poor American? Isn't there another side? I know somebody Black was doing something positive." One of my (Rita Teague's) students asked this question after we had done several months of reading, analyzing, and writing about American classics. It was one of the few times I was speechless; I really had no answer. I was teaching the prescribed curriculum for the American literature class. I knew it was important for students to have exposure to certain texts and authors, but my student's question reminded me about the many other American ideas and viewpoints that were missing. I discovered one solution to this problem with the strategy of pairing texts. In order to form a better picture of the social history and cultural context of a particular novel, it is helpful to read a contrasting novel from the same time period.

The student asking for another side, of course, was demanding that literary representations suit more than one audience and that characters speak from diverse sectors of the American public. By pairing an American classic text with a lesser-known text from a similar era, the reader/teacher/student hears a voice and learns of ideas not represented in the typical American classic text. For example, reading Huck Finn's lighthearted and comedic depiction of slavery contrasts sharply with Linda Brent's no-nonsense account of her experience as a slave—hers is the voice we never hear in *Huckleberry Finn*. The advantage of pairing texts is not limited to hearing the voices of African Americans; it also allows readers to access voices of Native Americans, Latinos, Asian Americans and other marginalized peoples.

I paired three sets of novels: *The Adventures of Huckleberry Finn* and *Incidents in the Life of a Slave Girl*; *Native Son* and *Their Eyes Were Watching God*; and *Passing* and *The Great Gatsby*. As each unit came to an end, I was anxious to learn what my students thought. One wrote in a reflective essay, "I loved the pairings. I really got a kick out of how a classic sees something and how it is viewed through the eyes of someone else in the same time." By setting two novels from the same era alongside each other, my students started comparing, critiquing, and engaging with two different views of the same world.

My students and I found great success in learning a more complete story of the 1920s when pairing *The Great Gatsby* by F. Scott Fitzgerald with *Passing* by Nella Larsen. These two texts cover the same decade and are situated in the same general locale. Fitzgerald presents an elitist, racist, and arrogant view of "colored" people through the words of Tom Buchanan and the thoughts of Nick Carraway. At a reacquaintance dinner, Tom and Nick have the following conversation: "'Civilization's going to pieces,' broke out Tom violently. 'I've gotten to be a terrible pessimist about things. Have you read *The Rise of the Coloured Empires* by this man Goddard?'" Nick remarks that he has not read this book and thinks to himself that he is quite surprised by Tom's tone. Tom continues, "'Well, it's a fine book and everybody ought to read it. The idea is if we don't look out the white race will be—will be utterly submerged. It's all scientific stuff, it's all been proved'" (17). This attitude is unanswered by Nick or any of the other characters, so the reader is left thinking this was a common view held by wealthy White Americans during the 1920s. Tom shares his feelings toward people of color again when he equates the sneering at family life and family institutions with intermarriage between Black and White. Thus a character that readers view as a representative of the wealthy White attitude during the flapper era voices the idea that Whites and Blacks marrying each other is as destructive to the American way of life as is ignoring the institution of the family.

How does *Passing* pair up with *Gatsby* when it comes to racial commentary and attitudes? I want to piece together references in each novel to a variety of dialogues and conversations that seem to have influenced each author on some level. For example, Fitzgerald's reference to a hypothetical work titled "The Rise of the Coloured Empires" looks like a condensed version of the racialist texts and speeches that girded up anti-immigrant sentiments and contributed to the idea of Anglo-Saxon supremacy. This reference resonates with concerns expressed by

Nella Larsen's characters regarding the necessity for middle-class African Americans to adhere to a strictly White, bourgeois model of American civilization in order to resist the popular perception that Blacks were "primitive" people and inherently unequal to Anglo-Americans.

By pairing *Passing* and *Gatsby*, I was in a much better position to answer questions like the one the student asked about Blacks doing positive things. Otherwise, what is a reader/student to think about how "Negroes" were perceived by Whites during the 1920s? Even though Nick did not comment on Tom's reading material or his racialist philosophy, he too makes racist comments later in the novel. As Nick and Gatsby are making a trip into the city of New York from "the Eggs" (i.e., an area of Long Island), they pass an interesting and, to them, unusual sight. "As we crossed Blackwell's Island a limousine passed us, driven by a White chauffeur, in which sat three modish Negroes, two bucks and a girl. I laughed aloud as the yolks of their eyeballs rolled toward us in haughty rivalry" (73). Why would Nick refer to the young men as "bucks," a derogatory term used to describe male African slaves? The minstrel stereotype of the Black man rolling his eyes in an exaggerated fashion was presented consistently in the films of this era. Need Fitzgerald have a character describe Black characters in this same stereotypical way? In the next paragraph Nick thinks, "'Anything can happen now that we've slid over this bridge . . . anything at all'" (73). Is this the kind of reasoning Nick consoles himself with as he marvels at Blacks in a chauffeur-driven limousine?

These racist stereotypes are further affirmed when the only witness to a hit-and-run accident is described as a "pale, well dressed Negro" (147). It's as if the only acceptable and credible witness is one who is as close to White as possible. With reference to Irene or Clare in *Passing*, one might ask students if this "pale Negro" is more trustworthy because his appearance is neat and dignified and because he is identifiable within a definite racial category. There is little doubt that he is a "good Negro." What would Fitzgerald's characters think of Clare and Irene, who use their light skin to their own advantage when they want the privileges of Whiteness? One doubts that either woman would be a credible witness in Fitzgerald's world.

We will use the following questions, which stem from the inquiries above, to focus the remainder of this essay:

1. What dominant social attitudes regarding race, class, and immigration are reflected in Fitzgerald's and Larsen's novels? What do these two novels tell us about race, class, and identity?

2. What can history tell us about the tremendous anxiety each
   writer imagines or reflects about the dangers of "passing" as
   he or she creates characters who cross the "color line" or infil-
   trate the ranks of the blue-blooded American aristocracy?

3. What is the effect of making sexuality a predominant concern
   in both of these novels?

This set of questions requires a bit more clarification by way of a
definition. The social phenomenon of "passing" is a practice wherein
an individual obscures some aspect of his or her identity (race, class
background, ethnicity, even gender or sexuality) in order to identify with
another race, class, or ethnic group. How many Americans have changed
their last names to sound more "Anglo" and pass themselves off as pure
descendants of our "mother" country, England? The assumption that
such behavior is threatening or disconcerting to many Americans is
evident in Tom's disdain for Gatsby, née Gatz, who tries to pass himself off as a man of high-enough status to earn the love of Tom's wife,
Daisy.

Just as Gatsby tries to pass for a man of high social status, Clare
Kendry (the tragic heroine in Larsen's novel) spends most of her life
successfully passing for White in a marriage to a prestigious White man
(Jack Bellew) who openly admits to hating Blacks. These machinations
by main characters appeal to students because they can identify with
the practice. Contemporary talk-show culture resonates with instances
where the audience and a frantic guest are presented with situations
where a supposedly clueless bachelor finds out that his fiancée is actually a man or the hapless boyfriend learns that his girlfriend is sleeping
with his sister. The phenomenon of passing stems from the fact that
many people will "put on" a new identity in order to fulfill their sexual,
social, or economic desires. The anxiety that the phenomenon generates
for the American public is evidenced by a recurrent obsession with social purity within American culture. Those who step outside the bounds
of a pure racial category or a European American national identity, of
gender norms, or even of the normative heterosexual paradigm are considered a social threat: They are viewed as corrupting our moral fiber
and weakening the body politic. As Tom Buchanan and Jack Bellew indicate through their attempts at policing racial and class borders, people
who "pollute" the "purity" of a society by diluting the ratio of European
American blood or by crossing boundaries of the status quo that define
the difference between men and women are perceived as dangerous.

Passing offers an alternative to the pervasive views articulated by
Fitzgerald's White male characters. Larsen's novel is narrated by Irene

Redfield, the wife of a respected and wealthy Black doctor, and she provides a fascinating contrast to Fitzgerald's Nick. Comparatively speaking, Larsen also produces rich White men somewhat analogous to Nick and Tom in the form of Hugh Wentworth and Jack Bellew.

Gatsby and *Passing* both reflect circumstances where a character enacts complex social and political ideas that have evolved in the history of making an American identity. Tom Buchanan cries out that "next they'll throw everything overboard and have blacks intermarrying with white" (137) when he realizes his wife has fallen in love with the upstart Gatsby and his "new money." Originally a member of the lower orders, Gatsby has crossed class boundaries to initiate an affair with Daisy, something Tom finds almost as repulsive as miscegenation. Jack Bellew, the husband of a biracial woman who is passing for White in Larsen's novel, constantly refers to Blacks as dirty. Hugh Wentworth, a rich White man sympathetic to the cause of uplifting the Black race, tells genteel Irene at a benefit ball that White women are enthralled by the opportunity to dance with an "Ethiopian," preferably the darkest one there. In his mind, sexual innuendo overshadows the "Ethiopian" man, as it corrupts the purity of Bellew's assumedly White wife because she is, in Bellew's view, a "dirty nigger" (76). Each character who tries to pass—Gatsby economically and Clare racially—poses a distinct threat to the supposed moral fiber and to the status quo. This brings us to the third question: why is sexuality the focused-on point of contact between individuals of two races or classes? How does sexuality get wound up with race and class when Tom spouts off about intermarriage or Hugh Wentworth comments on the Ethiopian's dancing abilities?

Certainly, the presence of men like Hugh Wentworth at a benefit for the Negro Welfare League or Harlem Hospital is exactly the kind of interaction that so upsets Tom Buchanan. Stereotypical suspicions that any collusion between Blacks and Whites has a sexually perverse motivation or is likely to challenge Anglo-Saxon supremacy resonate in different ways in the two novels. While Tom is clear about condemning interracial contact, Irene and Clare seek out contact with White men (though in different contexts) for racial or individual betterment. Irene gladly gives up her and her husbands' box seats so Mr. and Mrs. Wentworth can attend her fund-raiser, and Clare, married to a bigot who seems much like Tom Buchanan, is surprised that Whites would even want to attend "a Negro dance."

> This, Irene told her, was the year 1927 in the city of New York, and hundreds of white people of Hugh Wentworth's type came to affairs in Harlem, more all the time. So many that Brian (Irene's

husband) had said: "Pretty soon the coloured people won't be allowed in at all, or will have to sit in Jim Crowed sections." (69)

While Brian is not as optimistic as his wife Irene about the presence of elite Whites in Harlem, Irene is confident about the signs of the times. The social gatherings she plans and sanctions signal to her the sophistication and progress present in "1927 in the city of New York." Irene's vision paints race relations very differently from the smug superiority exuded by Nick and Tom. She looks upon the crowd at the benefit and is nonplused by Wentworth's teasing about the Ethiopian man's dancing:

> Young men, old men, white men, black men; youthful women, older women, pink women, golden women; fat men, thin men, tall men, short men; stout women, slim women, stately women, small women moved by. An old nursery rhyme popped into her head. She turned to Wentworth, who had just taken a seat beside her, and recited it:

> "Rich man, poor man,
> Beggar man, thief,
> Doctor, lawyer,
> Indian chief."

> "Yes," Wentworth said, "that's it. Everybody seems to be here and a few more." (75)

This picture drawn by Larsen of Black society and the Whites who also moved in it and enjoyed its pleasures is the opposite of the segregation and rivalry pictured by Fitzgerald. Here Blacks and Whites sit together, dance together, and eat together as they enjoy the evening festivities. One can just imagine the incredulous look that would appear on Tom Buchanan's face if he were in attendance at the Negro Welfare League Dance or even if he were made aware of its existence.

The sociohistorical evidence about race, class, and sexuality makes it difficult to imagine that Fitzgerald and Larsen could possibly have written any other way. Evidence is abundant, beginning as early as 1839, that sexuality was inextricable from views about race and class.[1] While several French writers, including the well-known Comte A. De Gobineau (whose racialist theory Toni Morrison quotes in *The Bluest Eye*[2]), became experts on eugenics and Social Darwinism, there were American leaders in the field as well. Dr. Josiah Nott, for example, responded to the Freedman's Bureau's taking over of the medical college in Mobile, Alabama, in 1866 by insisting that "history proves, indisputably, that a superior and inferior race cannot live together practically on any other terms than that of master and slave, and that the inferior race, like the Indians, must be expelled or exterminated" (9). In the interest of racial purity, Nott goes on to say, "In America, we have all the breeds of dogs and all the breeds of men almost of the earth, and no one believes that the Jew, Anglo-Saxon, Negro, or Indian will change types as long as blood is kept pure. The only fear is that we shall become a nation of curs, fit for no good purpose, if the doctrine of miscegenation[3] be carried out" (16). Irene Redfield and Clare Kendry are both living examples of miscegenation, and, for both, issues of sexuality are central.

Larsen is not only facing up to the kind of stereotypes that Fitzgerald seems carelessly to endorse; she is also making a bold statement about intermarriage that intervenes in popular medical and sociological debates as well. Nott claims that the only "negro" contributors to intellectual culture are in fact persons of mixed race who would not be extraordinary in intellect were it not for their black skin. He asserts that one biological distinction between races is that "the brain of the negro is nine cubic inches less than that of the white man, and the large headed races have always ruled the earth, and been the only repository of civilization" (26).

Primitivism, the belief that certain "low cultures" were more connected to nature, the sexual drives, and an unrepressed relationship to the body, cast the "primitive" as the opposite of "civilization" and often projected the "primitive" upon Blacks, the mentally ill, and (supposedly "deranged") gay, lesbian, and bisexual persons. For example, Nott's French colleague Paul Broca, an esteemed member of the London Anthropological Society, posited that what "Ethiopians" lacked in brains they made up for in pelvic dimensions.[4] Similarly, Nott quotes the American and Foreign Anti-Slavery Society as saying that "their moral condition is very far from being what it ought to be. It is exceedingly dark and distressing. *Licentiousness prevails to a most alarming extent among the people*" (25). Thus race was mixed up with sexuality, especially in texts produced by distinguished medical doctors.

The introduction to the most popular version of Larsen's novels includes critic Deborah McDowell's suggestion that we can read the relationship between Clare and Irene in *Passing* as lesbian. Dominant perceptions of biracial persons during the 1920s (probably originating one hundred years earlier) included the myth of sterility as well as the belief that such persons were frequently bisexual or gay or lesbian.[5] If McDowell is right about Clare and Irene's relationship, then Larsen's intentions in playing out this stereotype may never be discerned, yet the negative connotations of a lesbian relationship within that social context seem to indicate yet another way in which passing and admixture threaten the purity of heterosexual marriage and middle-class conventions, as well as racial solidarity.

The sexual innuendo in *Gatsby* is no less ominous or ironic. While Tom Buchanan himself is a libertine, he projects moral turpitude and the dissolution of civilization upon the "lower orders," especially the "colored races." While his affair with a working-class woman is his assumed birthright, the possibility that his wife could allow the blue blood of the family line to be contaminated by Gatsby's "upstart" blood is tantamount in his mind to miscegenation. Matthew Bruccoli, the editor of today's scholarly version of *The Great Gatsby*, footnotes Tom's reference to racialist scholarship by inferring that Fitzgerald erroneously refers to the wrong name of a single author whose works have justified Tom's opinions. Bruccoli names Stoddard, who most certainly might have been one of many "scholars" that Fitzgerald had in mind. What Bruccoli fails to explain is that there is also a man named Edward H. Goddard who writes about the downfall of Western civilization. Fitzgerald's conflation of Goddard and Stoddard probably means that Tom's reference to his reading material is skewed but not specific. He had many texts about supposed Anglo supremacy and about Anglo civilization to choose from. It is important for students to acknowledge this part of American cultural history because neither Tom nor his favorite scholar is an isolated or unique figure in the context of dominant beliefs regarding civilization and supremacy. Falling within the category of social Darwinism, these are common and recurring ideas about the inherent capacity for self-government, moral authority, progress, and economic control that many Anglo-Americans used as bases for fashioning themselves as they systematically excluded people of color, immigrants, and members of the working class from their social circles.

The dominant Anglo-American rendition of life in the 1920s proffered by Tom and Nick is but one small piece of the puzzle that makes up the social history of the decade. Pairing texts complicates the ways in which students read, but it does so productively. Students not only want to engage with each novel and learn more about the historical context; they can also choose from a range of voices and perspectives to learn more about themselves. Pairing *Gatsby* and *Passing* enables a study of contrasting worldviews within small parameters of space and time. The two novels probably had very different audiences, but in asking for "another side," the student mentioned at the beginning of this chapter was situating himself as a reader with a distinct place and identity. He was asking for a point of entry, a way to connect with texts that resembles the way he perceives himself in relation to the rest of his social world. He may have been looking for that slice of African American life that Nella Larsen or Zora Neale Hurston wanted to present to their readers. Most of all, he probably felt that he was a member of an audience located on "another side." Pairing texts not only includes diverse narrators from different novels in a conversation about their worldview; it also gives (at least) two sides of the same story, so that our students, too, can have more options for entering the conversation.

Notes

1. Consider, for example, Dr. Alexander Walker's treatise *Intermarriage: or, The mode in which, and the causes why, beauty, health, and intellect, result from certain unions, and deformity, disease, and insanity, from others.* Walker's basic premise is that intellectual and moral characteristics are inherited from the father and that physical strength and vital organs derive from the mother's genetic stock. This argument conveniently supports "breeding" between White men and Black women, certainly a boon to slave masters and overseers who were fathering a burgeoning biracial population in America. Conversely, since intellectual vigor is passed down from the (White) father, Walker sets the stage to demonstrate the inherent dangers of reproduction by a Black man and a White woman.

Having set up corporeal racial characteristics like bent thigh bones and high calves in the "negro" race, Walker begins the pseudoscientific process of defining racial differences that numerous "intellectuals" will pursue vigorously in the 1850s and 1860s.

2. In her description of Soaphead Church, the pedophile who convinces Pecola that she has blue eyes, Morrison writes: "They were industrious, orderly, and energetic, hoping to prove beyond a doubt De Gobineau's hypothesis that 'all civilisations derive from the white race, that none can exist without its help, and that a society is great and brilliant only so far as it preserves the blood of the noble group that created it'" (133).

3. This so-called "doctrine of miscegenation" appears two years prior in a pamphlet written by David Croly. Published in New York, the pamphlet argues that "Christianity, democracy, and science are stronger than the timidity, prejudice, and pride of short-sighted men; and they teach that a people, to become great, must become composite. This involves what is vulgarly known as amalgamation, and those who dread that name, and the thought and fact it implies, are warned against reading these pages" (1).

4. Broca insists that crosses between Black men and White women are not eugenic (i.e., are unlikely to produce offspring) because "one of the characters of the Ethiopian race consists in the length of the penis compared with that of the Caucasian race. . . . There results from this physical disposition, that the

union of the Caucasian man with an Ethiopian woman is easy and without any inconvenience for the latter. The case is different in the union of the Ethiopian with a Caucasian woman, who suffers in the act, the neck of the uterus is pressed against the sacrum, so that the act of reproduction is not merely painful, but frequently non-productive" (28).

    5. It is interesting to note that homosexuality also slips into the hyper-sexualized definitions of the "negro" race. Walker, for example, indicates that women with Sapphic tendencies, as well as nymphomaniacs, "have been ob-served to be of small stature, and to have somewhat bold features, the skin dark, the complexion ruddy, the mammae quickly developed, the sensibility great, and the catamenia considerable" (98). Equating hypersexual homosexual behavior with dark skin, insanity, and supposedly uncivilized races begins with Walker and is most fully fleshed out in Sanger Brown's 1908 medical text *The Sex Worship and Symbolism of Primitive Races*. Brown, like Walker and Nott, was a medical doctor. The introduction clearly states that "we may expect diseased minds to reproduce, or return to expressions of desire customary and official in societies of lower culture" (11).

    Homosexuality is still classified as a psychiatric disorder today, and it was viewed as no less pathological in 1908. Persons of mixed race, like the insane members of the White race and the low class in general, are predisposed to insanity because "the better ideas, which are constantly forming in the up-per stratum have not filtered through from the highest to the lowest minds" (Brown 95). Homosexual tendencies aside, the darker races who are "drilled by their betters into the appearance of civilization, remain barbarians or sav-ages at heart" (94). Like homosexual sex, intercourse between two biracial per-sons was considered nonreproductive: "if their unions were constantly between themselves, they would not be long before becoming extinct" (Broca, 31).

Works Cited

Broca, Paul. *On the Phenomena of Hybridity in the Genus Homo*. Ed. C. Carter Blake. London: Longman, 1864.

Brown, Sanger M.D. *The Sex Worship and Symbolism of Primitive Races; an Interpretation*. Boston: Badger, 1916.

Croly, David. *Miscegenation; The Theory of the Blending of the Races, Applied to the American White Man and Negro*. New York: Dexter, 1864.

Fitzgerald, F. Scott. *The Great Gatsby*. Ed. Matthew J. Bruccoli. New York: Collier, 1992.

Gobineau, Arthur Comte De. *The Moral and Intellectual Diversity of Races: with particular reference to their respective influence in the civil and political history of mankind*. Philadelphia: Lippincott, 1856.

———. *The Inequality of Human Races*. Trans. Adrian Collins. New York: Putnam, 1915.

Larsen, Nella. *Passing*. New York: Penguin, 1997.

Morrison, Toni. *The Bluest Eye.* New York: Washington Square, 1970.

Nott, Dr. Josiah. "Instincts of Races." 1866. *Racial Determinism and the Fear of Miscegenation.* Ed. John David Smith. New York: Garland, 1993.

———. "The Negro Race: Its Ethnology and History. By the Author of *Types of Mankind* to Maj. Gen. O. O. Howard, Superintendent, Freedmen's Bureau." 1866. *Racial Determinism and the Fear of Miscegenation.* Ed. John David Smith. New York: Garland, 1993.

Walker, Alexander. *Intermarriage: or, The mode in which, and the causes why, beauty, health, and intellect, result from certain unions, and deformity, disease, and insanity, from others.* New York: Langley, 1839.

15 Pairing William Faulkner's *Light in August* and Art Spiegelman's *Maus*

Barbara Brown
Fenton High School, Fenton, Michigan

Too many voices have been left out of my American literature class in the past, so I decided to broaden it by pairing canonical texts with less familiar ones. One of those new texts is Art Spiegelman's two-volume graphic novel *Maus*.

Maus is accessible to high school students in subject, content, and format. It ties in with European and American history courses, and its themes of search for self and the individual's place within society fit well with Faulkner's *Light in August*.

Light in August is pieced together in such a way that we must make out the patterns ourselves. The book's overall pattern does not become clear until all the varicolored and varitimed oddly shaped pieces of the narrative "quilt" are put together. Then we can hold up the finished reading, step back at the end, and see the pattern of each person's life and of the completed story. This is definitely an "Aha" novel. My graphic to help students understand this novel is a wagon wheel drawn on the board and left there for the duration of our study, with Joe Christmas as the center axle around whom the story revolves, showing that even as he moves around the country he winds up back where he started, with the other characters being spokes, the connectors, from him to the story of Lena Grove, who is the outside band of the wheel. She is the real mover; she starts in one place and then rolls through the town where Joe's life begins and ends and moves on, taking Byron and the baby (who gets confused with Joe in his grandmother's eyes) with her. There is more to this semipermanent graphic, and each week as we read further, I add items to it. This entire novel is "told" to us by Faulkner in flashbacks and flash-forwards as each character tells his or her experiences and remembrances.

Later, when we were reading *Maus I* and *Maus II*, my students noticed that both books represent oral language on paper. They speculated that Anja and the second wife might be the spokes connecting Art Spiegelman with his father. They also noted that on the last page of *Maus II*, where Art Spiegelman is portrayed as sitting and drawing/cartooning/writing/transcribing/interpreting from the tapes of interviews with his father, there appears to be a guard tower occupied by a rat outside his studio window. They did a quick comparison with the view outside the window of Faulkner's Reverend Hightower, a view seen just at sunset—the special light in which he "sees" his grandfather riding into Jefferson with his small marauding troop. Both of these perceived "scenes out the window" have a strong impact on the lives of the men sitting and watching. Both scenes also affected my students, many of whom wrote journal entries about what they "see" outside their windows, what is hanging over them and what they daydream about.

Several students showed how the life experiences of Joe Christmas and those of Anja and Vladek Spiegelman were formed, infringed upon, and changed by outsiders who believed them to be less human than the majority in power.

One student produced a comparison between the two books from the points of view of, on one hand, the disgusted White Jeffersonites who were appalled at Joe Christmas's affair with the White woman Joanna Burden (who, in their view, shouldn't have been the object of his attentions even though she was a Northerner) and, on the other hand, the disenfranchised Christian Germans who, during the worldwide depression in the 1930s, felt that their noses were rubbed in the wealth and well-being of their non-Christian, non-Aryan neighbors. The student concluded that both supposedly superior cultures—Faulkner's White Jeffersonites and the Christian Germans—would have left their supposedly inferior neighbors alone if the "others" hadn't overstepped their strictly assigned place in polite society. After showing the similarity between the two rationalizations, the student went on to condemn both.

When we turned to a board discussion and further analysis, my students generated both categories and ideas. They started with themes shared by the two books, noting in particular the quest for personhood and the individual struggle to find a place in society, as well as the strong memories being passed from one generation to the next.

My students speculated about how one person's (an author's or character's) voice can be passed on or heard. They said that one could compare the "inside" voice of Joe Christmas, or the narrator "overhearing" his character's inside voices, with that of Art Spiegelman interviewing his father.

Both of these authors use a distinctive narrative style and both are very visual. The students said that in reading Faulkner they could "see" Gail Hightower sitting in his study staring out the window and "watch" Lena's entrance into town, as well as Joe Christmas's final days of running and his death, just as easily as they could see the cartoons from Art Spiegelman's hand. The classes further noted the conversational style of wording, the oral history type of writing, and the use of language and references that they had to look up, as their cultural awareness had not included these words and events.

With both books, the reader becomes more aware of what is happening and what events mean as the characters simply live. The surface events resonate with deeper meanings, and when the students know about scapegoating, Black/White relationships in America through the years, the Civil War, World War I, and World War II and the Holocaust, they "see" more of what is going on.

Faulkner's Joanna Burden has survived her family and become a "friend" to all the Black people around. Joe Christmas can't decide if he is a survivor or not; when with Blacks he always says he is White, and when with Whites he always goes out of his way to tell them he is Black. He seems to feel guilt—imposed on him by his grandfather (as, in Joe's view, the Lord's avenging angel and as a guard at the orphanage), by the frightened dietitian, and by his foster father—and he doesn't know what to do with it.

Art Spiegelman, as a character in his own story, feels guilt because he has not ever had to suffer and doesn't understand his father and his hateful, embarrassing habits, so he searches his father's life to find out why he has them. In turn, his father feels guilt for having survived Auschwitz when so many others did not.

As they compared the two works, my students started a list of items common to both stories. That listing included stereotypes, family, community, clothing (especially, in both stories, the significance of shoes), smoke, habits, women's roles, men's roles, children's roles, the role of caregivers, religion, and escape.

My students also noticed that both authors use interviews. Faulkner includes those between Hightower and Byron Bunch at the Reverend's home, between Gail Hightower and Mr. and Mrs. Hines about what can be done for or about Joe, between the keepers of the orphanage and Simon McEachern, and between Joe and Bobbie Allen, as well as two notable interviews between Byron Bunch and the workers at the sawmill who talk to each other about Lucas Burch and Joe

Christmas. *Maus*, of course, is based almost entirely on interviews between Art Spiegelman and his father Vladek.

Remembrances or analepses are paramount in both narratives, and my students wrote about the effect of memory on specific characters in each book, using the author's words as evidence. Tonya wrote about this in both books as being a way to compare them: "Another similarity between the two novels, and again between the two main characters (whom she defines as Vladek Spiegelman and Joe Christmas) is that what happened in each one's past does affect each one's future." Tonya feels that Joe is so confused by what he remembers that he eventually kills Joanna Burden, confusing her wishes to "save" him with the same wish that his foster father, Simon McEachern, had held for him. She cites Joe's many flashbacks to support her claim and also says that the whole interview with Vladek constitutes an analepsis. She writes that Vladek, unlike Joe, does not kill anyone, but as with Joe his own freedom to move and enjoy life is killed by what he remembers and by the fact that he, like Joe, tends to superimpose his own memories onto outsiders, lovers, and sons.

Jake wrote that not only analepsis itself but also what is being remembered is important to the characters and to the readers: "Both of these authors deal with racism in their novels. They show it to us—not as a long written lecture against it, but more subtly, by giving us characters and flashing back in their lives and following the effects on them of how others felt about them."

Everybody in both stories is in search of self. How they search, what they find, and what happens to them through interaction with others can be easily compared as long as the writer confines himself or herself to one set. One student suggested a comparison between the two women, Joanna Burden and Mala Spiegelman (the second wife), who seem to be burdened with sad familial backgrounds and are trying to make their chosen mates happy but are unsuccessful.

Another student, Caleb, mentioned that both Vladek and Joe are in some type of trouble with an authority and that the authority helps to determine who these two men feel that they are. He also notes that both books are set in the summer of a remembrance by the authors, saying that "this is usually the season (for me anyway) when people can sit back and reflect on past events."

Laurie noted that the strongest central theme of the two books, an area of comparison for her, is the effect of a parent's actions on a child and on who he or she grows up to be. She felt that neither Joe Christmas's foster parents nor Art Spiegelman's parents intended to harm their children, but their unhappy influence led to personal conflicts for these children as adults. Laurie went further to say, "Joe Christmas struggles to find an identity lost with the premature death of his mother. With no father or family (who wants him), he is left alone, unwanted and uncared for except by an institution. The lack of birth parents and true family identity contributes to his frustration and eventually his death. The main character of *Maus* suffers similar frustrations due to the lack of stable parents. Scarred by abuse and racism the father of the author/main character is left unable to have normal relations with his son and with his own surroundings." She went on to add that abuse suffered by Vladek and by Joe due to racism and religious prejudice presents another correlation and point of comparison. She felt that these themes affecting the finding of one's place in the world are universal in character and speak to readers regardless of their own circumstances.

My students also saw similarities between the two books in the constant resurfacing of an "unmastered" past: Joe Christmas's constant drive to discover who he is, Black or White; Gail Hightower's drive to tie in with his "heroic" grandfather, as well as his confusion over what happened to his marriage and to his job as a Presbyterian minister in Jefferson; Lucas Burch ("Joe Brown") and his ongoing, seemingly unexamined and unstoppable penchant for womanizing, gambling, and sliding by on the job; Joanna Burden's relationship to her Northern father and brothers and her Southern neighbors; Art Spiegelman's contemplation of the death of his brother and the suicide of his mother, as well as the life of his father; Vladek's burning of Anja's diaries, his inability to get along with his living son, and his constant concern with the fears for survival he learned in the concentration camps. All are examples of a past that is neither mastered nor understood.

Writing about the "unmastered past," Amanda noted that "both pieces have characters who have been affected by war in some way" and went on to compare Percy Grimm and Gail Hightower but also commented that, "In pairing *Light in August* and *Maus I and II* one must realize that although both pieces contain fixations with war and reexaminations of war and longing for certain stirring events of those wars, they do not necessarily have the same outlook on war itself. In contrast to Faulkner and his characters who seem to believe war is glorious and provides opportunity for heroism, Art Spiegelman indicates that 'War is Hell,' and shows us the terrible side of war."

Looking at the past also led students to consider the lives of the authors. They mentioned that neither Faulkner nor Spiegelman was involved in the wars that had so strongly affected their parents and grandparents, but, even so, both felt resonances of war. Students cited Faulkner's relationship with his parents and grandparents and showed how this compared with what we can glean about Spiegelman's relationships with his family from the Internet. As Theresa wrote:

> [Both] William Faulkner and Art Spiegelman wrote books that were personally touching and a way for them to release pent up frustrations from their own childhoods, a way for them to look for their own lost identities. Both authors try to come to terms with issues that plagued them their whole lives. In *Light in August,* Gail Hightower may be the alter ego of William Faulkner. Hightower is constantly haunted by the image of his grandfather, a "hero" wounded in the Civil War while stealing chickens from a woman's yard. Faulkner had also had a traumatic upbringing based on images and memories of his "heroic grandfather" who was wounded in the Civil War, maybe while stealing horses which he then sold to his own side, who wrote a best selling novel, *The White Rose,* and who became rich and infamous for his money dealings when bringing the railroad to his home town. Faulkner believed as a child that his grandfather had done something noble and honorable. Art Spiegelman's alter ego, "Art the mouse," is trying to come to terms with his relationship with his father, and to come to an understanding of his father's behavior due to being a survivor of a World War II concentration camp. . . .
>
> Both authors use the quilting method, strewn about with characters coming in and out with great abandon, sudden flashbacks necessary to understand the background of the characters and extremely detailed descriptions of the action and characters. Faulkner shows us the upbringing of Joe Christmas so we can visualize this child of possibly mixed races' struggle and how it affected him as an adult. Spiegelman uses the same technique to show us with graphic description and drawings the horrors his father witnessed first hand and why this has made him so irritatingly peculiar to his son.

Michelle wrote that both stories are "true": "One is written from actual tapes of an Auschwitz survivor's voice—from an oral history, and the other is written by Faulkner from the 'mental' tapes of his own family's oral history, which he has heard all his life." She also wrote that "it is not until the end of the novels that one can truly understand the total meaning behind them. The final word picture of Joe dying in a crucifix position on the wooden table and the cartoon picture of the guard tower looking down over the present day Spiegelman shows the impact the stories had on their authors and makes an impact on the reader who vows not to let this discrimination and hatred happen again."

Jeff wrote, *"Light in August* by William Faulkner examines the problems facing society during the long period following the Civil War. His novel describes the crisis of young Joe Christmas who tries to find his place in the world, believing himself to be of mixed heritage. He encounters throwbacks to the beliefs at the time of the Civil War—people like Doc Hines and Joanna Burden—the representatives of the two opposing views show extremes taken by Whites regarding Blacks. *Maus I and II* by Art Spiegelman are similar in many respects: his books deal with the post–World War II period and his trying to find himself and come to grips with his Jewish background. Art Spiegelman attempts to extract from his eccentric father—another throwback or product of the war—his experiences in the concentration camp."

This discussion is not exhaustive. My students noted additional similarities between the two works, but this array shows how much insight high school students can bring to the pairing of texts. As they find commonalities between canonical and noncanonical works, they make the less familiar text more familiar. Another voice thus enters the American literature class.

Suggested Readings

Bohafner, Stephen J. "Comix as Art: The Man Behind the 'Maus.'" *St. Louis Post-Dispatch* 23 June 1991.

Harrington, Evans, and Ann J. Abadie, eds. *Faulkner and the Short Story: Faulkner and Yoknapatawpha, 1990.* Jackson: U of Mississippi P, 1992.

Leventhal, Robert S. "Art Spiegelman's MAUS: Working-Through the Trauma of the Holocaust." *Responses to the Holocaust: A Hypermedia Sourcebook for the Humanities.* http://jefferson.village.virginia.edu /holocaust/spiegelman.html (30 April 2001).

Ruppersburg, Hugh M. *Light in August: Glossary and Commentary.* Reading Faulkner. Jackson: UP of Mississippi, 1994.

Williamson, Joel. *William Faulkner and Southern History.* New York: Oxford UP, 1993.

Web Sites Addressing Art Spiegelman and *Maus*

A variety of articles can be found by searching the amazon.com and westword.com sites. Additional sites include the following:

http://arts.ucsc.edu/derek/Art.html

http://www.maths.tcd.ie/pub/mmm/Books/MausSurvivorsTaleI.html

http://youth.net/memories/hypermail/0708.html
http://www.mojones.com/mother_jones/SO97/spiegelman.html

16 Foreign Voices, American Texts: Translations

Alisa Braun
University of Michigan

Tracy Cummings
University of Michigan

Native American and Yiddish poetry, although commonly under-represented in the American literature curriculum, offer rich opportunities for diversifying our understandings of American literature. Most crucially, however, as we argue below, we need to address this poetry as *translated*. We hope that instructors will come away from this chapter with particular plans for classroom interaction, and also with a sense of the possibilities introduced by translated literature, so that they can choose from the vast literatures of the United States that are not written in English and offer them to students.

If we expect high school students to contend with complex works ranging from *Hamlet* and *Beloved* to *The Woman Warrior*, then surely they have reached the level of sophistication necessary to grasp the issues posed by translation. If, in their first "American Literature" course, these students are introduced to Native American and Yiddish texts, they will more readily accept the diversity of our country's indigenous and immigrant traditions and will gain skills for approaching translated literature. In this chapter, we will move from a discussion of using translations for furthering multicultural objectives to more specific discussions of Yiddish and Native American poetry.

One of the aims of multiculturalism has been to broaden conceptions of the term *America* and shift our attention to the presence of diverse cultures and traditions within our borders. This has meant opening up the American literature curriculum to encompass a more ethnically diverse range of writers. While these endeavors have succeeded (albeit to a varying and sometimes questionable extent) in introducing increasing diversity into the American literature classroom, the multicultural material being incorporated is generally literature written in English. Indeed, one scholar has noted that "with the exception of some discussions of Spanish, multiculturalism has paid very little attention to linguistic diversity" (Sollors 4). Such limited scope is not surprising, for writers are easier to place within the larger American literary context when they share the same language. In addition, shared language allows students to interact more directly with a work, fostering understanding and interpretation based on a common cultural background. And yet it seems inadequate to speak about "cultural diversity" without considering language as a fundamental fact.

We must thus question the effectiveness of maintaining an American literature curriculum that relies too readily on English language literature. The absence of linguistic (as distinct from ethnic) diversity among texts chosen for study merely perpetuates "false myths of a monolingual past," implying that English has been and will continue to be the language of the United States (Sollors 3). Such myths continuously deny the "historical significance and continuing presence of other languages" (2). The fact that such languages commonly represent those spoken by both immigrant and indigenous communities further limits the economic and racial breadth represented in the American literary curriculum.

Yet if linguistic diversity is to be incorporated, it must be done so effectively, because historical and cultural diversity are similarly obscured when we do not acknowledge that the literature has been interpreted or "rewritten" by an additional hand—the translator's. An awareness of the text's original language can initially combat the belief that English can fully capture the essence of the original work, especially when the translation is presented as a *secondary* representation.

The study of translation and transcription can also draw attention to the "making" of texts—how they are produced and selected for an English-speaking audience. When we analyze translations of American literature, we must account not only for the culture and the historical moment that produced the original but also for the translator's own milieu. Studying translation makes us aware of the linguistic and cultural differences that required the translation in the first place and simultaneously highlights continuities between cultures. Translation can be a bridge between cultures, making one culture accessible to another, and can actually help instructors present a variety of American literatures as distinct but as not completely alien. To focus on the moment of translation, a moment of mediation between cultures, is to focus on a moment when two cultures intersect.

The following discussions are meant to offer models for incorporating translated poetry into the classroom, and ultimately to offer suggestions for generating a more diverse and historically accurate American literature curriculum. We hope that our accounts of Yiddish and Native American poetry will inspire dynamic classroom interaction as students encounter a variety of alternatives for studying American literature.

―――――――――

The teacher of Yiddish literature is fortunate to have many resources available for introducing students to the rich and diverse nature of American Yiddish poetry. The extensive anthology *American Yiddish Poetry* (Harshav et al.) provides an excellent introduction to the history of Yiddish literature in the United States, though its selections (given in Yiddish and English) are limited to a few modernist poets, while *The Penguin Anthology of Modern Yiddish Verse* (Howe, Wisse, and Shmeruk), which is also bilingual, provides greater breadth. These bilingual editions provide a distinct sense of the culturally specific nature of the poetry by preserving the uniqueness of the language. In addition, one can find several volumes devoted to single authors such as Jacob Glatstein, Kadya Molodowsky, Moshe Leib Halpern, and Morris Rosenfeld.

Teachers can begin by having students consider the reasons why, despite linguistic barriers, Yiddish literature can be studied as part of an American literature curriculum. Students should be made aware of the fact that Yiddish writers were themselves multilingual and thus often had knowledge of the English-language literature being produced around them. Yiddish newspapers, fiction, poetry, and theater were themselves created in close proximity to English language literature, flourishing in New York City alongside the giant publishing houses. Several Yiddish writers also had connections with more popular English-language writers who took interest in their work and who often assisted in the translation and publicizing of their texts, and who were themselves influenced by Yiddish literature. Most significantly, the study of Yiddish poetry reveals that Yiddish writers were very conscious of their new status as Americans; much of their literature thus took "America" as its subject matter, addressing such familiar subjects as urban life, the pace of technology, and the American landscape. Their works express the hope with which the immigrants confronted their new homeland, as well as the disillusionment that could accompany this experience.

In his own day Morris Rosenfeld was one of the most popular Yiddish poets to write in the United States, and, since he is by far the most translated Yiddish poet, he will serve as an excellent case study for developing pedagogical strategies related to translation. While teachers can situate Rosenfeld's work in the context of Yiddish poetry (where Rosenfeld is classified as a "sweatshop" or "proletarian" poet and read in conjunction with poets who took social protest and revolutionary action as their subject matter), they can also introduce Rosenfeld in the context of American literary history. Rosenfeld was himself an immigrant who labored along with the masses in the sweatshops, and his poems dramatize the plight of the eastern European Jewish immigrant experience in the United States. Rosenfeld's verses vividly describe the horrors of turn-of-the-century sweatshops and the poverty that characterized life in the American urban setting. Thus one way to introduce Morris Rosenfeld's poetry in the classroom is with reference to late nineteenth- and early twentieth-century progressivism in America. Along with Upton Sinclair's *The Jungle* or Jacob Riis's photographs in *How the Other Half Lives*, Rosenfeld's poetry can be considered in terms of the effect of its commentary on working-class and immigrant life. Students can discuss the purposes this literature was designed to serve and whether it would function in the same way for different audiences.

In addition to considering Yiddish literature in the context of the period in which it was produced, students should also take into account the fact of its subsequent translation. In order to highlight the translator's role as interpreter, students can study the translators of Yiddish poetry as well as the writers. Teachers can have students conduct biographical research and arrive at a hypothesis as to what might have motivated the translator to choose a particular author. Students can consider the following questions: Were the translators writers themselves or were they assuming a new role? If they were published writers, what was the nature of their own work? What, if anything, else did these writers translate? And what can be deduced from the translators' selections? Students should also consider the date of the translation: When was the translation published and what was occurring in American culture at the time that might have prompted the translation or affected principles of selection? A study of the diversity of Morris Rosenfeld's translators would be particularly illuminating. They range from Rose Pastor Stokes (1914), the Jewish labor activist (and former sweatshop worker) who married millionaire John Stokes, to Aaron

Kramer (1955), the radical poet and anthologist of American poetry of protest, to Edgar Goldenthal (1998), a doctor and grandson of Morris Rosenfeld. Students can consider why Kramer wanted to reacquaint the American public with Rosenfeld's verse in the late fifties or whether Goldenthal's familial relationship to Rosenfeld produces any issues of interest.

If we think of the translator as one responsible for presenting a particular image of the writer to the audience, then students can examine individual volumes of translated verse to determine what idea of the writer this translator wanted to convey to his or her audience. Students can consider the poems selected for inclusion, or what the introductions to these volumes reveal about the motivations of the editors and translators. Students can also consider how titles shape the way in which the poems are received: what are the differing implications of a volume of Rosenfeld's poetry entitled *Songs of Labor* and another called *Songs of the Ghetto*?

Juxtaposing several translations of a single Yiddish poem and paying particular attention both to the poem's formal qualities (dialect, colloquialisms, register, style) and also to how culturally specific references are managed will allow students to observe the varied effects generated by different translations. Examples of the same stanza from one of Rosenfeld's best-known poems can demonstrate the utility of such a pedagogical strategy. Rosenfeld's "Mayn Yingele," which has been translated alternately as "My Boy" or "My Little Son," illustrates the grief of the working parent whose long hours keep him from spending time with his family. Professor Leo Wiener's 1898 translation of the third stanza reads, "My work drives me out early and brings me home late; oh, my own flesh is a stranger to me! Oh, strange to me the glances of my child!" (10), while, in their 1914 translation of the same stanza, Rose Pastor Stokes and Helena Frank wrote, "Ere dawn my labor drives me forth; / 'Tis night when I am free; / A stranger am I to my child; / And strange my child to me" (10). Finally, Aaron Kramer's 1955 rendition reads: "The time clock drags me off at dawn; / at night it lets me go. / I hardly know my flesh and blood; / his eyes I hardly know. . . ." (32). In the same poem, one could also consider the implications of the difference between a translator's use of "papa" or "daddy." A comparison of these versions will raise productive questions about differences between prose and verse translations, about differences between the use of antiquated language and the use of contemporary references, and, more generally, about how poetry is created.

Analyzing multiple versions of a poem also allows students to observe how translators handle culturally specific references and to consider the implications of different methodology. Irving Howe has written that Yiddish provides particular problems for the translator because of its association with the religious and cultural traditions of the Jews of Eastern Europe, for which English has no equivalents (137). Yiddish literature "carries a weight of historical associations and cultural assumptions that is not likely to be fully apprehended by the reader who is unfamiliar with the tradition of Yiddish . . . with the whole Yiddish cultural milieu" (139). For this reason, poems that include numerous culturally specific references are often less likely to be anthologized; they are assumed to be too distant from the general reader's experience, and translators are frustrated at their attempts to find satisfactory equivalents for Yiddish terms. In the case of Morris Rosenfeld, students can consider the different audiences implied by Leo Wiener's decision to preserve the Yiddish words in his translation and include a glossary of terms and Max Rosenfeld's decision to retain the title "To the Purim-Shpieler" (in *Morris Rosenfeld: Selections from His Poetry and Prose*) without defining the terms or explaining the reference to the Jewish holiday.

Finally, when linguistic difference, one of the most palpable signs of cultural difference, is erased, a poem can sound simplistic, primitive, or just plain bad. Much of Morris Rosenfeld's Yiddish verse adheres to strict principles of meter and rhyme because it was created with the intention of being performed, but such elements are essentially "lost" in translation. Several of Rosenfeld's poems were set to music and sung in the sweatshops by the workers and provided an important means of generating communal solidarity. While recordings of his poems are not easily accessible, Rosenfeld's poem "Mayn Rue Plats" ("My Resting Place") can be found on a recent compact disc, and the scores for several Rosenfeld poems can be found in the series of songbooks published by the Workmen's Circle. The use of a multimedia approach in conjunction with a reading of Rosenfeld's poems would allow students to consider the effect that the music has on the interpretation of the poem.

Including traditional Native American poetry as part of an American literature syllabus enhances the curriculum by adding historical accuracy and diversity as well as aesthetic breadth and depth. Although some major anthologies include sections on Native American poetry, the teacher working to establish Native American literature as part of the curriculum still faces several challenges. The students have often incorporated their own interpretations and images of "the Native American," and combating such stereotypes involves delicate classroom maneuvering. In addition, students are usually steeped in impressions of what poetry is and should be, and Native American chant and song might not readily fit into such models. Exacerbating student preconceptions, the material available to the instructor is often varied or misleading, so that teachers interested in moving beyond the limitations of popular anthologies must negotiate complex scholarly classification systems which often lead to dead ends.

Most scholars recommend beginning with stereotypes of Native Americans, suggesting that they must be elicited, addressed, and, to a certain extent, dismissed, before real progress can be made toward interpreting and appreciating American Indian literature. For example, in order to complement one's efforts toward providing historical background and contextualization, Andrew Wiget recommends showing a film such as *Winds of Change* in order to prompt discussion of stereotypical views of Native American culture (1985). A move toward recognizing Native Americans as a vast and varied group of tribes must also be made in order to instill a fuller appreciation of the complexity of what has fallen under the deceptively simple title "Indian." In addition, the variance between tribes should be explored, so that students can dispel generalizations.

Such discussions can lead to the conjunction of stereotypes and Native American literary reception, so that transcription and recording, as well as the attendant early translations, can be the next arena of exploration. The class can investigate early recorders, transcribers, or translators, from Frances Densmore to Franz Boas (perhaps through individual research assignments), examining methodology and impetus.[1] Class discussion can also address various ideological motivations, and how these might have affected what was selected and recorded—and *how* it was selected and recorded. For example, Brian Swann writes of Henry Rowe Schoolcraft that he collected materials "for converting Indians to Christianity" and because they "provided evidence of 'man's rise to civilization,' up the evolutionary scale from the Indians' 'child race'" (*Wearing* xii). The class can discuss the problems inherent in such approaches, and how they might have affected the impressions generated of Native Americans. Students should emerge with a sense of early recordings and transcriptions as mediated by prejudice and controlled by individuals and institutions.

Students should also come to see that even the most sincere act of transcribing involves altering the chant or song from its danced and/or sung form to that of a recording or written record frozen in time, and that such an act is a translation in and of itself. The idea that the written page represents a potential falling away from an oral and visual medium can be partially compensated for by introducing media beyond the printed page. Some films specifically treat Native American dance and song, although joining specific written texts with videos can seem next to impossible (see the extended bibliography for suggestions of films on dance and song). There are also numerous recordings available, although matching them with anthologized texts is a difficult task. You might try playing selections from the same tribe that employ similar language as specific poems.

While introducing students to the concept that Native American traditional poetry is necessarily mediated by a variety of historical and cultural precepts, you can include traditional concerns of translation. For example, you can introduce the dilemma discussed by Swann and Arnold Krupat, who write of "still literalism" versus "poetic" yet potentially "inaccurate free versions," presenting any translation as a compromise between aesthetics and accuracy (5). You can demonstrate this quandary by introducing students to multiple versions of a poem, although finding multiple translations of traditional poetry is challenging. Many poems share titles or have no titles, most anthologized volumes do not contain the original language, and some do not contain notes as to the original recording, so that comparison is difficult, with many translators still utilizing recordings and transcriptions made over fifty years ago. If you have the resources, you might try to work from articles that include dual translations, so that the work has already been done for you. For example, see *On the Translation of Native American Literatures* (Swann), *Smoothing the Ground* (Swann), *Traditional Literatures of the American Indian: Texts and Interpretations* (Kroeber), or the volume *Coming to Light* (Swann), all of which contain a few options for exploring the nuances of translation.

You can also utilize texts that include the original language or music scores, which will emphasize transcription and translation as intermediate acts between performance and reading. You might attempt to coordinate with a music department to recreate some of the selections, or work with a musically talented student or community member. One useful book in print is *The Hako* (Fletcher), which includes instructions for music and dance and contains the original language, translation, and explanatory notes.

Aside from using multiple translations, original language selections, and music scores, you can also introduce your class to aspects of textual production by examining different volumes. One very practical example is to have the students compare similar selections such as "Ghost Dance" songs (different versions can be found in the Norton and Heath anthologies). Students can discuss details such as the titles provided by the editors and the effect of illustrations and other aspects of presentation. You might split students into two groups, one per anthology, and have them write up a summary of the songs' origins and how they emerge from the anthology's presentation. The goal of these exercises is to have the students scrutinize anthologies as a filter through which they view the songs, a filter that ultimately parallels the filter through which Native Americans have been viewed in the United States over the years.

Some students will resist traditional Native American poetry, responding to a variety of aspects, from repetition to brevity, depending on the selection. Objections can actually be fruitful, however, when placed within the larger context of aesthetics. If the student objects to a particularly brief poem, the instructor might propose poems, such as some by Emily Dickinson or William Carlos Williams, for example, which employ similar effect. If repetition is the object of complaint, the student might be reminded that a variation in voice pitch might be an alteration missing from a printed page, or encouraged to explore just why repetition provokes an antithetical response. The student questioning whether oral art is poetry at all can be reminded of Homer, and then asked what it is about writing that establishes something so firmly in his or her mind as a poetic act. The idea is not that Native American literature needs non-Native literature for justification or comparison, but rather that the two together can help students contextualize their judgments and preconceptions. This approach takes preparation and quick thinking in the classroom, but it can provide students with a self-consciousness that can help them be more sensitive, critical readers and thinkers with a keener sense of history and of the diversity of poetic aesthetics.

The study of translation inspires active student participation, offering students an opportunity to develop their own literary criteria through the analysis of multiple versions of texts and volumes and motivating them to examine their own aesthetic judgments. By observing how definitions of poetry have evolved, students can question the notion that poetry can be defined in a singular fashion and thus they can find literature more open for their own exploration and less prescriptive. Finally, the study of translation prompts students to question appropriative movements in their own encounters with other cultures by observing the particular purposes for which translations were created (Venuti 95). The ultimate result is a more self-conscious and complex classroom interaction with American literature, as students are introduced to a variety of approaches to literary and historical analysis.

Note

1. One particularly useful tool for studying Frances Densmore is a Web site offering an extensive and balanced exploration of her life, with an optional section incorporating music and photographs. See http://news.mpr.org/features/199702/01_smiths_densmore/docs/index.shtml.

Works Cited

Fletcher, Alice C., with James R. Murie. *The Hako: Song, Pipe, and Unity in a Pawnee Calumet Ceremony*. 1904. Lincoln: U of Nebraska P, 1996.

Harshav, Benjamin. et al., eds. *American Yiddish Poetry: A Bilingual Anthology*. Berkeley: U of California P, 1986.

Howe, Irving. "Translating from Yiddish." *The World of Translation*. 1971. New York: PEN American Center, 1987. 135–143.

Howe, Irving, Ruth R. Wisse, and Khone Shmeruk, eds. *The Penguin Book of Modern Yiddish Verse*. New York: Viking, 1987.

Kroeber, Karl, comp. and ed. *Traditional Literatures of the American Indian: Texts and Interpretations*. 2nd ed. Nebraska: U of Nebraska P, 1997.

Rosenfeld, Morris. "My Boy." Trans. Rose Pastor Stokes and Helena Frank. *Songs of Labor and Other Poems by Morris Rosenfeld*. Boston: Badger, 1914.

———. "My Boy." Trans. Leo Wiener. *Songs from the Ghetto*. 1898. Upper Saddle River: Literature House, 1970.

———. "My Little Son." Trans. Aaron Kramer. *Morris Rosenfeld: Selections from His Poetry and Prose*. Ed. Itche Goldberg and Max Rosenfeld. New York: Yiddisher Kultur Farband, 1964.

Sollors, Werner. "Introduction: After the Culture Wars; or, From 'English Only' to 'English Plus.'" *Multilingual America: Transnationalism, Ethnicity, and the Languages of American Literature*. Ed. Werner Sollors. New York: New York UP, 1998. 1–13.

Swann, Brian, ed. *Coming to Light: Contemporary Translations of the Native Literatures of North America*. New York: Random, 1994.

———, ed. *On the Translation of Native American Literatures*. Washington, D.C.: Smithsonian, 1992.

———, ed. *Smoothing the Ground: Essays on Native American Oral Literature*. Berkeley: U of California P, 1983.

———. *Wearing the Morning Star: Native American Song-Poems*. New York: Random, 1996.

Swann, Brian, and Arnold Krupat, eds. Introduction. *Recovering the Word: Essays on Native American Literature*. Berkeley: U of California P, 1987.

Venuti, Lawrence. *The Scandals of Translation: Towards an Ethics of Difference*. New York: Routledge, 1998.

Selected Bibliography of Resources for American Yiddish Poetry

Volumes of Rosenfeld Translations

Cohen, Mortimer T., trans. *Poems of Morris Rosenfeld*. New York: Retriever, 1979.

Goldberg, Itche, and Max Rosenfeld, eds. *Morris Rosenfeld: Selections from His Poetry and Prose*. New York: Yiddisher Kultur Farband, 1964.

Goldenthal, Edgar J. *Poet of the Ghetto: Morris Rosenfeld*. Hoboken: Ktav, 1998.

Kramer, Aaron, trans. *The Teardrop Millionaire: And Other Poems*. New York: Manhattan Emma Lazarus Clubs, 1955.

Stokes, Rose Pastor, and Helena Frank, trans. *Songs of Labor and Other Poems*. Boston: Badger, 1914.

Wiener, Leo, trans. *Songs from the Ghetto*. By Morris Rosenfeld. 1898. Upper Saddle River: Literature House, 1970.

Poetry Anthologies

Harshav, Benjamin, et al., eds. *American Yiddish Poetry: A Bilingual Anthology*. Berkeley: U of California P, 1986.

Howe, Irving, Ruth R. Wisse, and Khone Shmeruk, eds. *The Penguin Book of Modern Yiddish Verse*. New York: Viking, 1987.

Howe, Irving, and Eliezer Greenberg, eds. *A Treasury of Yiddish Poetry*. New York: Schocken, 1976.

Whitman, Ruth, ed. and trans. *An Anthology of Modern Yiddish Poetry: Bilingual Edition*. 3rd ed. Detroit: Wayne State UP, 1995.

Selected Single-Author Volumes of American Yiddish Poets

Glatstein, Jacob. *I Keep Recalling: The Holocaust Poems of Jacob Glatstein*. Trans. Barnett Zumoff. Hoboken: Ktav, 1993.

————. *The Selected Poems of Jacob Glatstein*. Ed. and trans. Ruth Whitman. New York: October House, 1972.

————. *Selected Poems of Yankev Glatshteyn*. Ed. and trans. Richard J. Fein. Philadelphia: Jewish Publication Society, 1987.

Halpern, Moshe Leib. *In New York: A Selection*. Trans. Kathryn Hellerstein. Philadelphia: Jewish Publication Society, 1982.

Molodowsky, Kadya. *Paper Bridges: Selected Poems of Kadya Molodowsky*. Ed. and trans. Kathryn Hellerstein. Detroit: Wayne State UP, 1999.

Tussman, Malkah Heifetz. *With Teeth in the Earth: Selected Poems of Malka Heifetz Tussman*. Ed. and trans. Marcia Falk. Detroit : Wayne State UP, 1992.

Sources for Music

Di Goldene Keyt. *Mir zaynen do tsu zingen! We're here to sing!* New York: Di Goldene Keyt, 1997.

Mir Trogn a Gezang. Songbook. Ed. Eleanor Gordon Mlotek. New York: Workmen's Circle, 1972. ("Mayn Yingele" and "Mayn Rue-Plats.")

Songs of Generations: New Pearls of Yiddish Song. Songbook. Ed. Eleanor and Joseph Mlotek. New York: Workmen's Circle, 1997. ("Di Svet-Shap" / "The Sweat-Shop.")

Organizations

Two important sources for Yiddish books and resources include the Workmen's Circle and the National Yiddish Book Center. The Workmen's Circle can be contacted at 45 East 33rd Street, New York, NY 10016; (212) 889-6800; www.circle.org. The National Yiddish Book Center can be contacted at 1021 West Street, Amherst, MA 01002; www.yiddishbookcenter.org.

Selected Bibliography of Native American Resources

On Native American Literature

Bierhorst, John, ed. *Four Masterworks of American Indian Literature*. Tucson: U of Arizona P, 1974.

Gingerich, Willard. "Incorporating Performance and Oral Literature into the Literary Landscape: The Native American Case." *Multicultural Perspectives: New Approaches*. Council on National Literatures World Report VI. Whitestone: Council on National Literatures, 1993. 100–115.

Holland, Jean. "Teaching Native American Literature from *The Heath Anthology of American Literature*." *CEA Critic* 55 (1993): 1–21.

Hymes, Dell H. *"In Vain I Tried To Tell You": Essays in Native American Ethnopoetics*. Philadelphia: U of Pennsylvania P, 1981.

Ruoff, A. LaVonne Brown. *American Indian Literatures: An Introduction, Bibliographic Review, and Selected Bibliography*. New York: MLA, 1990.

Sherzer, Joel, and Anthony C. Woodberry, eds. *Native American Discourse: Poetics and Rhetoric*. Cambridge: Cambridge UP, 1987.

Tedlock, Dennis. *The Spoken Word and the Work of Interpretation*. Philadelphia: U of Pennsylvania P, 1983.

Wiget, Andrew. *Native American Literature*. Boston: Twayne, 1985.

———. "Native American Oral Literatures." *Heath Online Instructor's Guide*. Ed. Randy Bass. http://www.georgetown.edu/bassr/heath/syllabuild/iguide/nativetr.html (13 April 2001).

———. "Native American Oral Narrative: Major Themes, Historical Perspectives, and Personal Issues." *Heath Online Instructor's Guide*. Ed. Randy Bass. http://www.georgetown.edu/bassr/heath/syllabuild/iguide/nativeon.html (13 April 2001).

Historical Background

Murdock, George P., and Timothy O'Leary, eds. *Ethnographic Bibliography of North America*. 4th ed. 5 vols. New Haven: Human Relations Area Files, 1975.

Sturtevant, William C., ed. *Handbook of North American Indians*. 15 vols. Washington: Smithsonian, 1978.

Waldman, Carl. *Atlas of the North American Indian*. New York: Facts on File, 1985.

Internet Resources

Extensive resources can be found at the following three Web sites:

- http://www.cowboy.net/native/
- http://www.hanksville.org/NAresources
- http://www.jammed.com/~mlb/nawbt.html

The following site offers music, along with descriptions of the accompanying dances; it also offers representations in "English" syllables of pronunciation of words in several Native American languages: http://www.ohwejagehka.com.

Film Resources

Your wisest alternative is to check the Web sites listed above for video options, but we have also listed a few other ideas.

- The Web site of the UCLA American Indian Studies Center offers films on Native American dance, music, and poetry for purchase or rental at reasonable prices. The telephone number is (310) 206-7508. The address 3220 Campbell Hall, Box 951548, Los Angeles, CA 90095-1548. The Web site can be found at http://www.sscnet.ucla.edu/esp/aisc/.

- Norman Ross Publishing, Inc., offers selections on Native American dance and poetry at reasonable prices, although we have not checked the quality. The telephone number is (800) 648-8850. The address is Norman Ross Publishing, Inc., 330 West 58th Street, New York, NY 10019. The Web site can be found at http://www.nross.com/namwords.htm.

- *Winds of Change* (a PBS film) comes recommended by Andrew Wiget; it is available at www.shop.pbs.org. He also recommends an older film called *Hopi: Songs of the Fourth World* (1983) by Pat Ferrero.

Music

There are numerous options open for obtaining traditional Native American music. The best alternatives we see are to try amazon.com and to search the Web sites listed above (such as www.hanksville.org).

17 Dorothea Lange to "The Boss": Versions of *The Grapes of Wrath*

Anne Ruggles Gere
University of Michigan

What I hate about reading these books," wrote a student in my class, "is knowing that I'll never be able to write anything this good. It makes me want to stop writing altogether." Scott was a student in an American literature class that was designed to help students learn to write about literature as they became more conversant with their own literary heritage. We had just finished Sandra Cisneros's *The House on Mango Street,* and discussion had focused on her highly effective style. Students had noticed her powerful descriptions, such as the picture she draws of the family members' hair; the way she uses dialogue that sounds like real children would speak it; and the subtlety with which she reveals complex and difficult situations. We had talked about her growing reputation as a writer, and her contribution to an ever expanding definition of "American." It was in his reading log that Scott expressed his frustration. The effect of reading and discussing Cisneros had been to convince him that he could never do as well. He sounded like a playground hoopster who wanted to throw away his basketball when he realized that he would never be able to dribble behind his back and jam the way Michael Jordan could.

As I reread Scott's comment, I mused about what I wanted students to take away from my classes. Certainly I wanted them to know something about the historical sweep and variety of the American literary tradition; I wanted them to become familiar with the contributions of writers as diverse as Emerson, Dickinson, and Morrison. I wanted them to understand a variety of genres and styles. And, while I didn't aim to inculcate a particular standard of taste, I wanted my students to be able to distinguish between good and less good writing. But most of all, I wanted them to continue reading and writing. If reading Cisneros made Scott feel like throwing away his pen, then I needed to think again about what I was doing.

One of the words we English teachers often use is "appreciate." We want our students to learn to appreciate and value literature as we do. Thinking about that word "appreciate," I began to see one source of Scott's frustration. Appreciation implies passivity—seeing and valuing quality, understanding and prizing significance, recognizing and admiring certain features. Learning to admire a work has its importance, but I didn't want to achieve this goal at the price of convincing students that they should give up writing because they would never be able to achieve the effects of the published authors they were reading. If I wanted my students to understand fully the "making" of American literature, I needed them to see *themselves* as potential makers of literature.

This led me to think about pairing texts in new ways. I was already putting together combinations like *Gatsby* and *Passing,* but I realized that other forms of pairing might demythologize writing for students. I could create combinations of texts that would help students see how writers revise as they search for ways to tell a given story. I could show students how the same story gets retold by multiple authors. I could demonstrate how authors influence, quote, and borrow from each another. Perhaps I could sneak in the term "intertextuality" along the way, but mainly I'd show students how ideas circulate from one writer to another. Instead of seeing American literature as something to worship from afar, students might be able to imagine themselves as potential contributors to American literature, as writers who could add the next chapter to an ongoing story.

In response to Scott's complaint, I redesigned my American literature course to make a variety of authors and their work more accessible to students. One particularly successful part of the course focuses on John Steinbeck's *The Grapes of Wrath,* a familiar and frequently taught novel in American literature classes. The time devoted to this section varies depending upon what else I'm trying to accomplish, but it usually takes several weeks.

The first texts I show students are visual rather than verbal because so much of *Grapes* bears traces of images that made an impression on Steinbeck as he was writing the novel. Dorothea Lange's photograph of a young migrant mother nursing her baby was featured on the front cover of *Their Blood Is Strong,* a collection of Steinbeck's essays about migrant workers. Steinbeck knew Lange and her photographs well. He wrote affectionately to her shortly before her death, and six pieces in his seven-part article series on migrant workers were accompanied by Lange's photographs of migrant families, roadside scenes, and government camps. Indeed much of the attention Steinbeck's newspaper articles received can be attributed to Lange's compelling images. I also show students photographs by Horace Bristol, a photographer whose work appeared frequently in *Life* magazine. Steinbeck and Bristol worked together on relief efforts in Visalia, California, when floods stranded more than five thousand migrant families in 1938. We give particular attention to Bristol's pictures of a flooded boxcar home and of a young mother with her baby, because both a flooded boxcar and a nursing mother play such a significant role in the conclusion of the novel.

Initially, in looking at photographs by Lange and Bristol, the class focuses on narrating the stories told by these images. Both orally and in writing, students develop narratives about the people portrayed in the pictures. I ask them questions such as "What would this young mother say if you interviewed her right after this photograph was taken?" and give them prompts such as "Write a diary entry in the voice of someone who has been living in this boxcar home." After the class has begun to imagine itself in the lives of migrants, I provide some background on the relationship between these particular photographers and the author of *Grapes*. In addition to talking about the Lange-Steinbeck connection, I explain that Steinbeck and Bristol had traveled together throughout California, collecting stories and photographs among the migrant farm workers. They originally planned a picture-and-text book about migrant workers, but a few months after the Visalia flood, Steinbeck backed out of the project, explaining that he planned to write a novel instead.

Woody Guthrie's music enters the class next. Guthrie, the Depression-era folk singer known best for "This Land is Your Land," grew up in Oklahoma and, like the Joad family in *Grapes*, was displaced from the land and migrated to California. Guthrie gave voice to the struggles of migrant families with his songs and saw himself as one of "the people." He rewrote religious hymns and popular songs with lyrics rooted in the viewpoint of those who suffered most during the Depression. With lines like, "I'm just a wandering worker, I go from town to town / And police make it hard / Wherever I may go / And I ain't got no home in this world anymore" and "Rich man took my home and drove me from my door / My wife took down and died, upon the cabin floor," he called attention to the suffering of migrant workers (Klein 118 and 124). In March 1940, a few months after *Grapes* was published, Guthrie sang at a "Grapes of Wrath" benefit sponsored by the John Steinbeck Committee for Agricultural Workers in New York. In addition to developing support for migrant workers, this concert introduced folk music, and Woody Guthrie in particular, to a mainstream audience, so that his protest songs began to enter the popular consciousness at the same time that *Grapes* was emerging as a best-seller.

Later in 1940, Steinbeck wrote this description of Guthrie as part of an introduction to a book of protest songs:

> Harsh voiced and nasal, his guitar hanging like a tire iron on a rusty rim, there is nothing sweet about Woody, and there is nothing sweet about the songs he sings. But there is something more important for those who will listen. There is the will of the people to endure and fight against oppression. I think we call this the American spirit. (qtd. in Klein 118)

Listening to some of Guthrie's lyrics in his harsh voice offers my students another version of the story told by the photographs of Lange and Bristol. In addition to providing my students with some background on Guthrie, I ask them to compare the visual and musical versions of the migrants' stories with questions such as "What differences and similarities do you notice between the two stories?" and "What, if any, significance do you attach to Guthrie's life experience as compared with Lange and Bristol, who looked at migrant families from the other side of a camera?"

The next texts I share with the class are drawn from *The Harvest Gypsies*, the collection of seven essays Steinbeck wrote for the *San Francisco News* in 1936. In addition to observations drawn from his travels to migrant worker camps with Tom Collins, manager of the first government camp for migrants, Steinbeck drew upon the reports that Collins submitted to the Resettlement Administration and upon documents collected by the Farm Security Administration. We talk about the interaction of Lange's photographs with Steinbeck's words in this series, and look again at the image of the nursing mother that appeared on the cover of the 1938 collection *Their Blood Is Strong*, the volume in which Steinbeck's seven essays were first collected. We pay particular attention to the choice of Lange's photograph for the cover and to the implications of the title, given that the migrant labor force included Mexicans and Asians as well as White people from Oklahoma. We speculate about why the later edition of the same collection of essays changed the title to *Harvest Gypsies*. The class is occupied by questions about the imagined audience for *Their Blood Is Strong*, the goals for its publication, and the effects it might have had.

Turning to the language of these essays, we look at the way Steinbeck describes the migrants. Careful to distinguish them from the Filipino, Japanese, and Mexican people who preceded them, he writes, "It should be understood that with this new race the old methods of starvation wages, of jailing, beating, and intimidation are not going to work; these are American people" (*Gypsies* 22–23). I ask my students to consider what Steinbeck means by "American" here. We look at his use of quotations such as this one from a young boy he interviewed in a squatters' camp: "When they need us they call us migrants, but when we have picked their crops, we're bums and we got to get out" (23–24). We discuss the impact of the food eaten by migrants: "when the family is making money . . . biscuits, fried potatoes, dandelion greens, pears . . . dinners during lay-offs . . . oatmeal mush" (49).

We continue looking at the relationship between images and words in the photojournalism of publications like *Life* magazine, where Horace Bristol published much of his work, and in books like Agee and Evans's *Let Us Now Praise Famous Men: Three Tenant Families.* We also consider documentary films and look at clips from Pare Lorentz's *The Plow that Broke the Plains* (1936). Lorentz, who helped transform the American documentary, was a friend and collaborator of Steinbeck's. They shared an interest in calling attention to the plight of migrant farm workers. Lorentz read and praised early chapters of *Grapes,* and, for a time, they considered working together on a film about migrants. Eventually, however, Steinbeck withdrew, as he had from Bristol.

We compare the story Lorentz tells in *The Plow* with those told by the photographs, music, and essays we have already examined. In turn, we consider an account that begins, "It will be interesting to trace the history of one family in relation to medicine, work relief, and direct relief. The family consisted of five persons, a man of 50, his wife of 45, two boys, 15 and 12, and a girl of six. They came from Oklahoma, where the father operated a little ranch of 50 acres of prairie" (*Gypsies* 46). This story goes on to recount the father's injury, the daughter's illness and subsequent loss of eyesight, the older son's death from a burst appendix, the truck's being sold for food money, and the father's loss of his job.

By this time students have begun to understand the depth of the material that was available to Steinbeck as well as the multiple ways in which the stories of homeless migrants were told. With this background, we turn to the novel itself. I provide a little information on its reception, highlighting the controversy that *Grapes* aroused when it was published in 1939, including quotations from both critics and fans. Comparing these readings of *Grapes* with quotations from newspapers that attacked it as dangerous and untrue, with descriptions of it as obscene, and with words of praise from President Franklin Delano Roosevelt, Eleanor Roosevelt, and author Upton Sinclair (see Wyatt 3) leads students to see the heightened emotions that *Grapes* aroused. This information on initial responses to *Grapes*, in combination with some of Steinbeck's own expressions of uncertainty about whether *Grapes* should be fiction or nonfiction, shows the challenges faced by the book and its author—often a revelation for students accustomed to thinking of canonical American literature as uncontroversial.

In reading the novel, we look, of course, at the alternating accounts of the Joad family and of the forces that surround them, and I ask my students to consider how the two stories work together, what each contributes to our understanding, and how each connects with the other versions of the story we have already considered. We look, for example, at a sentence like "suddenly the road will be filled with open rattletrap cars loaded with children and with dirty bedding, with fire-blackened utensils" (*Gypsies* 19), comparing it with the description of the Joads' household goods in Chapter 10 of *Grapes*. We compare the listed diets of migrants with the *Grapes* account of the Joads eating stew in Chapter 20. We look at Casy's union organizing in Chapter 26 in light of Guthrie's lyrics as well as sentences like this from *Gypsies:* "The migrants are hated [because] . . . if they are allowed to organize they can, simply by refusing to work, wipe out the season's crops" (30).

John Ford's 1940 film of *Grapes* provides another text to pair with the novel. Available on video, it offers a different representation of the homeless migrants whose story we have seen in multiple versions. Students usually begin by observing the differences between the film and the novel, noting features such as the change in the ending; the omission of sexuality in the lives of Al, Rose of Sharon, and Connie; and even small details like the shifts in language and in the keepsakes Ma Joad fingers before the family leaves the farm. From there, conversation often moves to issues of genre, of what is and is not possible in a film, and of how Ford uses the resources of camera angles, documentary, and more intimate styles, as well as powerful imagery, like the woman accidentally shot in Hooverville.

One good place to start is the introduction of Tom Joad in both film and novel. We begin by looking at Chapter 2, paying particular attention to the novel's description of Tom in his ill-fitting new clothes, the conversation he has with the truck driver, and the references to the landscape they pass. Turning to the film, we consider Ford's use of long shots and shadows to render Tom as a threatening figure and talk about why Ford might have chosen to portray Tom this way. Fast-forwarding to the end, we discuss Ford's portrayal of Tom in the final scenes, and, of course, we consider what is gained and lost by the different endings of the novel and film.

The genre of photojournalism reenters the classroom as we turn to Dale Maharidge and Michael Williamson's *Journey to Nowhere: The Saga of the New Underclass* (1985). In addition to showing that Steinbeck's story of people displaced by social and environmental change continues to be retold, this book reminds students that the social problems illustrated in *Grapes* did not magically disappear in 1940. For students living in relatively protected circumstances, the Maharidge-Williamson accounts of families living in tents and of individuals unable to find work often come as disturbing surprises. Like Steinbeck, Maharidge and Williamson spent several years following the lives of people driven from their homes by unemployment, but the 1980s focus was on the closing of steel mills rather than drought in farmlands. Maharidge and Williamson traveled with jobless and homeless people who left Youngstown, Ohio, to find work. I tell my students that Maharidge had Steinbeck in mind when he wrote *Journey,* and we compare some of its images and text with selections from *Gypsies* and *Grapes.*

The final text in this long series of pairs is another musical one, Bruce Springsteen's 1995 CD *The Ghost of Tom Joad.* In an interview, Springsteen explained that after someone gave him a copy of *Journey to Nowhere,* he stayed up all night reading it. Two of the songs on the Springsteen CD, "Youngstown" and "The New Timer," refer directly to *Journey,* but the title song owes its origins to *Grapes.* As the class listens to Springsteen's account of Tom Joad, we talk about it in relation to Woody Guthrie, the photographs of Lange and Bristol, Lorentz's and Ford's films, the journalism of Steinbeck and Maharidge, and, of course, *Grapes.*

Pairing or connecting this array of texts—visual, verbal, and oral—shows students how many different ways a story can be told. One student wrote in her reading log as we finished with *Grapes,* "I see so many layers to this novel now. It combines history, geography, economics, and all kinds of social issues, and it's still a good book." This more complicated understanding of how a novel develops and the many materials that feed into it gives students a broader perspective on the research that is frequently part of fiction writing. Many find it reassuring to know that a writer like Steinbeck didn't just sit down and write *Grapes;* they take comfort in knowing that he drew upon interviews, reports, and pictures as well as his own imagination.

Because this unit of instruction introduces students to so many different versions of the same story, they come away from it ready to compose yet another account of the plight of displaced and/or homeless people. Soup kitchens, shelters, social service agencies, churches, and street corners, along with libraries and the Internet, offer resources for their composing. Given the freedom to choose from the various kinds of texts studied, students produce songs, essays, photographs, videos, photojournalism, and fiction that represents their own investigation into and understanding of families like the Joads. I find their final products interesting and informative to read. Best of all, since I began using this way of pairing texts, I have not had a student echo Scott's comment that reading discouraged him as a writer.

Works Cited

Agee, James, and Walker Evans. *Let Us Now Praise Famous Men: Three Tenant Families.* 1941. New York: Houghton, 1989.

The Grapes of Wrath. Dir. John Ford. 20th Century Fox, 1940.

Klein, Joe. *Woody Guthrie: A Life.* New York: Knopf, 1980.

Maharidge, Dale, and Michael Williamson. *Journey to Nowhere: The Saga of the New Underclass.* New York: Hyperion, 1996.

The Plow That Broke the Plains. Dir. Pare Lorentz. U.S. Resettlement Administration, 1936.

Springsteen, Bruce. *The Ghost of Tom Joad.* Columbia, 1995.

Steinbeck, John. *The Harvest Gypsies: On the Road to the Grapes of Wrath.* 1936. San Francisco: Heyday, 1996.

Wyatt, David, ed. *New Essays on* The Grapes of Wrath. New York: Cambridge UP, 1990.

V Professional Learning; or, What Happens When Teachers Ask, "What Happens When . . . ?"

Jeremy Wells
Indiana University

One of the things that contributes to the success of collaboration between veteran and new teachers is a willingness to share experiences. New teachers bring fresh experiences, expectations, and approaches to literature, opening up new avenues for inquiry and reshaping the teaching in exciting ways. It can be a nice trade-off. In the summer of 1999, this notion of synergy between novice and veteran teachers was put to a test and produced noteworthy results. Going around the room and introducing ourselves on the first day of a summer workshop, we learned that among our first-timers were two teachers who worked in special education, two who taught science, and one who taught social studies. We also included middle school teachers, and we could count among our numbers a teacher who worked in elementary education, as well as graduate assistants and a university professor.

Together, we were working to expand the literary canon beyond the "classics"; to read more minority and women writers; to think about the theories that undergirded our approaches to texts; to consider literary works in historical context; and to attempt other, similarly "expansive" ventures. Yet we weren't so much interested in historicizing the Pythagorean Theorem, deconstructing the difference between igneous and sedimentary rocks, or imagining new ways of teaching the bicameral legislature.

It surely occurred to each of us on that first day that we were an odd bunch, and, admittedly, the introduction of new subjects and new grade levels made the going a bit rocky at first. By the end of the first week, however, we had come to concern ourselves with a different set of questions—questions that had less to do with differences that separated us and more to do with what we had to learn from each other. How, for example, could we make available to a fifth grader the idea that was central to our project—that the category "American" was not a single, stable, eternal thing? What did the elementary school teacher have to teach the rest of us in turn about pedagogical process and student resistance? What would happen to the science and social studies teachers' classrooms if they started to think about the "literariness" of the texts they were using? What would happen if they tried to get their students working together with first-year college students on a subject both had been studying? What happens when these college students get the opportunity to become teachers? How does it affect their conceptions of what it means to teach? To learn? Above all—and in keeping with the central terms of the project—what happens when we admit teachers outside of English and language arts departments into the process of making and remaking the language arts classroom in general and American literatures in particular?

"What happens when . . . ?" thus became a kind of refrain during our two weeks together. It could even be said to be our motto, for so much of our time involved the kind of speculative, suppositional, even hazardous thinking inherent in the words. What *does* happen when . . . ? It's a question teachers do not always have the luxury of asking. This is especially true of the K–12 teachers who teach several classes each day, serve as yearbook advisor, help out with the school play, prepare students for standardized tests, chaperone the prom, and, presumably, lead lives of their own that they must attend to from time to time. For these teachers especially, the questions are often much more immediate: What are we going to do tomorrow, and how will we do it? We afforded ourselves the luxurious space to consider the speculative questions (What happens when . . . ? What if . . . ? Why do it this way?) alongside the more material, more immediate ones (How will we do it? When will we do it?). So, too, for the college teachers, for if the university, by design, offers a bit more space and time for reflection and revision, we nonetheless came to think about the material conditions of teaching and learning in ways to which we are not always accustomed. Too often, we occupy ourselves with abstract questions of how we're going to introduce the topic of race into our discussion of *The Scarlet Letter*, or colonialism into discussion of *Moby-Dick*, or sexuality into discussion of *The Color Purple*, or linguistic failure into discussion of *Ariel*—and we do these things without asking our students how much poetry they had studied before college, how much African American literature they had encountered, whether they liked Hawthorne when they first read him, or whether they still read him in high school at all.

The essays in this section comment in various ways on the types of professional learning that professional collaboration affords. This section features essays by authors including a high school teacher and two former University of Michigan Ph.D. students. These pieces offer different perspectives on how collaboration can shape one's teaching and one's self-understanding as an educator and lead to significant professional development and reform. They also suggest the wide range of insights and even feelings that participation in this type of project can yield, from exhilaration and heightened awareness to productive confusion to real frustration. Diverse as they are in both subject matter and tone, the essays are nonetheless linked by the question, "What happens when . . . ?"

This question is central to Jennifer Buehler's essay "When It Doesn't All Go Smoothly." An English teacher at Plymouth Canton High School in Canton, Michigan, Buehler describes what happened when her enthusiasm and her revolutionary intentions ran headlong into the exigencies of school teaching. She left the workshop ready to become a visionary, but, as she says early on in her essay, she soon felt like she "couldn't see." Many of her students were reluctant to read, and of those who did, many did not know how to read closely or to write cogently about their responses to the texts. Buehler thus found herself pulled by several competing imperatives: trying to excite students into becoming readers versus having to threaten them with bad grades if they don't, for example; or trying to get students to think critically about *any* text, regardless of whether it's a "classic," versus teaching them that some texts are more important than others. As such, her essay represents an important deviation from published scholarship on teaching, much of which ignores or quickly glosses over the frustrations in order to celebrate the successes and moments of inspiration. At the end of her essay, Buehler offers a list of the practical lessons she has gleaned from her experiences. In addition to providing guideposts to teachers who would follow her example, the list reveals that, very often, it's the frustrating moments that can prove the most educational of all.

Buehler's essay ends by quoting a fellow project participant who once observed that "making American literatures" is all about making teaching harder, and hence more valuable, than it has been before. By coincidence, Michael Sowder and I conclude our essay "Ex Libris: Graduate Student Collaborations with High School Teachers" with the same quotation. We note that the harder high school teachers make it for themselves and their students, the harder it's going to become for us to think of ourselves as revolutionaries who open our students' eyes to issues of close reading, literary history and historicity, feminism and multiculturalism, and so forth. "Ex Libris" discusses what happens when graduate student teachers pull their noses out of their books and library cubicles long enough to think of themselves as part of a much larger community of teaching language, literature, and writing. Both former Ph.D. students at the University of Michigan, Sowder and I enumerate the benefits that graduate students have enjoyed as a result of participation in the project. Some of these were obvious and expected, such as learning about the nuts and bolts of each others' classrooms and being able to share specific assignments and teaching strategies. Other benefits caught us a bit more by surprise, such as learning that the work we do as graduate students might actually have an audience (and, fantasy of all fantasies, an *impact)* outside of the academy. Paraphrasing a poet's description of publishing a book, we liken "our solitary efforts" as scholars and teachers to "dropping a petal into the Grand Canyon and waiting to hear it hit bottom." We learned that the work we do can have a resonance—that, figuratively speaking, it can echo—outside of the walls of the university.

18 When It Doesn't All Go Smoothly

Jennifer Buehler
Plymouth Canton High School, Canton, Michigan

At some point in the fall semester, I realized I was driving without a road map in my tenth-grade American literature class. I couldn't see. I had thought that I knew what I was doing, and that I knew my students. A number of my sophomores had previously been in my ninth-grade reading and writing workshop, and I was delighted to have them back. I had made a commitment to broadening the selection of texts in my classroom to include voices previously unheard in our readings. My students were going to write a range of original works in response to the literature. If all of this went well and, if my enthusiasm lasted, we might conduct research in the University of Michigan archives. If I got a grant from the local arts council, we could have a local drama troupe come out and take us through a role-play reenactment of the Underground Railroad. I had started out with no idea what would really happen during that school year, but I had known that we faced exciting possibilities.

I had settled on an organizing principle for the curriculum gleaned from one of the articles I read during the summer as a workshop participant in the Making American Literatures project (see the Introduction for a description of this project). I would organize the readings around historical contact zones, moments in which voices of different groups in society came together around a contested issue. The historical backdrop I wanted to create required that I embark alone into an interdisciplinary model since I was not already part of a teaching team, but I was willing. On the beach in August after our workshop ended, I read *A People's History of the United States* by Howard Zinn, trying to brush up on history and get a better handle on who the competing voices in those contact zones might be. The article I had read on contact zones didn't come with an accompanying syllabus, but I didn't mind. Every year in August I tell myself I will reinvent the wheel in the interest of creating a class better than any I've taught before. The problem was, that article was written by a college professor for a college audience, and I found myself in over my head soon after school started.

Plunging In

One of the most embarrassing moments of the school year can be parent open house. It's always the Thursday of the second week of school, and I always want to make a good impression, providing an overview of the material I'll teach and my approach for the year, and identifying the things I hope the students will be able to do by the end of the course. After open house I usually feel I have spoken pretty well. I hope to convey the impression that the course will be both challenging and accessible for students, that I am enthusiastic and that they're getting cutting-edge teaching. The embarrassing part is not what happens at open house, but what happens after. Around midwinter I begin to imagine all the parents sitting at home, charting lists of what I said their children would do at open house against what we have actually done, and the gaps between the two imaginary lists mortify me.

In the fall, I told the parents about the contact zone concept for studying American literature. I also told them that I was committed to developing readers in my classroom, so that, as in the ninth-grade reading workshop, students would have some choice in their reading, but this year the choices would be linked to core books that we all read in class together, such as *The Crucible* and *The Adventures of Huckleberry Finn*. I held up books that I had bought at Borders just before school started—young adult novels, literature for adults, nonfiction, and children's picture books set in historical periods from the Salem witch trials to the Civil War. I had *A Break With Charity* by Ann Rinaldi and *The Slave Dancer* by Paula Fox. I had *I, Tituba, Black Witch of Salem* by Maryse Condé, an adult novel. I had *From Slave Ship to Freedom Road*, a picture book by Julius Lester that posed "What would you do?" questions about slavery to young readers. I had a book of drawings called *The Middle Passage* in which Tom Feelings portrayed what it would be like to come across the ocean packed in a slave ship. My assortment of books was hastily assembled, but I believed that I would find a structure for using the books and expand the collection as the school year continued. I thought it was enough for me to be making this important effort to broaden whose American experience gets talked about and to position students as active readers by providing a choice of texts in a variety of genres and ability levels. We were still starting from the traditional place of peoples coming to America and we were still preparing to move chronologically through history, but I believed we would be breaking new ground.

There were problems, however, and they were deep-seated ones that only needed time to come out. I planned to begin by having students choose excerpts from contemporary American novels and memoirs to read in literature circles. This activity would introduce some of the guiding principles of the course: choice in reading selections, student-centered discussion groups, and a diversity of American experiences represented in literature. Students seemed to listen with interest as I ran down the choices in brief book talks. They could find out about an assembly line worker in *Rivethead* (Hamper), the daughter of a Black father and an American Indian mother in *Yellow Raft in Blue Water* (Dorris), the son of a Holocaust survivor in *Maus* (Spiegelman), a Black teenage girl in *Sugar in the Raw* (Carroll), Mexican immigrants in *The House on Mango Street* (Cisneros), or a Japanese American woman in *The Dream of Water* (Mori). They chose their texts and formed their groups, and we were off to a good start.

Right away, however, problems emerged. I had asked the students to react to the reading in their notebooks, which would contain responses to literature and, I hoped, ideas for writing throughout the year. I didn't give them a specific prompt, though, and I didn't model what a good response looks like. We didn't talk about close reading of the text, incorporating quotes into the response, or reading to emerge with a point of view about the text and a readiness for discussion. I didn't even have students prepare discussion questions or literature circle roles for their groups. As a result, some students read those packets I had so carefully assembled, and some did not. Some groups discussed—the fourth-hour conversation over *Sugar in the Raw* extended into lunch, and fifth-hour students from the same lunch table came in charged up and ready to talk about that passage. Other groups were disengaged and inattentive, unable to get a conversation going. Even so, when the groups reported back to the whole class about their discussions, we heard a number of thoughtful comments about the narrators they had met and the kinds of American lives they had been exposed to.

We changed gears abruptly after that. I liked what we had done for the most part, in spite of the flaws in my approach and the unevenness of the kids' skill and engagement, but with the framework I had in mind, those first literature circles were a prelude to the real curriculum. We needed to get into *The Crucible*, and I wanted to find a way for us to examine the experiences of a diverse range of early Americans using a similar model. I turned to McDougal Littell's *The Language of Literature: American Literature* and chose excerpts from *Of Plymouth Plantation, The Interesting Life of Olaudah Equiano, Women and Children First,* and *Blue Highways*. Of course, *Blue Highways* is in no way about early Americans, yet I chose it because I wanted to pay attention to the experiences of

American Indians and I was more comfortable discussing a contemporary piece than a folktale, a creation story, or a song. In an attempt to focus on images as texts and elicit responses from students to nonprint sources, we also looked at and wrote about Tom Feelings's drawings from *The Middle Passage*. Alongside our whole-class readings of these texts, I asked students in their existing literature circle groups to research in more depth the experience of one kind of early American, then create a first-person narrative to be presented orally in the voice of that early American. I handed out a list of American literature Web sites from our Making American Literatures summer workshop group, hoping it would lead kids to sites containing archives, photos, and audio selections.

Once again, I thought I was onto something good. We found narratives by slaves taken from Africa on slave ships, by American Indians in the New England forest, and by colonists on Plymouth Plantation. We were still paying attention to the multiplicity of American experiences. Students used what they had learned and wrote about it in original voices, taking center stage to demonstrate their knowledge and creativity. Looking back on that project, though, now I see the ways in which we stumbled. Much of the students' research was terrible. I made a chart that students used to report which sources supported which pieces of information in their narratives. That turned out to be a weak tool. It was not enough to prevent them from doing cursory research for narratives based on superficial understandings of their subjects. I think one group out of two classes used the Web sites I listed. Embarrassingly, too much of their research came from an encyclopedia. I took photographs of the speakers and made audio recordings on presentation day, but I never shared those with anyone. The students never asked for them, either. I knew by then that what we were doing sounded better than it actually was.

We rounded out the first marking period by listening to *The Crucible* on audiotape and watching the Nicholas Hytner film version. I began having students use their notebooks to write more focused responses to what they read and heard, but some students still failed the test at the end because they couldn't explain the significance of the quotes I provided or write essays using evidence from the text. The deficiencies I saw on that test were evidence that my students needed both greater skill for writing about literature and deeper engagement with the subject matter, but I couldn't stop and reassess my plans at that point. Instead, I asked students to spend the last three weeks of the marking period finishing what I had set out for us to do in the beginning. They were to read a book of their choice from the small collection I had assembled about early America and also develop original writing in any genre that linked to the issues we had examined relating to early Americans.

Students met again in their literature circles to discuss their reading and share their writing, but some groups had read the same text while others were reading a variety of different texts. I had bought multiple copies of books when I could, but I had limited control over the collection because I had bought what was on the shelves of the local bookstores rather than ordering ahead. I rationalized this by thinking of my purchase as the seed for a much larger American literature classroom library similar to the young adult one I have for the ninth graders, but it was a weak rationalization for a last-minute purchase. Consequently, giving directions for literature circles was a disaster—I didn't know what to tell students to talk about, and they hadn't been trained to talk well independently. I told myself it didn't matter since those discussions are supposed to arise from student interest, but that was an excuse for a poorly planned activity. When the marking period finally ended, students turned in portfolios that contained their responses to independent reading (many had not read the books) and their writing about early Americans, which consisted mostly of five-paragraph essays, diary entries, poetry, and epilogues to *The Crucible*. I graded those portfolios using a rubric I had designed (but never fully explained) to evaluate their work for the marking period. When I turned in grades, I felt exhausted, and there were still three marking periods to go.

Pulling Back

As the year went on, I backed off significantly from the approach I had used in the fall. The idea of contact zones fell by the wayside, as I realized I simply did not know enough to create that syllabus on my own. We returned to traditional units on the novels that tend to be taught every year in the American literature course at my school, and day after day I emphasized individual written response to the text but also close reading of certain scenes as a whole class. Students read *The Adventures of Huckleberry Finn* next, but again they read badly. Even though they wrote responses to the reading several times each week; even though they met regularly in literature circles to discuss their reactions to the book; and even though we discussed the significance of certain scenes and quotes in detail, large numbers of kids failed the test. It was clear from the vagueness of their essays and their inability to put quotes in context that, again, many had not read the book. While this should have come as no surprise to me, it did. I discovered that I now had two problems on my hands. The problems in my approach to the course design paled in comparison to the students' problems as readers. They didn't read; they read but didn't finish; they read but fell behind; they read but not closely. I was so disappointed in their indifference as readers that I decided to make reading well the focus of the course, and that decision set us on our path for the rest of the year.

We went on to read excerpts from *Walden* and full works including Salinger's *The Catcher in the Rye*, Kesey's *One Flew Over the Cuckoo's Nest*, Wright's *Native Son*, and Wilder's *Our Town*. Students filled hundreds of pages in their notebooks, never answering study questions, even though some kids wanted them—attempting day after day to articulate some original reaction to issues they identified as important in the text. I asked students to underline quotes that seemed significant in the reading, and we talked about those quotes in class. Gradually quotes started showing up more often in their responses. Their literature circle questions began to focus on specific passages and scenes. Our discussions got better, and sometimes I knew it was because I had shown the kids ways to be better readers. Sometimes it was because I'd found the right questions to challenge and engage them. From time to time we watched movies as introductions to the readings: *Dead Poets Society* introduced *Walden*, and *Rebel without a Cause* introduced *The Catcher in the Rye*. We would finish a book and spend two days writing about quotes and thematic issues on the test, and on the third day I would be ready to hand them the next novel. In the spring, kids began commenting on how much they had read—more full-length books than their friends in other sections, they told me. This surprised me. I look back and count six complete works that we read as a whole class, along with anthology excerpts, independent reading, and films. Students created a couple of pieces of writing for their portfolios during each marking period, most of them creative writing and personal essays. To me that seems small. Why to some students did it seem big?

Putting My Thinking on the Table

I know that when I set out to teach American literature in the fall, I gave myself a tall order. The most effective and realistic classroom change is usually incremental, but I plunged into change wholesale, thinking that the momentum I'd gain from trying a new approach with my students would carry me through to the end of the year. I thought I could keep inventing change as I went, disregarding what I already knew about how tired teachers get as the year wears on.

I realize now that, before anything else, I have to balance my desire for change with an ongoing and careful assessment of what my students can do. Things began to fall apart in my mind when I saw that the student-centered activities I'd tried to design did not prepare kids to demonstrate the skills of reading and writing about literature which I still wanted to measure on the tests. If students read literature but could say nothing insightful or specific about it, then something needed to change in my approach. Not only were kids not insightful about literature; many kids just weren't reading. As I began considering the unevenness of my students' skill levels and motivation, I arrived at the two questions I should have been asking all along: What is the purpose of an American literature class, and what should students be able to do once they've read the literature? These are obvious questions and they certainly get bandied about my department each year, but we never come to a consensus on the answers. Inconclusive discussions have allowed us to keep doing what we've always done in our classes, sometimes because that's easiest and sometimes because that's what feels most comfortable. As a result, there are as many ways of teaching American literature in my department as there are teachers who teach it, and kids get entirely different experiences of the course depending on the teacher of their section.

I've been a listener during many debates among my colleagues about the American literature class. They would disagree over whether to teach the course chronologically or thematically; whether to read "dead White men" or multicultural authors; whether to study history through these texts or study the texts themselves; whether to build cultural literacy or produce more tolerant Americans. I usually kept a low profile in these debates, as I was trying to figure out what I believed: whether the American literature course should be a multicultural endeavor or should be focused on the canonical tradition. In the Making American Literatures summer workshop, my inquiry group's task was to address the issue of silenced and marginalized voices in American literature. Throughout our discussions during those two weeks, the need to include those silenced voices on our reading lists became a given to me, and our conversations primarily addressed the kinds of opposition we might face in our departments on the subject of broadening the canon.

What we should read became my biggest concern in the weeks when school was starting. I was painfully conscious of the girls, the Filipinos, the Koreans, the Indians, the Pakistanis, the Blacks, and the working-class students in my room, and I thought nothing was more important than choosing readings which included characters who resembled my students. It took a while for me to realize that the reading list mattered far less if my students were unprepared to be engaged as readers—or worse, didn't bother to read. By the third marking period, I stopped feeling so bad about what I wasn't doing to draw kids in, and I decided I just needed sharper teeth in my grading policies. My rubric was allowing kids to pass because "they did all the work," even if their work was extremely poor in quality. I resolved that if a student failed both tests during the marking period—always open-book, open-note, essay and quote-interpretation tests—then he or she would fail for the marking period. I had to laugh bitterly when my vexation over the teaching of American literature ultimately came down to a rule about what you had to do to pass. More kids started reading the books after I made that policy.

Communicating to students what it meant to be engaged as readers and how to demonstrate engagement was a harder problem to solve. It's common that students are expected to read a chapter and answer study questions, or read a novel and write a five-paragraph essay on the theme. I wanted my students to develop the skills involved in doing those assignments, but those weren't the assignments I wanted to give. Rather than focus on study questions, I wanted students to fill their notebooks with responses that would demand independent thinking and push them to find the significance in what they had read. I would guide them to find meaning, but I wanted the process to begin with the students. I wanted my students to write essays, but I didn't want essays to be the only kind of writing we did. I settled for open-book, open-note essay writing on the tests while students generated draft-writing approaches of their own (based on minilessons by me) for their portfolios. They wrote parodies of *The Catcher in the Rye* and modern-day *Huckleberry Finn* stories in the vein of *Rule of the Bone* by Russell Banks. They wrote dialogues, vignettes, and editorials. They co-authored drafts. Their work was uneven, but at least I wasn't reading thirty drafts of the same paper at the end of each novel.

Students couldn't be engaged as readers, however, if they were unable (or unwilling) to read the material I gave them. My students are not illiterate, but most are not sophisticated readers, either. Reading comprehension ranges widely among the tenth graders in my heterogeneous classes, and, when I ask students to read tough "classics" like *Gatsby* or *Huckleberry Finn*, I want them to do more than just comprehend or struggle to get through the assigned pages. Students are supposed to read deeply, to find symbolism, to pick up on social criticism. Ideally, at times they will even find themselves in the pages they are reading. Not everyone is able to do this. If the reading is on a high level and is assigned in large chunks each day, it is no wonder that my students fall behind, fall asleep, or read and don't remember anything. If students have never been hooked on reading or immersed in a book they love, it is unlikely that they will be developmentally ready to read the classic American novels I am prepared to present—novels that were written for adults, not teens.

I have been an avid reader of young adult literature for years, and much of what my ninth graders read is young adult literature in the reading workshop. For some reason, I had never found a way to incorporate young adult books into my American literature course. After the summer workshop, however, I realized how imbalanced and, for some, inaccessible, my American literature reading list had been, and how much it could be helped by the addition of young adult literature. I've done some research on teenage readers; G. Robert Carlsen's work in *Books and the Teenage Reader* gave me a sense of how young readers become more sophisticated over time and how gradual that process is. Developing readers move through stages, beginning in elementary school by reading for sheer pleasure and becoming unconsciously absorbed in the story. Around middle school, students who have read well for pleasure are ready to begin reading for a different purpose—to experience vicariously the worlds their characters inhabit. By ninth grade, teenagers who spend most of their time thinking about themselves begin reading literature to meet people like them and to discover characters in situations similar to their own. It is not until students reach the highest stages of reading development that they begin reading to grapple with philosophical issues and to appreciate the aesthetics of the text.

These stages are not discrete units; rather, they provide overlapping satisfactions in reading, and, in the classroom, students are sure to be reading at different stages. Some students may be so weak as readers that they have never experienced the early stages. By expecting young high school students to read only classic novels, and by expecting them to read primarily on the philosophical and aesthetic levels which most readers don't reach until the end of high school or the beginning of college, we are fighting a losing battle with a large number of students in our classes. Everyone loses.

I have known each year I've taught that the books we read as a whole class were too hard for some, that the pace was too fast for others, that the books were at times too long, and that the issues the books addressed were often too abstract or remote from the students' lives to generate real engagement. Still I kept assigning the classics, thinking there were certain books that kids had to read if they were going to say they had taken an American literature class. I felt backed into a corner by my own ultimatum, but I was determined to keep assigning those books until kids toughened up and learned to read them. I'm afraid now that my rigid beliefs merely set kids up to fail, or to come back later and tell me they never read the books I assigned.

As a result, I am no longer sure of what I thought at first—that the central purpose of an American literature class is to deliver the classical literary canon to teenagers—and my uncertainty places me in a terrible dilemma. It puts me at odds with many of my colleagues in the English department, who focus almost exclusively on the canon, teachers who have far more experience than I do. It puts me at odds with my own academic training, at least that which I received in high school, where we were assigned Hawthorne, Hemingway, Fitzgerald, Faulkner, and Dreiser, although, even in that advanced level program, not all the students read the books. My uncertainty also places me in a standoff with those advocates of cultural literacy who speak so convincingly about our students' lack of knowledge and the need to "fill them up" with literature.

My undergraduate training in American studies, however, tells me different. The American studies program at Yale University placed differences of race, class, and gender at the heart of all our discussions about American life. Texts included novels as well as diaries, photographs, films, paintings, and musical works, and we also did "readings" of material culture such as furniture and other physical artifacts of American life. The canon was something we approached critically, and we sought not only to challenge but also to expand it in the interest of emerging with a more complex picture of American culture. It was exhilarating work which taught me to approach reading in a new way, and items that once seemed innocuous, like magazine advertisements, became texts for study.

It seems that I forgot this complex and expanded approach to reading and to American literature when I became a high school teacher. In the desire to adapt my ideas to the American literature classes my colleagues were already teaching, I returned to the notion that some texts are more important than others, and that the delivery system of pouring literature into my students' heads was what teaching American literature was all about. My students resisted. Their resistance provided me with clues for further rethinking of my teaching. I can't expect to keep kids engaged, or to transform their ideas about texts and reading, if we only study the classics.

Now I am striving for more of a balance in what we read and in how we read it. I still want to expose my students to some "classics" so they will have read books that "culturally literate" people know about. But I am willing to weigh those books now with other kinds of reading that students may find more accessible—including, but not limited to, young adult novels—which I hope will also broaden students' notions of what it means to read. Recently, my class read Richard Wright's *Native Son*, a classic novel (albeit one that is not taught frequently in high school), but we read it alongside the documentary film *Hoop Dreams* and the National Public Radio audio diary "Ghetto Life 101," all of which were set on the south side of Chicago. The grouping of these texts gave us a more complex portrait of poverty and of African American life than Wright's novel alone could have provided. The real people we encountered in the film and in the audio diary gave us a portrait of dignity and hope in the face of adversity, which may have tempered the impressions that students absorbed from reading about Bigger Thomas. Neither *Hoop Dreams* nor "Ghetto Life 101" is part of the literary canon, but I think they helped raise a greater range of issues than Wright's novel alone could have, and they helped me to straddle the gulf that separates the canon from more nontraditional texts.

I'm still in the process of negotiating and reconstructing my sense of what American literature is supposed to be. In my evolving version of the course, students may not read as many classics as we would like, but I hope the ones we do read will be meaningfully grounded in a context that challenges students' notions of the literary and of what counts as literature. Regardless of the context, what we will do is keep reading all the time. Readers improve by being immersed in the act of reading. If students read adolescent books, too, then maybe reading all the time won't be so painful. Maybe at some points in the year they will be reading for pleasure and to find characters who are like them. With that groundwork laid and with help, maybe they can go on to read harder books on a more sophisticated level—when they are ready for it. By the end of the year, I hope to have helped empower students who will remember the things we read together, and, more important, I hope those students will want to read something on their own in the future. I hope their training in American literature will help them go on to approach reading, and the culture all around them, with greater sophistication and engagement.

Determining what students should be able to do once they've read the literature is an equally difficult challenge. Students in language arts classes traditionally develop skills in reading, writing, listening, and speaking. I keep those language arts strands in mind, but my real concerns are about what assignments I should give, how I should evaluate, and what we should spend class time doing. I still struggle with those issues, but I have a clearer sense now than I did a year ago of the experience I want to provide in my class. I also know a little more about what kinds of standards I want to adhere to so students will not be able to get away with coasting through the class by listening to the discussions instead of reading the books.

Students should have to talk. If I provide good focus questions and a framework for approaching the books, students should be required to express a thoughtful opinion about what they've read. They should be able to refer to something they noticed in the reading and react to something someone else has said. That kind of participation shouldn't happen by chance or good will. It should be an expectation that everyone will talk, and there should be a range of opportunities for that to happen. Some days everyone should have to talk, even if it means going around the room for a single comment, read out of a notebook, from each person. Some days a group of students should run a discussion in the center of the room while the class observes, forcing the small group to sustain conversation on their own and allowing the others to follow how a conversation can become engaged or how it can break down. Some days students should meet in literature circles—small groups that remain consistent over time—to discuss in more detail the issues that came up in whole-class discussions or in their notebooks. Those groups should have to account for the discussion at some point to the whole class, and they should be evaluated on how focused they are in their group. Finally, whole-class discussions will help to pull all of us and our thinking together, and they should happen periodically during our reading of a book, but not every day. There should be elements on the rubric to evaluate all these kinds of talk; that way, I can be sure that every day or every week we hold a discussion, everyone is accountable for saying something.

Students should write in meaningful ways. Responses in notebooks and analytical essays should be central, since future teachers will expect my students to be able to organize evidence and argue effectively, but there should also be room for pieces of writing that students structure on their own. Again, they need a rubric and a sense of how those pieces will be graded. What qualities or themes should those pieces of writing have in common with what we just read? What kinds of writing about literature will best engage fellow readers? Carefully crafted assignments that are designed at the outset to pull together paired texts or foster development of certain skills and ideas are important, too. There should be room in those assignments for flexibility, though, so students won't feel like their work is expected to fit into a formula identical to everyone else's. Models for writing are necessary, as are instructions on process and craft. Writers need time to work in class in a focused environment where they can get help and write as part of a community. They need a chance to share what they've written during the process and at the end. They may need a peer-response group. Maybe they should be required to read finished work on stage using a microphone. Maybe we should publish an in-class magazine. We (teachers) raise the stakes when we require students to take risks even while we go to great lengths to make it safe to do so.

I know there are many more things that my students can do besides read, write, and talk about literature. I have tried some other kinds of activities, some of which I liked a lot at the time: time capsules and teenage diaries with *Our Town*, a Quaker reading with *Blue Highways*, performances in the voices of early Americans, letters to the producers of *Hoop Dreams* and "Ghetto Life 101," essays and narratives on each student's own American identity. My students have also written themselves into the text of *As I Lay Dying*, interviewed people about coming to America as a complement to reading immigrant literature, created their own archives from junk in the family basement after visiting the local historical society. The hard part is figuring out which activities are worth doing and what they might add to the experience I want to help students create in the course. Having a picture in my mind of who my students are when I meet them in the fall, what I want them to do throughout the year, and what I want them to be like as readers and writers when we finish in the spring will make planning for a better American literature class possible. I'm still straining my eyes to see a clear outline of that picture. Maybe after another year of teaching American literature, I'll be able to write more definitively about my vision and the real kids who came to give it life.

Only after struggling through a year of attempts at change do I really understand that change is hard. Here is some of what I've learned:

Lesson 1: Have the road map clearly laid out before school starts. In the desire to change my curriculum immediately on the basis of what I had learned in the Making American Literatures project, I thought I could make up my syllabus as the year went on, but I found that exhaustion makes careful planning impossible. I made a chart in my notebook starting with a circle around each of the anchor texts I generally teach each year. Outside each circle, I wrote the titles of potentially related texts we could read alongside the anchor text. For instance, when we read *The Catcher in the Rye*, we could also look at stories in young adult novels of teenagers in conflict with the world around them, such as Ellen in *Finding My Voice* (Lee), Jeremiah and Ellie in *If You Come Softly* (Woodson), Hallie in *Someone Like You* (Dessen), or the real teenage girls who wrote about their lives in the collection *Ophelia Speaks* (Shandler).

Thinking first about the texts I already teach and then building in new texts around the anchors makes it easier for me to envision a gradual reshaping of the curriculum. In the future I also hope to begin each year with some broad focus questions that we'll use to approach the course as a whole and each group of texts we read. I won't teach the class chronologically, but good focus questions will provide us with a different kind of structure, and the questions may help us find out what these texts together are saying about the American society we live in.

Lesson 2: Buy just a few new texts at a time. Choosing a few new texts that you know well is better than buying a huge stack of unfamiliar books that will sit untouched on the shelf all year. I learned that lesson at the expense of a generous allotment of departmental book money. None of the books I bought for independent reading in American literature went directly to waste—most of the titles were young adult historical fiction, and when they didn't work well in the American literature course, I put them in the ninth-grade classroom library. But it would have been more practical to spend the money on a class set of one single text that I knew would pair well with an anchor text. The problem was that I could never make up my mind on that one text.

Lesson 3: Know what you're going to do to teach reading. Just because the students can read doesn't mean that they *will* read or that they will read well. Know what you want students to do to demonstrate a careful, thoughtful approach to reading. How will they learn the difference between a plot summary and an analytical reading response that reveals insight? Will they keep a list of significant quotes as they read? Will they write their own questions about significant moments in the text? What can they do, besides taking a quiz, to demonstrate that they have done the reading? What other things can they "read" besides a novel or a selection from the anthology? What do paintings, advertisements, photographs, or architecture reveal about America in connection to written texts?

In the future, I will emphasize during the first week of school the skills that I want students to demonstrate as readers, and I know I will use some of the discussion strategies mentioned above to model the kind of reading I am looking for. I believe that a focus on reading is essential, no matter what kind of English class it is. If I'm not striving to engage kids as readers, even kids as old as tenth graders, then I'm doing them a disservice and adding to the literacy problems in our culture.

Lesson 4: Keep the focus on literature. Historical background may help immensely to put texts in context, but an American literature class should be more than just a vehicle for teaching American history. What students learn about history from the novels shouldn't overpower what they learn to find in the texts themselves. It was Anne Ruggles Gere who pointed out that there are experiences with texts that can only be had in an English class, and I have pondered since then what those experiences should be, especially as I have moved away from the historical approach I envisioned for my curriculum when the year began.

Literary texts, novels, short stories, poems, memoirs, documentaries, interview transcripts, and radio diaries, among other texts, should provide students with models of narrative voice which foster the development of students' own voices. Literary texts should capture the range of voices in American life, helping students to form a sense of personal identity within the larger culture. Literary texts should ultimately provide a model of competing ways in which to narrate the American experience, highlighting how many ways there are to live as an American and to approach American culture. Helping students to have these kinds of interactions with texts is very different work from having them read novels to learn about history.

Lesson 5: Vary the routine, but maintain high standards. At some point during the third marking period, James, one of the boys in my fifth-hour class who had been struggling—not keeping up with the reading, writing poor responses, and subsequently failing tests—complained to me that "all we ever do is read and write in here." At the time I disregarded his comment as the familiar complaint made by kids who don't like the kind of work done in English class and are too lazy to make a real effort. Now I am embarrassed that I didn't pay more attention to his concern. He was right. We did focus exclusively on reading and writing because those were the things I knew best. I used class time in predictable ways for silent reading, in-class response writing, whole-class discussion, literature circle meetings, and tests, in that order. Sometimes we broke things up by watching a movie. Jee Yoon Lee, one of the graduate students in our summer workshop, described her approach to planning by saying she tries to keep her class unpredictable. I hope to do more of that this year.

I have tried to create a more interesting balance of activities during the first marking period by having kids try research and performance and having them choose their own books alongside the traditional reading and writing activities. I gave up on that approach, however, because I was afraid that what I planned in the interest of student-centered learning was just gimmicky and superficial. I wanted my class to have rigor, and I'm not sure if that concern revealed a desire to measure up in the eyes of my colleagues, the parents, the kids, or myself in an attempt to be the quintessential "good teacher." I wanted my class to be challenging, meaningful, and worthwhile. I wanted the challenges to be within reach for kids, but I also wanted them to feel they had to stretch themselves in order to do well. I didn't care so much about whether the class was fun. Now I think I should have. I hope in the future to keep a balance in mind so that students are challenged in lots of different ways, held to a high standard but also enabled to have fun through much of what we'll be doing.

It's ironic that after a summer workshop on American literature, I feel in some ways that I know less than ever about the teaching of American literature. That assessment isn't entirely fair—I've thought harder about the teaching of this course than I have about any other, and I have more ideas for teaching it now than I ever did before. But as one of my colleagues, Mary Cox, a teaching veteran of twenty years, said, "You've taken what was easy and made it hard." That is what has happened for me, too. Teaching American literature becomes hard when one realizes the potential of the course to create a new culture, to help thinking citizens shape themselves within that culture, and to make language arts a purposeful venture for teenagers coming of age in this society. Allowing students to "make" literature means allowing them to read, write, and discover for themselves, albeit with (sometimes heavy-handed) guidance along the way. What students do may surprise you. What you are able to do as a teacher may surprise you, too. Taking what was easy and making it hard seems exactly what I want to do for my students. It's only fitting that I also do that for myself.

Acknowledgments

For the Lessons Learned model, thanks to Sherman Alexie's approach in commenting on the making of Smoke Signals. For the concept of keeping experience with text central in English class, thanks to Anne Ruggles Gere. For supporting my professional development and giving me freedom to develop as a teacher, thanks to Sharon Strean. For information on stages of literary development in reading and arguments for the use of young adult literature in the classroom, thanks to G. Robert Carlsen in *Books and the Teenage Reader,* Linda Robinson in *Into Focus*, and John Bushman in *Using Young Adult Literature in the English Classroom.*

Works Cited

Stand-Alone Books

Banks, Russell. *Rule of the Bone: A Novel*. New York: HarperCollins, 1995.

Carlsen, G. Robert. *Books and the Teenage Reader: A Guide for Teachers, Librarians, and Parents*. New York: Harper, 1971.

Carroll, Rebecca. *Sugar in the Raw: Voices of Young Black Girls in America*. New York: Three Rivers, 1997.

Cisneros, Sandra. *The House on Mango Street*. New York: Vintage Books, 1989.

Condé, Maryse. *I, Tituba, Black Witch of Salem*. Charlottesville: U of Virginia P, 1992.

Dessen, Sarah. *Someone Like You*. New York: Viking, 1998.

Dorris, Michael. *Yellow Raft in Blue Water*. New York: Warner, 1987.

Faulkner, William. *As I Lay Dying*. 1930. New York: Vintage Books, 1964.

Feelings, Tom. *The Middle Passage*. New York: Dial Books, 1995.

Fox, Paula. *The Slave Dancer: A Novel*. Scarsdale, NY: Bradbury Press, 1973.

Hamper, Ben. *Rivethead*. New York: Warner, 1991.

Kesey, Ken. *One Flew Over the Cuckoo's Nest*. New York: Signet, 1962.

Lee, Marie G. *Finding My Voice*. Boston: Houghton, 1992.

Lester, Julius. *From Slave Ship to Freedom Road*. New York: Dial, 1998.

Miller, Arthur. *The Crucible*. 1952. New York: Penguin, 1981.

Mori, Kyoko. *The Dream of Water: A Memoir*. New York: Fawcett, 1995.

Rinaldi, Ann. *A Break with Charity: A Story about the Salem Witch Trials*. San Diego: Harcourt, 1992.

Salinger, J. D. *The Catcher in the Rye*. 1951. New York: Bantam, 1986.

Shandler, Sara. *Ophelia Speaks: Adolescent Girls Write about Their Search for Self*. New York: HarperPerennial, 1999.

Spiegelman, Art. *Maus: A Survivor's Tale*. New York: Pantheon, 1986.

Twain, Mark. *The Adventures of Huckleberry Finn*. 1884. New York: Bantam, 1981.

Woodson, Jacqueline. *If You Come Softly*. New York: Putnam's, 1998.

Wright, Richard. *Native Son*. 1940. New York: Harper Collins, 1991.

Zinn, Howard. *A People's History of the United States*. New York: Harper, 1980.

Anthologies

McDougal Littell. *The Language of Literature: American Literature*. Evanston: Houghton, 1997.

- Bradford, William. *Of Plymouth Plantation*.
- Equiano, Olaudah. *The Interesting Narrative of the Life of Olaudah Equiano*.
- Heat-Moon, William Least. *Blue Highways*.
- Thoreau, Henry David. *Walden*.
- Williams, Alicia Crane. *Women and Children First*.

Harcourt Brace Jovanovich. *Adventures in American Literature*. New York: 1980.

- Wilder, Thornton. *Our Town*.

Audiovisual Materials

The Crucible. Dir. Nicholas Hytner. 20th Century Fox, 1996.

Dead Poets Society. Dir. Peter Weir. Buena Vista Pictures, 1991.

"Ghetto Life 101." Prod. David Isay. *All Things Considered*. Natl. Public Radio. 8 June 1993.

Hoop Dreams. Dir. Steve James. First Line Features, 1994.

Rebel without a Cause. Dir. Nicholas Ray. Warner Brothers, 1955.

19 Ex Libris: Graduate Student Collaborations with High School Teachers

Jeremy Wells
Indiana University

Michael D. Sowder
Idaho State University

Doctoral candidates in literary studies often complain that the work they do leaves them feeling isolated: isolated because they spend so much time holed up in libraries and office spaces working on their dissertations; isolated because their dissertations are likely aimed at audiences of fewer than fifty (and perhaps as few as five) specialists in their fields to begin with; isolated because they only rarely get to meet and work with their colleagues from other campuses who share their particular interests; and isolated, above all, because they have no way of gauging whether their work proves interesting to people outside of the academy. They—that is, we—are urged to narrow our fields of study early on in our graduate careers. At the same time, we are encouraged to master a highly specialized academic vocabulary. Learning how to explain our work to people outside of the academic loop, much less learning how to work collaboratively with them on projects of mutual interest—these skills rarely receive the attention they deserve.

For a fortunate group of Ph.D. candidates at the University of Michigan, however, things are at least beginning to change. More than fifteen graduate students thus far have been involved in conversations about American literature with secondary teachers as part of the Making American Literatures project (see the Introduction for more about the project). A number of us have had the chance to be more extensively involved through summer workshops, follow-up meetings, and classroom visits. All of us specialize in American literature, though our dissertation topics span a considerable range (from Walt Whitman to Jewish

American women's literature to Southern literature). All of us have also taught (or are currently teaching) first-year writing and literature courses that incorporate American texts. All are deeply invested in the project of rethinking the central terms of American literary studies, focused as we are on such issues as race, gender, class, religion, region, ethnicity, and nationality, and the roles they play in the texts we read and teach. Last, all of us are committed to making ourselves better teachers.

Our collaboration with secondary teachers is helping us to rethink our roles as teachers at the same time that it is suggesting to us that the work we do can, in fact, have an impact outside of the academy. In the interest of publicizing our experiences, and in the hope of encouraging others to develop similar projects elsewhere, this article summarizes several of the ways we have found ourselves benefiting thus far.

Making Our Work More Public

Perhaps the main benefit of the project has been the most obvious. By meeting regularly with secondary school teachers, we have begun to gain a better sense of what it is that we do in our respective classrooms. Simple though this may sound, its implications have been considerable. Graduate student instructors at the University of Michigan have typically been out of high school some seven to twelve years (and some considerably longer) by the time we begin teaching our own undergraduate literature courses. Many of us remember our high school English classes as having encouraged our love for literature and our desire to study it, but few of us can recall exactly how those beloved high school teachers taught us *The Catcher in the Rye*, *Death of a Salesman*, or *My Ántonia*—what it was they *did*, in other words, that fostered our literary interests. We only vaguely recall what it was like *not* to know the essay strategies we needed to take the AP test, what it was like *not* to be able to read a poem closely. Working with these teachers has reacquainted us with what happens in secondary school classrooms, providing us in addition with the teacher's perspective that, as high school students, most of us were not yet ready to grasp.

In turn, we are providing the school teachers with a sense of what goes on in our classrooms: what sorts of courses we get to teach as graduate students (mostly first- and second-year writing courses, some of which have a literary bent); what sorts of assignments we give (lots of papers, of course, and relatively few quizzes); and what sorts of abilities we expect, or at least hope, that our students will possess when they enter our classrooms (a wide-ranging curiosity, an interest in reading something unfamiliar, a willingness to think critically, a knowledge of some of the basics of essay writing). Just as important, we provide an idea of what we *don't* expect, namely, a prior knowledge of this or that specific text. Students can do just fine in our classrooms even if they haven't read *Julius Caesar* or *The Scarlet Letter*, for example, though everything they have read presumably helps. Knowing this, the teachers have told us, helps them to construct better college prep courses: ones that foster the kinds of critical thinking and writing strategies we value rather than ones that insist upon the inclusion of particular texts because we, as college teachers, are supposedly going to "expect" students to have read them already. Much of what scholars have been doing at the university over the past fifteen years is to destabilize the idea that certain texts must be read because of values presumed to be inherent within them. The emphasis is now as much upon *how* and *why* we read certain texts as it is upon *what* we read, with questions of literary value being recontextualized alongside questions of history, power, identity, and so forth. This knowledge proves useful because many of the teachers with whom we're working are at least as far removed from their own undergraduate classrooms as we are from our high schools. Learning about the nuts and bolts of each other's pedagogical practices helps us as graduate students to know where our students are coming from, and it helps the secondary school teachers to know where their students are going.

By exchanging knowledge in this manner, both groups are, in effect, working to overcome the barrier that separates us from each other. That barrier has seemed increasingly artificial to us as graduate students as we have realized two things about the teachers with whom we're working. First, we have learned that they are willing to engage (and, in many cases, are already engaging) literary texts in much the same ways we do—asking questions about a particular novel's status as "classic" or canonical, for example, and working to uncover the circumstances that made the novel seem "timeless" at some point in its history. (*The Scarlet Letter* is a good example here, for it did not become central to an American literary tradition until well after its initial publication.[1] In a related vein, we discussed Nathaniel Hawthorne's status as "major American writer" in one of our collaborative seminar meetings this past fall.) Together, we have also raised questions about the historical conditions that make certain literary works possible in the first place, studying, for example, the regionalist fiction that exploded in the United States after the Civil War, a time when magazine publishers were eager to give their readers a more harmonious view of the different regional populations in the United States. We have studied such nontraditional texts as Harriet Jacobs's *Incidents in the Life of a Slave Girl*, Art Spiegelman's *Maus II*, and a series of nineteenth-century sailor songs from Michigan's Upper Peninsula. Such texts have forced us to consider questions of literary canon formation (Why is it that we must label these texts "nontraditional"?) and questions of pedagogy (How can we incorporate these texts into our classrooms, and how might they change our perspectives on the texts we're already teaching?). The simple fact that we were pursuing these questions *together*, contributing what we could based on our own backgrounds and experiences, suggests that collegiate and high school English teaching need not be thought of as altogether separate. The teachers we're working with have educated us, in other words, about the possibilities of what can be discussed in precollegiate classrooms.

The second realization has to do more directly with students themselves. The barrier that seems to separate high school teachers from graduate student teachers seems all the more artificial when considered from a student's vantage point, for students, after all, are often entering classes taught by graduate students only three or four months after having left high school. This is especially true in academia today because graduate students handle more of the first-year undergraduate teaching load than ever before, a result of declines in the numbers of tenured and tenure-track faculty at most colleges and universities. Most Ph.D. candidates at the University of Michigan teach first-year undergraduate courses at least three times before finishing their degrees. Understanding better where our students are coming from and what they are capable of helps us to design more challenging courses and to frame the materials we present in them more effectively. We know, for example, that some of our students will come to our classes having already dealt with the difficult race and gender politics (not to mention the difficulties in language) in such novels as *Light in August* and *Beloved*. Realizing this, we can be more comfortable in giving our first-year undergraduates similarly complex reading assignments, and we can expect to be able to identify a few discussion leaders in each of our classes who are already familiar with, say, Faulkner's writing style or Morrison's oblique mention of historical events.

On an even more concrete level, we have profited from our secondary school colleagues' vast pedagogical experience by listening to (and often borrowing wholesale) the kinds of assignments they have devised in the past. We often end our large-group discussions of particular texts by brainstorming assignments, units, and text pairings in small groups. Quite often, this means, for the graduate students, learning about the innovative projects that the secondary school teachers have already initiated in their classrooms (such as one teacher's having his students "perform" poetry in groups, or another's having her students interview members of their community in order to produce alternative local histories) and adapting these assignments to the texts we're considering with our undergraduates. Doing so makes us better teachers and, on a broader level, it demonstrates to us how collaboration can reshape participants' teaching. We learn that we can teach American literature more effectively when we understand our teaching as a communal (rather than simply a collegiate) affair.

The particular community we're building in this project involves professors from the University of Michigan and from Oberlin College as well. Another advantage for us as graduate students has been to encounter our professors in this setting. The University of Michigan offers better and more extensive pedagogical training for its graduate students than many similar schools, but, for most of us, that training is supervised by professors who are not on our dissertation committees. Rarely do we discuss our teaching with our dissertation committee members, and only occasionally do we get a sense of what they do in their classrooms, what issues and what problems they face. Encountering them at the seminars as fellow teachers rather than as advisers opens up the teacher-student relationship and allows us to learn from each other's experiences. We find that we share many of the same problems and concerns; we have the opportunity to learn how they have addressed certain problems; and we discover that our teaching experience can have value for them as well. We also sense among them the same excitement that comes from reaching beyond the academy, thus finding ourselves once again in a larger community of teachers than graduate school might sometimes lead us to believe.

Discovering the Relevance of Graduate Work

At the first seminar of the academic year, project director Anne Ruggles Gere asked us to reflect for a few minutes in writing about one of the three terms: *making, American,* or *literatures.* As we took turns speaking about the associations and ideas the terms evoked, the scope and importance of our project was brought more and more into focus. One secondary school teacher began by noting how his spell checker highlighted "literatures" as a misspelled word. Another spoke eloquently about how the inclusion of voices like Harriet Jacobs's and Leslie

Marmon Silko's enabled students to come to new understandings of the term *American* in her course called "America Dreaming." Another spoke about how the idea *American* carries ineluctably alongside it ideas of history, and of how she brings history into her literature classes. Toward the end of the sharing of ideas, one graduate student spoke about how listening to the participants' reflections brought her to the realization that, through our teaching, reading, and writing, *we* are the ones making American literatures—one of those startling surprises about the obvious which seemed all the more startling because of its obviousness. *Of course*, as teachers and scholars we are making American literatures.

But the blindness and forgetting giving rise to this insight about the work of teachers, especially the work of secondary school teachers, should come as no surprise given the character of graduate school life. After several years of study, graduate students easily begin to feel themselves not only isolated but also irrelevant to the larger society, powerless subjects laboring with minimal impact within institutional limitations and pressures. The image of the irrelevant, cloistered student-scholar was already a cliché when Chaucer imagined his pilgrim "clerk." And favorite writers of graduate students, like Michel Foucault, can provide ready theoretical affirmation for such feelings of powerlessness. What difference can a graduate student instructor really make in a semester of English composition? In terms of the larger issues we seek to address in our research and writing—issues about what counts, and has counted, as American, as literature, as making—can semester-long composition and introductory literature classes really matter? Our research and writing itself seems to have little appreciable impact outside the academy. And even literature, the ostensible purview of our discipline, can seem, with its entrenched canon, like a linguistic edifice we must both master and change. Labor in the library, at our desks, even in our seminars, can feel ephemeral, if not elitist. Graduate students thus often feel alienated within their own profession.

And so, hearing secondary school teachers speak with passion and commitment to the very literary, cultural, and historical issues upon which we spend solitary hours and intellectual labor presents an opportunity for remembering again what we are doing in grad school. We begin to see that, perhaps unknowingly, we have been participating in a larger community of educators struggling to transform the canon, bring new voices into the classroom, and alter what counts as American literature. Secondary school teachers—at least some of them—are also struggling with how to open up the canon, how to teach Jacobs's *Incidents*, Silko's *Ceremony*, Kingston's *The Woman Warrior*, whether and how to teach *Leaves of Grass* as a gay poem or Rebecca Harding Davis as a radical feminist. Outside the university, too, educators are taking up questions of American identity, nationality, race, class, and gender. They wrestle with what principles we can say designate the literary—questions of aesthetics, history, and politics. We found surprising congruity in the texts we teach, the knowledges we share, the issues we bring to the classroom, and the questions we bring to each other. Like the laborers in the field whom Robert Frost wrote of as working together, though unseen and apart, we have discovered each other as allies working together, though apart, to transform the field of American literary studies.

Meeting allies outside the academy thus helps us see that our work in literary studies may already be having material effects in the real world. Stated differently, it counters the lingering fear that our solitary efforts may be, to paraphrase from one writer's description of publishing a book of poetry, like dropping a petal into the Grand Canyon and waiting to hear it hit bottom. And just as important as the feeling that our labor may be relevant outside the academy, we have realized that we do, in fact, know something about American literature, that we can contribute usefully to the debates currently surrounding it. So much of graduate school moves us in the opposite direction, for when we spend time in the library, we mostly come to realize how much more there is to read, and when we work with other specialists in our fields, we realize how much more there is to think about. For several years, however, we have been engaged with many of the seminal theoretical works that first raised questions about the canons of American literature, and we have been reading widely about particular moments of U.S. history and culture as well. The Making American Literatures project has taught us that our specialized backgrounds and our insights into certain questions do enable us to contribute to a larger community.

But the realization that we are allies making American literatures led quickly to discussions of the obstacles and challenges this work presents. Several graduate students noted that the meetings have made clear the extent of the material obstacles faced by secondary school teachers in making changes in courses and canons. We heard about the limited choices among anthologies that for the most part replicate traditional approaches to literature. We heard that administrators, faculty, and even students can be resistant to opening the canon and taking on the work of historical grounding necessary for doing so. Community pressures sometimes mandate teaching or not teaching particular books. In other words, high schools are "public" in ways that the university is not. One school system insisted on using an abridged version of Maya Angelou's *I Know Why the Caged Bird Sings* in which the pivotal molestation chapter had been removed, rendering the book largely incoherent. These are challenges that graduate students generally do not face in bringing new voices into the university classroom.

But we also discovered many challenges that we share. Much of the resistance on the part of teachers to opening the canon comes from limitations in their own education. We all find it easier to teach familiar texts. Bringing in new and newly recovered voices requires educating ourselves both about the books and about the historical contexts out of which they emerged. This is no small task. One professor involved in the project remarked, for example, that teaching certain Asian American literary texts without knowledge of the history of Asian American immigration would be like teaching *The Red Badge of Courage* without knowledge of the Civil War. We explored the difficult issues the comment raised—issues about our own competence and authority to teach literatures we were not trained in. How much historical knowledge is necessary? Should a lack of special expertise mean not teaching a compelling, rediscovered text? And, perhaps more fundamental, how effectively can a person of one racial identity teach the literatures of another? Or even of one's own—one African American professor spoke of how racial identity always affects one's authority in the classroom. How might she most effectively persuade students that she doesn't teach African American works simply because she shares the racial identity of their authors?

Consequently the project has, on the one hand, encouraged us to see that our graduate work may have relevance outside the academy. On the other hand, a new understanding of the different challenges that graduate students and high school teachers face provides an appreciation of how the issues we approach from a theoretical perspective get played out in different arenas of pedagogical practice. This understanding should then inform our thinking when we return to our research and writing, and it should also make us better teachers. Finally, the understanding that we have been unknowingly working with other educators in the same fields of change has created the conditions of possibility for thinking new ideas about collaboration with recognized allies.

Conclusion

One participant, a high school teacher from Detroit, summed up her experience in the project as follows: "This used to be so much easier," she observed after we had spent several days together, pursuing the same kinds of troubling questions raised in this chapter. "Now we've made it so difficult." Dealing with complex disciplinary concerns—concerns about the canon, identity politics, the nature of the literary, and so forth—can leave one a bit exhausted at the end of the day, to which any graduate student in literary studies can attest. But this teacher's response suggested enthusiasm more than exasperation, for "making things difficult" had become, by that point, the enterprise that kept bringing us together. Forcing oneself to rethink the texts one teaches is difficult. So, too, it is difficult to reconceptualize the community in which one operates. But if collaboration has demonstrated anything to us at this stage, it is that these tasks are worth pursuing in spite of the difficulties they entail.

Graduate student instructors often assume that their role is to open students' eyes, so to speak, about questions of canon formation, disciplinary boundaries, historical circumstances, and the complex nature of identity as it pertains to literary texts. We assume, in other words, that it is up to *us* to encourage students to rethink the foundational categories of their own educations. How much more difficult is it going to be for us, then, when more of our students come into our classrooms already thinking along these lines? When we must therefore rethink our responsibilities as educators? We hope that, when these questions become more prominent, we will still be able to have conversations across institutional lines in order to be able to pursue the answers.

Acknowledgments

We would like to thank the following University of Michigan graduate students for sharing their insights: Alisa Braun, Colleen O'Brien, Sondra Smith, Scott Heath, Joshua Lavetter-Keidan, Valerie Moses, Jee Yoon Lee, and David Anthony.

Note

1. See the first chapter of Jane Tompkins's *Sensational Designs: The Cultural Work of American Fiction, 1790–1860* (New York: Oxford UP, 1985).

Afterword: Where Do We Go from Here? Future Work for Making American Literatures

Sarah Robbins
Kennesaw State University

The contributors to this book have been engaged in a multidimensional and generative project. In that spirit, it seems fitting to close this collection with a multilayered reflection that looks ahead to future goals. Accordingly, this afterword will add a bit of context from my own perspective as a longtime secondary school (and, more recently, university) teacher of American literature, but also as a university professor engaged in several related programs promoting teachers' professional development. I will also highlight recurring elements in the project-based learning described here and offer some suggestions for ways in which teachers and students can continue to benefit from collaborative American literature teaching.

Because this book's contributors shared an association with Making American Literatures, a project originally funded by the National Endowment for the Humanities, we began to see our teaching in a broader cultural context than we might ordinarily do. Being part of a national enterprise challenged us to think about the broad social implications of our daily decision making as instructors. I hope that our stories may encourage others to tap into the heightened awareness of teaching as public intellectual work. That is, I think these essays exemplify how productive it can be—for teachers, their students, and the larger community—when educators are encouraged to view and critique their daily classroom lives as *publicly* significant.

Committed as we were to bringing diverse (new and traditional) voices together in the American literature canon for secondary schools, we also began to see such efforts as questions of value beyond solely aesthetic or narrowly disciplinary concerns—to consider the curriculum in universal as well as local *human* terms. This aspect of our work, in turn, prompted the kind of self-consciously humanistic, classroom-level enterprises described by Anne-Marie Harvey in this volume—seeing literary study as an opportunity for all students to "grapple productively with all of the identities that define them, however mysterious and difficult they may be."

Like the NEH-funded Making American Literatures project, this collection includes a geographical range appropriate for exploring the dynamic content of a discipline that has so often constructed itself as being concerned with a "national" literature. In fact, the transcontinental reach of the initial project helped prompt instructional efforts like those David Anthony described in his essay here—inviting students in an American literature course to examine "the relationships between narrative, national historical myths, and national identity," to see "that the historical narratives we rely on to anchor us in our understanding of ourselves (as the children of immigrants, as 'Americans,' and so on) are subjective and often decidedly unstable," and to interrogate individuals' complicated positions in the national community through research and writing grounded in literary study. Having come to understand the influential part that learning about a literature labeled as "national" can play in students' self-constructions, the contributors to this volume and their colleagues in other classrooms involved in the original project hope that other teachers will join in further explorations of this issue.

Seeing literature *as* writing, viewing ourselves and our students as potential literature makers, and using writing to reflect upon our classroom practices as a crucial source of pedagogical knowledge—all these have come quite naturally to this group of contributors, most of whom have ties to the National Writing Project. The NWP's self-identification as a *project*, in fact, is worth underscoring in this context. Linked to a professional organization conceiving of its mission as an ongoing *venture, endeavor*, or *undertaking* (to name just a few of my thesaurus's synonyms for "project"), our contributors may have occasionally joked about how our work was making teaching more difficult and complicated, rather than providing clear-cut answers to our overarching questions, but we never really intended to come up with a stable formula for teaching American literatures. The unsettled and unsettling quality of our ongoing work seems crucial to emphasize in an "afterword," since this is the moment when some readers might be expecting to find a definitive list of literary texts, a patterned system for organizing course curricula, or a precise set of replicable strategies for teaching American literature based on a synthesis of our volume's earlier essays. Instead, the topics we explore keep generating more questions than answers.

Nonetheless, reading and rereading this collection of essays has suggested a broad group of concepts emerging from these reflective stories of classroom practice. Perhaps the best way to highlight these themes would be to describe how the original terms—*making, American,* and *literatures*—have led us to identify more complex issues worthy of further examination.

Making Choices for Principled Teaching

As Anne Ruggles Gere observed in her introduction to the collection, we set out in part to explore "the forces that deliver certain texts to our classrooms"—to see American literature as a dynamic discipline that is constantly being redefined by shifting cultural tastes, the economics of publishing, and teachers, along with their students. We began by questioning how, at the level of individual learners and within institutions, disciplinary formation for American literature might be seen as an ongoing process. More important, we were asking how teachers and students could participate self-consciously in that process of defining and refining or continually reformulating those various literatures. On one level, a number of the essays in this volume have provided some specific examples of instructional activities involving students and teachers in literature making—whether in their own writing or through informed critique of others' literary texts. So, for example, Anne-Marie Harvey details strategies she has used to promote comparative analysis of cultures by having students interview world travelers and generate their "own list of associations with American Whiteness" as a way of rendering the dominant culture's normative activity more visible. Man Martin describes an assignment that encouraged his students to "make" popular culture texts literary by re-viewing them through interpretive frameworks of Carl Jung and Joseph Campbell. Students in these classrooms are highly engaged learners, interacting with texts to explore how specific pieces of literature can be made and remade in multiple contexts of composition and consumption.

Useful as we hope such particular ideas for instruction will be, however, on another level the essays as a group provide a potentially more significant resource for teachers. As Jennifer Buehler points out, however many involving ways she and her colleagues might come up with to "read, write, and talk about literature," even these energizing kinds of activities do not insure meaningful, grounded learning unless she confronts the "hard part" of "figuring out which activities are worth doing and what they might add to the experience [she wants] to help students create in the course." As I consider the particular classroom practices vividly recorded in my colleagues' essays here, I see them guided by tentative outlines for a broad reconceptualization of literary production and study growing out of the "making" dimension of our project.

A number of the essays emphasize an important instructional implication of seeing literature making as a historically situated social process that calls (in disciplinary terms) for sustained collaborative examination. That is, we have begun to develop teaching practices that are self-consciously communal in their focus and their application. Like the shift in composition instruction from an emphasis on product to an enactment of process, the "making" vision of literature (as an action and as a school subject) moves from demanding that students master a specific set of facts or skills *about* literature to inviting them to create social knowledge *through* literature—both imaginatively via their informed analyses of others' texts and literally in their own "making" processes.[1] Teachers who conceive of literary production and literature instruction as *text-based, community-building processes* can, as suggested by the stories in this collection, imagine the course content and the instructional approaches in their literature programs as specifically situated in a social context, productive of communal values (for the classroom or the larger society), and grounded in writers' and readers' intertextual exchanges. Aware of their school disciplines as necessarily responsive to shifting community values such as those described by Dave Winter in his history of American literature at Wheeler High School, these teachers expect rather than fear shifts in the curriculum, and they ask questions to make those shifts (and the influences behind them) visible. Like George Seaman, for instance, they urge students to imagine the different audiences anticipated by different textual representations of "literature"—to unbuild the seemingly stable text (or textbook) assigned to them, to undo the process of social construction that *made* a piece "literary." Like Rita Teague and Colleen Claudia O'Brien, they may promote such recovery of complex literature-making processes through comparisons of texts in historical context (e.g., *Gatsby* and *Passing* in light of the 1920s). Like Tim Murnen, they might invite students to examine two versions of the "same" text on/by Cabeza de Vaca, uncovering ways in which the context of presentation can remake literature. Or, like Mimi

Dyer, they might ask students themselves to identify and organize literary pieces into a curriculum—while emphasizing how their decision making fosters shared understandings grounded in their social engagement with text.

Parallel to the decidedly community-oriented turn in composition studies, with its insistence that all writing is potentially collaborative or, at the least, social, the literature-teaching practices described here affirm textual production of all kinds (whether generative or analytical) as a self-consciously communal enterprise. Another important element in both of these social conceptualizations (of writing and of literature) is that they are not simplistically and predictably linear. I still cringe every time I recall visiting classrooms with "THE writing process" represented in a line of steps on the blackboard, from a "prewriting" brainstorming activity to a "final" copy's static "publication" for the teacher. Culturally situated views of writing and of literature making cannot be reduced to a sequence of "steps" followed in the same predictable way on all occasions. As Anne Ruggles Gere's discussion of varying "literary" responses to Depression-era American culture indicates, author, subject, medium, and audience can all constitute shifting forces that shape varying textual productions, and students' social examination of such variations in an intertextual context can provide them with a reservoir of cultural capital on which to draw for shaping their own "literary" pieces within a critically literate classroom community. Taken together, then, the essays in this volume not only show our project teachers' view of literature as reflecting, in the words Tim Murnen invokes from Jane Tompkins, "the way a culture thinks about itself"; they also envision students and teachers as informed, activist participants in those socially meaningful processes.

American Meanings in an International Age

The contributors to this volume conceived of the middle term of our title as more global than national. Convinced that appropriating the broad term *American* to designate only U.S. literature was too limiting, we forcefully extended the boundaries of the discipline to include Canadian, Caribbean, and Central and South American texts. We paid attention to cross-national exchanges as notable forces in American literature making—whether in the journeys from England to the United States by Charles Dickens and his serialized narratives, or in the imaginative journeys to Africa and Italy by a "Canadian" writer (Michael Ondaatje, born in Ceylon, now Sri Lanka), resulting eventually in an

"American" film, *The English Patient*. We accented the complex literature making of immigrants—published writers, classroom teachers, and
students Americanizing themselves. As indicated by Alisa Braun and
Tracy Cummings, we sought out spaces and techniques for using translated literature in our classrooms. Overall, we viewed *American* as an
inclusive term, and we constantly questioned the very concept of a national literature in a global culture (Ruoff and Ward; Pérez Firmat).

Yet we also noted that ideas about nationhood, civic responsibility, appropriate goals for "American" communities, and the distinctive
socializing role of a national literature seemed central to many of the
traditional and new texts we were studying. As we devoted increasing
consideration to the positive impact that learning about "American"
literatures *could* have on our students' lives, we sought ways of blending reading and writing to foster students' examination of their own
positions in national culture. So, for instance, David Anthony crafted
an integrated assignment that prompted his student Amy's moving
story of her grandmother and herself in relation to ideas about American hunger. Meanwhile, our collaborative inquiry into questions of literary value and the cultural work that texts do made us increasingly
sensitive to student critiques of our courses as irrelevant or as inad-
equately representing their own aspirations for America.

As the anecdotes from the classrooms of Kara Kuuttila Shuell and
Rita Teague illustrate, revisions of our courses in response to student
needs were often as intellectually invigorating for us as for the class.
Sometimes they were also unsettling—revealing and challenging as they
did our otherwise unexamined personal investments in various icons
and ideologies of American life. For example, even though Shuell sym-
pathized from the outset with her student Sean's complaint that the
Puritans had nothing to do with his life, her first efforts to justify their
inclusion in his study of American literature were admittedly more
defensive than productive. A collaborative reconstruction of her curriculum has reaffirmed Shuell's lingering wish to keep Plymouth Rock on
her map for the nation's literature. Now, however, she not only has an
engaging coming-to-America framework for studying the Puritans *with*
her students; she also has an enhanced awareness of the associations
and beliefs that she herself had developed for the period and its texts.
Better equipped through critique of her teaching to question what her
personal values may affirm or exclude, she is also better prepared to
help her students use their reading and writing of American literatures
as a way to define communal visions for an inclusive national future.

Teachers have not always been encouraged to position their curricular decision making within such a purposefully sociopolitical framework, of course. In fact, as Dave Winter's incisive history of 1960s and 1970s versions of American literature at Wheeler High in Marietta, Georgia, demonstrates, even when such a purportedly powerful cultural force as a school district mandate enters the classroom, other socially constructed ideas about what and how to teach may carry greater weight. Along those lines, in reminiscences of their decades-old decision making, Dave's interview subjects struggled uncomfortably with their own reevaluations of the school's shying away from "relevance" and diversity in choices about what to teach and how to teach it *as* American literature. Noting discrepancies between the teachers' personal commitments to diversity and their reluctance to choose an available multicultural anthology over one decidedly more "White" and traditional, Dave highlights his classroom ancestors' sense that their responsibility to safeguard and pass on classic texts in the ways they had been taught outweighed other factors that tend to promote curricular reform, including their own intense consciousness of (and constructive participation in) key social issues of the day, especially integration.[2]

One of the benefits of Winters's research, of course, is its demonstration that teachers' daily activities, like literary texts themselves, are historicizable social practices meriting the same kind of cultural critique usually reserved for more publicly visible work (see Shumway). Winters's research also shows that it is especially important to examine critically the literature making which is bound up with our *national* identity. When Roger Hines was genuinely inspiring many students with his heartfelt teaching of Robert Frost, the question Rita Teague's students could raise later about how "the Black man" figures in representations of American literature did not yet seem askable at Wheeler High School. But Patsy Musgrove was quietly laying the groundwork to help make such an exchange possible, even likely, in Dave's classroom there today, by rescuing and treasuring a compendium her colleagues had rejected— an anthology including African American voices—and thereby anticipating the truly multicultural student body that is learning together at Wheeler today.

Making *Literature* Plural in Multiple Ways

Adding an *s* to signal our vision of American literature*s* as inherently plural, we contributors to this collection were thinking about including underexamined genres in our classroom canons, as represented by

Jennifer Buehler's astute grouping of *Hoop Dreams*, the NPR audio diary "Ghetto Life 101," and Richard Wright's *Native Son*. We were also anticipating expanding our particular school curricula to represent the rich ethnic and linguistic diversity evident in American classrooms today, by viewing student writing as potentially literary (McQuade). In practice, these have been very productive elements of our work, but, like the other organizing elements in our project title, the term *literatures* proved to be even more generative—and more richly complicated—than we anticipated. Studying literature in the context of a program that was also examining issues of place and identity led a number of us to "make" literatures in, with, and for our local communities. Jim White's efforts to have his students write themselves onto their own local maps represents just one example of this social dimension. As Laura Schiller's essay shows, such projects were often collaborative, allowing our students to create texts for authentic audiences and substantial purposes—to become self-conscious agents of community formation.

As one of the reviewers of this collection observed, many teachers face constraints when they seek to expand their curricula to include ethnic and linguistic diversity. District-level (or state-level) adoption of anthologies can create many of these constraints, especially when combined with the selection of "American literature" as a core language arts content area to be "covered" in a high school exit exam, as contributors from Georgia discovered. Whether we liked it or not, defining forces that often seem beyond an individual teacher's control were coming to bear decisively on local versions of the discipline we had chosen to examine. In this case, though, teachers were ready to act as informed participants in processes that, before, might have appeared remote and inaccessible. While calling upon their university colleagues for support, Georgia teachers ably served on districts' textbook adoption committees and responded to the state exit exam by resisting the elimination of teacher and student choice from syllabi construction. At a time when pressure for standards could have resulted in disciplinary standardization, teachers worked to maintain a pluralist commitment to American literatures in their classrooms.

Although Georgia teachers called upon their university colleagues in discussions of textbook adoption, support does not flow in only one direction between the university and school contributors represented here. University faculty members who have collaborated with this book's contributors report that their own teaching has been influenced by interaction with their secondary school colleagues. Similarly, as Jeremy Wells and Michael Sowder's essay in this volume attests, these collaborations have acted as a significant influence on the American literature teaching of graduate students at a point when their professional identities are often formed more by what they are reading in seminars and what they are doing in research than by collegial models of reflective practice in action. When David Anthony designed course plans *with* Michigan schoolteachers, and when Anne-Marie Harvey's California college students corresponded via e-mail with Dave Winter's high schoolers in Georgia, they helped dissolve boundaries that often separate disciplinary formations as experienced by students at different levels of the education process. These exchanges wrought new American literatures, fostering more of an integrated progression from secondary school to university, rather than a frightening leap across a great divide.

Along related lines, as this essay collection has certainly illustrated, participants in this project—whether secondary teachers or university faculty—have acquired a more pluralistic sense of the American literature field in large part by coming to see their work as connected to other classrooms through colleagues engaged in similar, even if necessarily different, work. As Peter Shaheen indicates in his introduction to the second section, these ongoing exchanges have invited teachers to view themselves as prepared to change their own practices but also able to reform "the practices of the institution." Linked through their collaborative learning, teachers have found ways to re-form themselves as makers of American literature, thereby enabling their students to become active agents in the development of the field and the cultural values it inevitably represents.

Notes

1. See Pradl's discussion titled "The Impasse of Reader Response" in *Literature for Democracy.* Pradl observes that "literary texts are central to democratic education. They affirm and confirm—through the personal acts of aesthetic evocation that are necessary to access them—the uniqueness of the individual, even while insisting that such acts are inevitably related to sharing and participating in the actions of a larger community" (80).

2. I do not mean to criticize 1960s and 1970s Wheeler teachers for their choices, but rather to emphasize their *historically situated sense* of what then seemed crucial to maintain as the rightful aim of literary study. As Richard Brodhead has said in an evaluation of today's calls for cultural studies of literature, "For this aspect to monopolize consideration—for a newfangled 'far' reading to replace the once-mandatory 'close' reading—would not represent an escape from limitations of knowledge, only a restructuring of their bounds" (11). Winters's research suggests, in this context, that we need to explore the

social forces which made close reading seem mandatory just as carefully as we might assemble reasons that other approaches could, if we ignored Brodhead's advice, become equally limiting today.

Works Cited

Brodhead, Richard H. *Cultures of Letters: Scenes of Reading and Writing in Nineteenth-Century America*. Chicago: U of Chicago P, 1993.

Jay, Gregory S. *American Literature and the Culture Wars*. Ithaca: Cornell UP, 1997.

McQuade, Donald. "Composition and Literary Studies." In *Redrawing the Boundaries: The Transformation of English and American Literary Studies*. Eds. Stephen Greenblatt and Giles Gunn. New York: MLA, 1992. 482–520.

Pérez Firmat, Gustavo, ed. *Do the Americas Have a Common Literature?* Durham: Duke UP, 1990.

Pradl, Gordon M. *Literature for Democracy: Reading as a Social Act*. Portsmouth: Boynton/Cook, 1996.

Robbins, Sarah, Janet Edwards, Gerri Hajduk, June Howard, David Winter, Dede Yow, and Sandra Zagarell. "Linking the Secondary Schools and the University: American Studies as a Collaborative Public Enterprise." *American Quarterly* 50.4 (September 1998): 783–808.

Ruoff, A. La Vonne Brown, and Jerry W. Ward, Jr., eds. *Redefining American Literary History*. New York: MLA, 1990.

Shumway, David R. *Creating American Civilization: A Genealogy of American Literature as an Academic Discipline*. Minneapolis: U of Minnesota P, 1994.

Editors

Anne Ruggles Gere teaches at the University of Michigan, where she directs the Joint Ph.D. Program in English and Education. She began her teaching career at the high school level and has taught American literature to a variety of students. Along with Sarah Robbins and Donald McQuade, she served as a founding director of the Making American Literatures project, and she has continued her rethinking of American literature in her ongoing work with teachers from the University and from secondary schools. In her recent book *Intimate Practices: Literacy and Cultural Work in U.S. Women's Clubs 1880–1920,* she explores several aspects of American culture at the turn of the century.

Peter Shaheen started teaching in 1978. He has worn a variety of hats, including debate and forensics coach, humanities teacher, creative writing teacher, and American studies teacher. He has been published in a number of journals on a variety of topics ranging from the history of elocution in America to his daughter's fifth-grade graduation. He teaches at Seaholm High School in an interdisciplinary team program called Flexible Scheduling.

Contributors

David Anthony is assistant professor of American literature at Southern Illinois University at Carbondale (SIUC). He is currently working on a book manuscript entitled "White-Collar Gothic: Debt, Affect, and Masculine Interiority in Antebellum Sensationalism." The focus of this project is the representation of gender and emotion in nineteenth-century mass culture, an interest that extends to his teaching, especially in courses on the Gothic and sentimentalism in both the United States and England. His work on the Making American Literatures project continues to inform his teaching at SIUC, where he now works closely with students from rhetoric and composition, as well as the school of education.

Alisa Braun is a doctoral candidate in the Department of English at the University of Michigan, where she has taught courses in American literature and composition. Her dissertation examines the involvement of American Jewish writers in relationships of patronage during the late 1800s and early 1900s. Her research interests include American literary history, Yiddish literature, and translation theory.

Barbara Brown has been an English and social studies teacher in Michigan since 1961 and currently teaches writing, literature, and history courses at Fenton High School. She graduated with a B.A. from Central Michigan University and has done extensive graduate work at other Michigan universities.

Jennifer Buehler is a teacher at Plymouth Canton High School in Canton, Michigan, and has been a member of NCTE since 1995. She makes presentations on young adult literature in southeast Michigan through the Eastern Michigan Writing Project. She graduated from Yale University with a degree in American studies and now lives in Ann Arbor.

Tracy Cummings received her master's in English from the University of Michigan. Her research interests include twentieth-century literature, women's writing, and literary theory. She teaches at the Art Institute of Portland where her American literature courses focus on portrayals of the artist and the visual arts in works by Hawthorne, James, Faulkner, Black Elk, Malamud, and Dickinson, among others.

Mimi Dyer, a graduate of Duke University (B.A. in French) and Kennesaw State University (M.A. in Professional Writing) is the Web master for the Kennesaw Mountain Writing Project. A veteran of several programs associated with the NEH and the Georgia Humanities Council, Dyer currently teaches English at South Forsyth High School in Cumming, Georgia. She was a presenter at the 1999 NCTE Convention and the 1999 and 2000 Georgia Council of Teachers of English conventions. She is also active in the National Writing Project and has received grant funding through its Rural Sites Network.

Anne-Marie Harvey teaches in the UC Berkeley English department, where she recently received her Ph.D. She has taught reading and composition, literature seminars, and a graduate-level course on pedagogy. She currently coordinates the California Making American Literatures research group, which is studying better ways to teach writing in literature classrooms. She is also a freelance writer.

Emanuel (Man) Martin teaches English at Stephenson High School in Stone Mountain, Georgia. A former syndicated cartoonist, he enjoys integrating popular culture with more traditional literatures, and he takes special interest in comic books and cartoon figures in American culture. In addition to teaching and coaching high school debaters, Martin writes extensively. He has produced a novel manuscript and several short stories, as well as an interactive Web site.

Tim Murnen is a Ph.D. candidate in the Joint Ph.D. Program in English and Education at the University of Michigan (UM). As a high school English teacher and department chair, he taught literature and composition, directed the drama program and the writing center, and sponsored the literary magazine, the cheerleading squad, and the African American Club. Currently he is teaching undergraduate courses in literature and composition at UM.

Colleen Claudia O'Brien received her Ph.D. in the University of Michigan's Joint Program in English and Women's Studies. Her research incorporates social history archives and medical texts in a study of Progressive Era American women's literary dialogues about race relations and citizenship. Colleen's undergraduate English classes at the University of Michigan collaborate with secondary school classes to present their own work on literary texts.

Sarah Robbins, director of the Kennesaw Mountain Writing Project, was a K–12 teacher of English and language arts for more than fifteen years, working in public and private schools in Georgia and Michigan. Sarah is currently teaching classes in American literature and culture, professional writing, and women's literature at Kennesaw State University. In the past several years, she has co-directed a number of professional development programs for teachers and received several master teaching fellowships for developing interdisciplinary courses using new technologies to teach writing and literature.

Laura Schiller is a literacy consultant for the Southfield Public Schools in Southfield, Michigan. Prior to taking this position, she taught sixth graders in the same school district. After participating in the Oakland (Michigan) Writing Project, she served as co-director. One of the first Michigan teachers to be certified by the National Board for Professional Teaching Standards, Laura is in frequent demand as a presenter to teachers of the English language arts.

George M. Seaman is an English teacher at Lassiter High School in Marietta, Georgia. He has been involved with several programs offered by the Kennesaw Mountain Writing Project, including the summer teacher institute and a summer honors program for high school students. He has also worked at the district level in drafting a plan for using student portfolios in assessment.

Kara Kuuttila Shuell graduated from Albion College in 1989 with a B.A. in English and French and in 1993 received an M.A. in English from Oakland University. As a high school English teacher in Southfield, Michigan, she has also been involved in the MELAF project (Michigan English Language Arts Framework), working as a demonstration site teacher. With this initiative, she had the opportunity to work with Michigan's content standards and benchmarks before they were released to all school districts in the state.

Michael D. Sowder, assistant professor of English at Idaho State University, received his doctorate from the University of Michigan, where he wrote a dissertation on Walt Whitman. His scholarship has focused on the relationship between poetic and religious discourses in the nineteenth century. He is also a poet, and his teaching focuses on nineteenth- and twentieth-century American and international poetry. He has found that the accessibility and diversity of voices speaking in contemporary American poetry prepares students well for encountering diverse voices in earlier periods.

Rita Teague has been teaching in Southfield, Michigan, for twelve years. Previously she taught in an urban area where African Americans were bused in for integration, in a rural historically Black university, and in several inner-city high schools. She became intrigued by the Making American Literatures project as a result of her experience of teaching in a variety of venues and, at the same time, her similar experiences when encouraging students to connect with American literature. The strategy of pairing texts to expose students to voices not heard in American classics has added a needed dimension to her students' and her own teaching and learning. Presently Teague is pursuing a doctorate in educational policy and leadership.

Linda Templeton teaches ninth- and twelfth-grade English at East Paulding High School in Kennesaw, Georgia. She is a member of the Kennesaw Mountain Writing Project, serves as chairperson of the National Writing Project's Rural Sites Network, and was a participant in the 1998 Making American Literatures NEH project. Currently, Templeton is participating in the Keeping and Creating American Communities project through Kennesaw State University. She is a lifelong learner and encourages all teachers to be lifelong learners.

Jeremy Wells recently completed his Ph.D. at the University of Michigan, where he studied and taught American literature and college writing. His research focuses on race, regionalism, and imperialism in American literature, especially in late nineteenth-century texts about the South. Originally from Huntsville, Alabama, he has lived in Texas and North Carolina, and he graduated from Vanderbilt University in Nashville, Tennessee, with a degree in English. He joined the Making American Literatures project in the summer of 1998 and served as an assistant director in 1999.

Jim White has taught English at Farmington High School for ten years. Before becoming a teacher he was a reporter for a weekly newspaper. He and his wife Denise, who teaches third grade, live in downtown Farmington, a suburb northwest of Detroit.

Dave Winter, a geographic mutt who has called three states home, felt very comfortable with the teachers from California, Georgia, and Michigan in the Making American Literatures project. A native of Detroit who began his teaching career at Mayfair High School in Lakewood, California, Winter has taught American literature and journalism at Wheeler High School in Marietta, Georgia, for the past eight years. Winter has held a variety of leadership positions in professional development programs offered by Kennesaw State University.

This book was typeset in Palatino and Helvetica by Electronic Imaging.
The typefaces used on the cover were Bookman, Helvetica Narrow,
and Universe Condensed.
The book was printed on 60-lb. Williamsburg Offset by Versa Press, Inc.